Introduction to Fen
Thought and Action

Introduction to Feminist Thought and Action is an accessible foundation that whets appetite for further study. It provides a non-US-centric introduction to gender studies, covering topics like 19th-century African, Chinese, and Arab movements, and foregrounds Black and Indigenous feminisms. Several case studies—the Aztecs and the Spanish, Agriculture and Gender, Beauty and Authority, Racial Stereotypes, and US Voting Rights—reveal how the interconnected architecture of privilege and oppression affects issues like globalization, media, and the environment. Feminist theories about race, sexuality, class, disabilities, and more culminate in step-by-step instructions for applying intersectionality and practicing activism. Rich with 19 diverse first-person voices, it brings feminism to life and lives to feminism.

Menoukha Robin Case holds a master's degree in English with a concentration in creative writing; a master's degree in Women's and Gender Studies; and a PhD in English with a focus on women in Yoruba culture, traditionally and in diaspora. Her postdoctoral work has been in Indigenous Studies, with an eye toward Indigenous feminisms. She has taught relevant topics at several colleges (University at Albany, Simons' Rock of Bard College, and Skidmore College), such as Race, Class, and Gender; Introduction to Women's and Gender Studies; Native American Women's Studies; Black Feminist Thought; and Feminist History and Theory. In addition, she brings feminist analysis into a wide variety of classes, from Mythology and Modern Life to Water: Local and Global Issues to Roots & Routes of African Diaspora Resistance. She is currently an Associate Professor at SUNY Empire State College, where, along with teaching and mentoring, she develops online courses, including Introduction to Women's and Gender Studies.

Allison V. Craig holds a master's degree in English with a focus on feminist theory from Virginia Tech and a PhD in English with a focus on gender and crisis from the University at Albany (UA), State University of New York (SUNY). Her dissertation, "'Only a Girl Like This Can Know What's Happened to You': Traumatic Subjects in Contemporary American Narratives," examines the difficulty of representing traumatic experience and the problem of seeing violence and exploitation as natural and inevitable functions of social life. Dr. Craig currently teaches in the Writing and Critical Inquiry Program at UA, using her expertise on trauma and empathy as tools to foster critical awareness through writing. She also teaches at SUNY Empire State College, focusing especially on issues of social injustice and genocide.

Introduction to Feminist Thought and Action

*#WTF and How Did We Get Here?
*#WhosThatFeminist #WhatsThatFeminism

**Menoukha Robin Case
and Allison V. Craig**

Routledge
Taylor & Francis Group

NEW YORK AND LONDON

First published 2020
by Routledge
52 Vanderbilt Avenue, New York, NY 10017

and by Routledge
2 Park Square, Milton Park, Abingdon, Oxon, OX14 4RN

Routledge is an imprint of the Taylor & Francis Group, an informa business

Library of Congress Cataloging-in-Publication Data
Names: Case, Menoukha Robin, editor. | Craig, Allison V., editor.
Title: Introduction to feminist thought and action: #WTF and how did we get here?: #Whosthatfeminist: #Whatsthatfeminism / edited by Menoukha Robin Case and Allison V. Craig.
Description: 1 Edition. | New York, NY: Routledge, 2019. | Includes bibliographical references and index. |Identifiers: LCCN 2019017943 (print) | LCCN 2019020756 (ebook) | ISBN 9781315183114 (Master Ebook) | ISBN 9781138740969 (hardback) | ISBN 9781138740976 (pbk.) | ISBN 9781315183114 (ebk)
Subjects: LCSH: Feminism—History. | Women's studies—Cross-cultural studies. | Women's rights—History.
Classification: LCC HQ1121 (ebook) | LCC HQ1121 .I587 2019 (print) | DDC 305.4209—dc23
LC record available at https://lccn.loc.gov/2019017943

ISBN: 978-1-138-74096-9 (hbk)
ISBN: 978-1-138-74097-6 (pbk)
ISBN: 978-1-315-18311-4 (ebk)

Typeset in Bembo
by codeMantra

Visit the eResources: www.routledge.com/9781138740976

Contents

Preface: What's This Book?

This book will mean different things to different readers. Some may have already experienced what we describe; at least part of it (racism, classism, or sexism) is likely a direct part of your daily life. For others, much of this will seem new or an indirect part of your life. Whether your experiences are direct or indirect, we live together and need to consider how to act in our shared world. We hope to illuminate the value of our connectedness, the importance of listening and learning from each other.

What this book is not: This book is not a survey of Women's, Gender, and Sexuality Studies (WGSS) as an academic field. Many excellent books provide that important institutional history (e.g., *Women's Studies: The Basics*).

We discuss some of but do not provide in-depth information about the many forms of feminism that have arisen over the past centuries. If you're interested in learning more about a particular feminism, seek books on that topic (e.g., *Native American Women's Studies: A Primer* by Stephanie Sellers; *Feminist Theory: From Margin to Center* by bell hooks, regarding Black feminism).

This book is not a collection of primary documents—speeches, lectures, treatises—by prominent feminist thinkers, although we do quote some. Collections, such as *The Essential Feminist Reader*, edited by Estelle Friedman, and *Women's Voices, Feminist Visions: Classic and Contemporary Readings*, edited by Susan Shaw and Janet Lee, make fine accompaniments to this book.

This book does not include advanced scholarship, that is, analyses that utilize but don't explain feminist theories. There are excellent books that collect such studies (e.g., *Feminist Frontiers*, edited by Verta Taylor and Nancy Whittier).

All the above approaches are valuable in and of themselves, and we recommend them for future studies. Our experiences suggest that they'll be more valuable to you if you have a clear understanding of how your own story relates to the stories of others and a toolbox of clearly defined concepts and methods to delineate those relationships. Together, these can prepare you for the vast array of resources and scholarship that contributes to WGSS as an exceptionally rich academic field.

What this book is: This book offers tools (definitions, concepts, and methods) that you can use to dismantle assumptions.

Audre Lorde, whose brilliantly constructed bridges across differences give us all a place to stand together, was a poet who knew how to create a packed statement in just a few words. Her much-quoted "The master's tools will never dismantle the master's house" raises many questions.

Who is the master? What is the master's house? What purpose does it serve? Whom does it shelter? What happens in there, anyway? Why do people want to dismantle it (the word "master" is a clue)? Hammers, saws, and screwdrivers can either build or dismantle an ordinary house, so what's so special about the master's tools that they only construct, but never take apart, "his" house? Why won't (notice that she didn't say can't) these tools dismantle the master's house?

We'll identify the master's tools and help you learn to use feminist tools.

This book provides historical premises so you know how and when to use feminist tools. Several premises shape how we present historical context. We'll expand on some in upcoming chapters, and you can research others according to your interests.

First, we keep in mind that patriarchy (a system in which males have power over females) is only a few thousand years old—it's the mere skin of human history. Older traditions, like gender-balance and matriarchy, are still very much alive in groups here and there around the globe. Such traditions understand greed, which drives that desire to have power over another, as fear-based. We affirm that fear is not meant to be the foundation of a culture or a way of life. As cutting-edge science increasingly tells us, humanity's deepest ancestral wiring for daily life is for empathy, compassion, equity, care, and cooperation. Therefore, ranking systems such as sexism, classism, and racism violate the core of our biology.

We also keep in mind that wherever and whenever there's inequity, people resist.

Finally, we keep in mind that grassroots movements generated the contemporary academic field, not the other way around.

This book provides a toolbox of concepts and methods. Because WGSS is an interdisciplinary field, we make use of every academic discipline, from anthropology to zoology. Concepts and methods allow integration of that range of possibilities.

This book introduces theories from the ground up. Concepts and methods have been developed into theories by feminist thinkers, both in grassroots and in the academy. The three legs of the cauldron—history, concepts, and methods—cook up theories that will give you a basis for studying whatever is important to you personally.

This book situates feminism in the present. The contents of the cauldron you'll encounter here, developed over a wide-ranging history, have worked together to answer questions from many different angles, shaping diverse kinds of feminism, from 17th-century Indigenous American actions to contemporary social media sites. And so we ask: #WTF: who's that feminist, what's that feminism? Global connectors like social media allow all kinds of feminists to converse, debate, and act together when they find common cause, so the cumulative answer is #feminisms.

What to do with this book: Use it to acquire a foundation that will help you in future WGSS studies. We hope it also sparks abiding engagement with issues of equity and justice.

We want to convey how gender, race, class, age, ability, sexuality, and associated ways of measuring social worth intertwine to construct hierarchy so that you gain an understanding of the architecture of oppression. We want to provide reflective tools that will help you locate yourself in and among the various rooms of that architecture. Finally, we want to provide tools that did not construct the master's house that are suitable for liberating projects.

You'll learn more about all these ideas in the upcoming chapter, so don't worry if they're surprising or confusing right now. We hope you'll bring your learning to various issues you encounter and care about as you pursue your studies and work for change.

Acknowledgments

Those we owe thanks—for our lives, our hearts, our unfolding and changing thoughts, and our sustained will to act—are too numerous to name.

We're grateful for the openness and generosity of all who shared their Entry Stories. They enrich this book illimitably. They're the voices that speak to readers.

Rhianna Rogers was exceptionally generous, sharing stories that connect her life and scholarly achievements.

Thanks to former students, PhD candidates, and professors whose researched contributions offer inspiration for students' future studies.

Thanks to Alice Lai and Chimine Arfuso, exceptional readers who helped clarify the text.

Thanks also to Katharine Ransom and Sarah Riddington, who shared family photos of activism.

Part One

Stakes and Stories

Introduction: Welcome! Are you a Feminist?

2017 was a big year for women in the US. From a women's march that outnumbered attendance at the presidential inauguration to #MeToo revelations about sexual misconduct, to Black women voters ousting accused pedophile Roy Moore, movements led by women seized the spotlight after the 2016 election. In response, Merriam-Webster made "feminism" the word of the year. This is nothing short of amazing given that feminism has often been belittled as the F-word. Equally interesting is that not all the women participating in these various movements would call themselves feminists.

2017 saw both a sustained rise in 'feminism' lookups and a number of event-driven spikes.

'Feminism' is our #WordOfTheYear.

Merriam-Webster's 2017 Words of the Year
Feminism, dotard, gaffe, syzygy, and 6 more of the top lookups in 2017
merriam-webster.com

9:32 PM - 11 Dec 2017

4,701 Retweets 8,649 Likes

88   4.7K   8.6K

Figure 1.1 Word of the Year.[1]

What is at stake if you say you're a feminist or not? Whether you claim the name or not, you may be thinking or acting like a feminist if you share feminist goals and values. How can those identifying as feminists find common ground and work together with those who don't?

Part One

1   Stakes

Inequity

Merriam-Webster defines feminism as: [1] "the theory of political, economic, and social equality of the sexes" and [2] "organized activity on behalf of women's rights and interests."[2] Because inequality isn't determined by sex alone, this popular definition is incomplete. Activists (those who organize activity) have broadened this incomplete definition, including many reasons and ways to be a feminist. If you value respect, empowerment, and freedom for everyone, you share feminist values. If you want equity regardless of race, class, gender, or sexuality, you share feminist goals.

By definition, inequity exists when something is given to someone or some group and kept from others. It can be as simple as giving someone you like a bigger slice of cake or as extreme and horrific as treating people as property. Inequity of any kind elicits protests and a fight for fairness, often called "equal rights." When something is quantifiable like a piece of cake or pay, "equal" means "the same," but when it comes to less measurable qualities, there's a common misconception about what "equality between the sexes" actually means. It does *not* mean we should treat women as if they are *exactly the same* as men but instead that neither should be treated as superior or inferior. Similarly, people of different ethnicities have distinct histories and cultures but should not be treated as more-than or less-than because of these differences. Equity, therefore, accords equal respect, not identical treatment that erases our valuable differences. Feminism is part of the struggle for equity.

First, let's look at why inequity awakens a drive for equal rights. According to recent science, the desire for fairness is biological. Primatologist Frans de Waal studied how some animals empathize with one another, cooperate to achieve goals, and value reciprocity and fairness. They even protest when witnessing inequity that doesn't affect them directly, as did Capuchin monkeys who refused their favorite food, grapes, when their partners were given bland cucumbers.[3] Evolution was once thought to be driven by competition (survival of the fittest), but scientists now understand cooperation is the key drive.[4] Humans, like other animals, respond to caring. Our compassion-based biology floods the body with chemicals that offer a sense of well-being. It seems reasonable, then, that humans are driven more by reciprocity (fairness), empathy (compassion), and cooperation (sharing) than violence, threats, and conflict.

Any fight for equal rights usually meets resistance. People who protect, promote, and believe in inequities may be motivated less by compassion chemicals and more by chemicals released by another biological drive: fight, flight, or freeze. Research since 2008 has found correlations between political attitudes, physiological traits, and the brain. Fear-based responses can turn anyone into an enemy and anything into a competition. Habitual fear leads to desire for control and authority over others. Authority may be justified with a sense of superiority and expressed as the right to have more than others (greed). Self-esteem tied to belief in superiority can destroy the desire for mutually beneficial relationships (sharing).

Brain development is affected by culture. Neurologically, fear is designed to be a momentary response to a threat, not a way of life, but some cultures promote the latter. Compare the cooperative "We're in this together" to the competitive "Whoever dies with the most toys wins." Battles between fear- and compassion-based drives duke it out in cultural ideas and social practices. Fear emphasizes the slim differences between us such as race, class, and gender over our shared experiences as human beings. Collectively, this draws nations and religions into the fray. Feminisms and feminists may focus on any part of the resulting tangle of problems.

Inequity comes in many forms: economic, educational, unequal treatment under the law, and media misrepresentation or lack of representation. We know that women don't get equal pay for equal work, but did you know this inequality is affected by ethnicity? This table, based on $56,000, the approximate US median salary in 2016, lists what people were paid for the same job.

Table 1.1 Wages for Work[5]

Race/Ethnicity/Gender	Portion of $1.00	Median Wage Gap
Asian men [a]	1.12	+$6,720
White men	1.00	$0
Asian women	0.87	−$7,280
White women	0.80	−$11,200
Black men	0.73	−$15,120
Native American men	0.70	−$24,200
Latino men	0.69	−$17,360
Black women	0.63	−$20,720
Native American women	0.59	−$22,960
Latina women	0.54	−$25,760

Earnings within each category vary: for example, many Asian men earn less than white men. However, as a group, they are the most highly educated category, often leading to higher income.
a Median means half earned above and half earned below.

To earn as much as a white man, a person needs a second or third job earning minimum wage and working between 30 (white women) and 68 (Latina women) additional hours a week. Another household member could work but would have expenses too, so part of the additional wages goes toward basic needs such as housewares, food, clothing, and medical care. Two-worker families may also need to commute and juggle schedules. For the household to afford a car, earnings have to be higher. The gap is impossible to bridge if a family has children or elders to care for.

If you find it unfair that different people get different pay for performing the same job, you share some feminist values. If you find it unfair that families of color have less chance to build security for their children, you share some feminist values. If you think all people, regardless of race or gender, should get equal pay for equal work, you share some feminist goals.

Institutions like schools and churches can support a better life. Educational opportunities vary globally; within the US schools are supported by property taxes, so neighborhoods where people earn the least have poorly equipped and maintained schools, creating a cycle of low earnings that's difficult if not impossible to escape. Also, not everyone can attend school or church safely. Girls may be threatened or even killed going to the very community venues they rely on for support and advancement.

Table 1.2 Girls Attacked in Public Venues[6]

Ruby Bridges	Ruby Bridges was the first African American child to attend an all-white public elementary school in the American South. She was met by violent mobs.
Cynthia Wesley, Carole Robertson, Addie Mae Collins, Denise McNair	These African American girls, aged 12–14, were killed while attending Sunday School when the KKK bombed the 16th Street Baptist Church in Birmingham, Alabama, in 1963.
Aisha	Aisha, a Nigerian student, was captured from her school along with many female students by Boko Haram. She was raped and impregnated.
Malala Yousufzai	At age 11, Malala, Pakistani, wrote a blog advocating for girl's education. The Taliban attempted to have her killed. At age 15, she was shot in the head on a public bus. Malala survived and continued her activism. She was awarded the International Children's Peace Prize in 2013 and the Nobel Peace Prize in 2014.

If you believe all girls should have equal opportunities to learn, you share some feminist values. If you want all girls to be able to safely attend public institutions regardless of their race or religion, you share some feminist goals.

Another significant feminist value is respect for one's body. In 2017, *Time* magazine named the global #MeToo movement a collective "person of the year." The fact that a "person" can be a group says a lot about feminism. The December cover pictures iconic "Silence Breakers" who ripped the lid off systemic sexual harassment and misconduct.[7] If you're distressed that the highest office in the US could be occupied by someone who said "grab 'em by the pussy. You can do anything," you share some feminist values.[8] If you think men should be held accountable for abusing their authority to force sexual contact with women, you share some feminist goals.

We've made progress and have problems to overcome. Notably absent from *Time's* "Silence Breaker" cover was Tarana Burke, a Black woman who started the Me Too movement "to [build] solidarity among . . . survivors of harassment and assault."[9] Although she was discussed inside the magazine, many were concerned with her absence from the cover image. If white celebrities become the face of the #MeToo movement, people may overlook the fact that women of color are disproportionate victims of sexual violence.[10]

If passing over Black women's challenges and accomplishments seems wrong to you, you share some feminist values. If you find it wrong for elected officials and doctors to call Harvard Law graduate Michelle Obama, the 2008–2016 First Lady of the US, an "ape in heels" or "monkey face," you share some feminist values.[11] If you think all accomplishments should be respected regardless of race, you share some feminist goals.

Does sharing feminist values and goals make you a feminist? Why is the answer important? Why do people come to call themselves feminists? Does everyone mean the same thing when they say this? If not, what kinds of feminisms are there? Throughout the book, we'll look at why feminisms differ and how we can bridge differences to make a difference together. We'll also learn what it means to "think as a feminist" by taking a deeper look at taken-for-granted terms such as words, beliefs, and values.

Feminist Toolbox: Begin with the Basics

In the upcoming chapters, we'll go beyond common knowledge to examine how thought works. We'll take the first steps by getting to the bottom of taken-for-granted concepts, such as "words," "beliefs," and "values," redefining them according to specialized academic uses. The ability to examine how our thinking is actually produced is a powerful tool that can help dismantle the master's house.

Words are the basic building blocks of thought. Yet they can mean different things according to context. Boot means one thing in a shoe store, another in a computer lab, another in the armed forces, and yet another in a membership venue, so you can buy boots, re-boot your computer, go to boot camp, or be given the boot by a club. Similarly, the terms "belief" and "value" are commonly used in various ways. For the purposes of our study, we'll use cultural studies definitions of these words.

Belief refers to stories, called narratives, that shape the way people understand the world: they tell us "this is what is true: this is how it works."

Beliefs can be formed and shared in many different contexts, from religion to popular culture to science, and shift from one context to another.

For example, in medieval times, Europeans believed the Sun circled the Earth. They also believed that only men could be creative geniuses and that women should confine themselves to painting mundane domestic images such as flowers and food. It was believed unseemly for women to study anatomy, so the human body was an improper subject for women painters. Galileo Galilei and his friend, Artemisia Gentileschi, challenged these beliefs.

Values differentiate thoughts and behaviors that are thought to be right and good from those that are thought to be wrong and bad. Generally, judgment is based on whether thoughts and behaviors accord with beliefs.

Belief and Value Systems: Values (right/wrong, good/bad) are associated with beliefs (this is true: it works like this) and work together as cultural systems. They are in a continual state of change. By going against the grain, we can intervene and direct them.

The medieval belief that flowers were a fitting subject for women shifted when flower paintings became trendy. Men, to cash in on their popularity, stopped describing them as mundane domestic images and called them philosophical statements on the impermanency of life.

Most readers are familiar with Western ways of thinking. Even if you were raised in a non-Western culture, Western beliefs and values are known throughout the world due to conquest and media. Therefore, we'll start with an iconic Western example, and because the roots of Western cultures are patriarchal, Galileo, the main character in our story, is male. We'll consider him along with Artemisia Gentileschi, who, although she pre-dated the term, is now considered a feminist. Their stories demonstrate how individual beliefs and values change yet leave lingering traces behind.

The belief that the Sun circled the Earth gave way to the belief that the Earth circles the Sun. This is an example of a belief shifting from the religious to the scientific sphere. But science as we understand it today didn't yet exist; it took Galileo's challenge to create it. Galileo is called the father of modern science because his heretical finding initiated a new cultural context in which beliefs about the cosmos and nature could be explored with particular methods. The way he himself was valued changed as beliefs changed: He went from scholar to criminal by violating religious beliefs, and when his discoveries finally gained credence, from felon to a new category, scientist.

Artemisia's painting, *Judith Slaying Holofernes* (1620), depicts the widow Judith slaying an Assyrian general who had been planning to destroy her village. Most paintings of this Biblical story show a demure Judith with a look of distaste on her face, but Gentileschi's women are strong and determined. It was considered unseemly in her day but is now an icon of early female empowerment. Perhaps this connects to how she was blamed for being raped: If women are believed to be delicate, then strong women are not valued—they are unwomanly.

The pre-Galilean belief that the Earth was the center of the universe was part of a complex religious system that affected not only Galileo's discovery but also who could be king, queen, lord, scholar, peasant, and criminal. Medieval beliefs about the nature of man and woman affected not only Artemisia's artistic and personal life, but also what any woman could

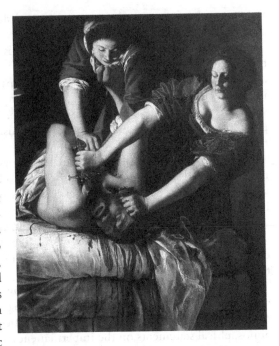

Figure 1.2 Judith Slaying Holofernes.[12,13]

learn, master, and contribute to society. Systems are built around beliefs and values that are subject to change. Change is part of the work of feminisms.

#WTF: What's That Feminism?

Women of all genders, ethnicities, and nations can be feminists, and so can men. Today, many people tell their stories on internet blogs. Whether you tell your story in person, in print, or on the net, it adds to our collective knowledge. In the e-zine *Roots*, Byron Hurt explains "Why I Am a Male Feminist." The story is introduced with: "The word turns off a lot of men (insert snarky comment about man-hating feminazis here)—and women. But here's why black men should be embracing the "f" word."[14] His story is retold along with those of other Black male feminists on the *Msafropolitan* blog.[15] Some of them relate to what Trevor Noah, a South African comedian who hosts *The Daily Show*, wrote:

> I never thought to call myself a feminist because of branding," he explained. "I had this skewed idea of feminist: I thought it meant being a woman who hates men. When I read Chimamanda Ngozi Adichie's *We Should All Be Feminists*, I was like, "Oh, this is what my mom taught me. This is simple. I don't understand why everybody is not this.[16]

You probably noticed the wide variety of reasons people associate with the F-word, which is how some people refer to feminism or feminist. What is your reason? We invite you to consider your own story as a bridge to a feminist landscape where you can locate yourself among diverse groups in our interconnected world. Once you have passed the threshold into feminism, the journey isn't over. There is a lot to learn to navigate in the complex feminist landscape and find productive ways of interacting with diverse feminists along with justice-seekers who don't identify as feminists.

Claiming the F-word can help us make connections today, but women's movements throughout the world pre-date the word "feminist" and people throughout history have had what we now call feminist values and goals without ever using the word. Sojourner Truth never called herself a feminist, but her women's rights and abolitionist speeches are posted on many feminist websites because they exemplify feminist goals and values.[17]

Suffragettes adopted the term feminism, and its earliest recorded use can be traced to 1841, when *Webster's American Dictionary of the English Language* defined it as "the qualities of females." It would not be popularly equated with sexual equality until 1913, when Rebecca West famously said, "I myself have never been able to find out precisely what Feminism is: I only know that people call me a Feminist whenever I express sentiments that differentiate me from a doormat or a prostitute."[18] The next year, Carrie Chapman Catt wrote an article in *The New York Times* that began, "What is Feminism?" She described a leaderless "evolution, like enlightenment and democracy" comprised of all who support women's suffrage (the right to vote) and global emancipation of women.[19]

Figure 1.3 Backlash.[20]

To one degree or another, in one way or another, the F-word has always been derided. Depending on the time, feminists have been accused of man-hating and subject to the archaic accusation that they are "not feminine," called manly, feminazis, bitches. It isn't surprising if people hesitate to call themselves feminist when doing so means derision. And the stakes of derision go beyond misunderstanding: The simple truth is that inequity directly benefits those in authority, and they will act to maintain their benefits. The person who pays $44,800 to a white woman instead of $56,000 to a white man gets the same job done and pockets the difference. If he can pit men against women, and white, Black, and Latina women against each other, he profits from all of them. It's easy to do if you make the F-word a slur and launch it as a weapon to divide those who could fight together for equal rights.

Let's look at different stakes and shifting concerns and try to identify some core principles. We begin with feminist responses to Western cultures. The idea of Western culture, or Western society, is not limited to Western Europe but includes other countries heavily shaped by Western European thinking, which is why much of the Americas as well as Australia and New Zealand are considered "the West." Western cultures have been patriarchal for several thousand years.

Patriarchy is a social system that maintains that males are superior to females and reserves men certain privileges. Privilege has taken many forms, from fathers owning daughters and husbands owning wives to how much a woman earns when she does the same work as a man. The sense of male superiority saturates media and artistic depictions of men and women and affects our laws and rights today. Since the 19th century, movements that responded to Western male control over females have been called feminist.

Although contemporary feminists are concerned with all inequities, this original limited association with the word feminist or feminism still looms in the average person's imagination. In the past few decades, the titles Gender Studies and Gender and Sexuality Studies were added to and sometimes displaced the title Women's Studies. Sexuality Studies adds the range of ways that people may share intimacy. Gender Studies has worked to include the experiences of people of all genders. Still, the title Gender Studies itself emphasizes gender as if it were the most important consideration for all cultures. Because Western ideas of gender are fairly rigid, many people find them oppressive. Gender oppression is surely a battle worth fighting on your own ground.

A Pantene ad entitled "A Man's Boss, a Woman's Bossy" encourages women to "be strong and shine," words cleverly related to hair and designed to sell shampoo.[21] Unanswered questions include: Why is hair more important to women than men? Why are women expected to spend more money on beauty than men? And gender alone can't reveal the whole picture. Is Pantene's shampoo good for non-white hair types? Is it affordable, or does it cost so much to "boss" that most women will remain subordinate? These kinds of questions expand feminist concerns.

Different Entry Points to a Shared Journey

Mainstream responses to patriarchy are important, but since ideas about gender and sexuality vary from culture to culture, we also need to look at non-Western ideas and responses. The belief that specific character traits or behaviors are natural to a male or female body is a **social construction**. This means that societies put together—build or construct—a set of expectations for what is masculine and what is feminine, promoting these through many modes, ranging from arts to politics, from advertisements to science. What happens when cultures with conflicting gender ideas meet?

There's a passage in Linda Hogan's novel *Solar Storms* about Tulik, an elderly leader of his Native tribe. During negotiations with white businessmen, he pauses to comfort a crying child. In his culture, both men and women do whatever is necessary for a child's well-being. The white businessmen, seeing the baby in his arms, no longer considered him "manly" enough to be a leader and stop negotiations. They decide the tribe has no strong men and that they're entitled to destroy their land. They are later surprised to be faced by male *and* female warriors.

Non-Western cultures highlight how Western ideas of gender are just that, ideas that Westerners believe. Some cultures maximize gender's importance (it's built into language and entrenched in customs; social roles and behavior are sexed) while others minimize its importance (it's barely visible in language and customs; social roles and behaviors are not sexed).

Analysis of Western gender is highly relevant; after all, Western culture has infiltrated (though not utterly overtaken) most global media. Yet there are many reasons we cannot make Western culture or gender our sole perspective. For most Native Americans, patriarchy is something Europeans brought with invasion. Many Native Americans shun the term feminism, while others redefine it. They talk about women's responsibilities instead of women's rights. All who act against inequities don't call themselves feminists and may even actively dislike the word. Still, they may inspire feminist values or contribute to feminist goals. Always at stake in the heart of such goals are concerns about one form of inequity or another.

As we read on, we'll encounter movements aligned with feminist values and goals from different eras, from the US and abroad (you can read essays, speeches, or stories by their proponents in other texts). For now, let's look at how the stakes of a few well-known feminisms differ and overlap. In alphabetical order:

- **Black feminism** includes the work of Audre Lorde, Barbara Smith, Kimberlé Crenshaw, Patricia Hill Collins, and bell hooks, among many others. It began when grassroots Black feminists critiqued white feminists for dismissing the effects of racism on non-white American women. The main stakes of Black feminism are community liberation and personal and social empowerment for Black women, men, and children through freedom from racism. This can be achieved through legislative, cultural, and/or radical social change. It often includes the idea that no one is free until everyone is free. Women of color have further developed this theory as Latinx[22] feminism, Womanism, and other non-white feminisms. Born from grassroots, Black feminist theory became the backbone of academic feminism, but some texts apply it without ever explaining why it was developed, how it works, or giving credit to the women who created it.

- **Ecofeminism** includes perspectives ranging from Sherry Ortner to Vandana Shiva. Some state domination of nature and domination of women go hand in hand; in woman-positive cultures, nature is treated with respect. The main stakes of ecofeminism are restoration of mutual respect—between all people and between people and the rest of nature—to repair the ecological balance that supports all life. There is advanced discussion in academic feminist journals[23] of how Indigenous principles have been appropriated and altered for use by academic ecofeminists. These principles are held by many who would not identify as feminists but whose groups are led or inspired by Indigenous women. Like Black feminism, ecofeminism has a very mixed presence with tensions between the academy and grassroots. Winona LaDuke, as a Harvard educated Native American, bridges both worlds.

- **Liberal feminism**, from Elizabeth Cady Stanton to Betty Freidan to Gloria Steinem to Hillary Clinton, focuses on the personal, political, and cultural liberation of women. The main stakes of liberal feminism are women's social empowerment, psychic well-being, and personal freedom through legislative and cultural change. Though in its early stages it was grassroots, liberal feminism largely came from educated white women and easily became academic.

- **Radical feminism**, including the work of Mary Daly, Robin Morgan, and others, is based on the idea that sexism is so entrenched that we need to completely dismantle social structures. Modes range from abolishing the very idea of gender to establishing separate male and female societies. The main stakes of radical feminism are women's social empowerment and personal freedom through radical social change. Radical feminism started "on the streets" but quickly entered mainstream studies in the academy.

- **Socialist feminism** originates with activists such as Emma Goldman and includes a wide range of work, from Barbara Ehrenreich's *Nickel and Dimed: On (Not) Getting by in America* to Donna Haraway's *Cyborg Manifesto*. It focuses on analyses of economic systems. It looks at issues such as public and private sphere, and ties patriarchal beliefs to financial systems and their branches (such as who funds what scientific research) that oppress or short-change women. The main stakes of socialist feminism are personal economic empowerment and social freedom for women through legislative and structural change. Its beginnings are rooted in early union activism, and while related branches, such as Marxist feminism, are now better known in the academy than on the streets, it has recently gained new visibility in politics through figures such as Alexandria Ocasio-Cortez.

We'll add more feminisms in upcoming chapters. This brief survey isn't meant to be exhaustive or definitional, but we hope it provides a sense of how wide-ranging feminist concerns, scholarship, and activism is. We hope it empowers you to craft your own definition based on your experience, learning, and concerns.

Feminism can take place anywhere—in the streets, in entertainment and media, in Congress, in churches, and in classrooms. It can take many forms. Some academics derive feminist theories from grassroots experiences. Others develop them in colleges and universities. Divisions can occur between the "streets" and the "ivory tower," when members of educational institutions appropriate (borrow without permission or credit, or inappropriately apply) grassroots activists' theories. But the academy can also support activism and contribute to grassroots movements. You can find many peer-reviewed journal articles about academic feminisms, while grassroots feminism tends to reach out through actions and social media. Most often, though, locations and forms blend and borrow.

We can see that feminist concerns are connected. Reference to core principles can be located through words like "liberation," "equity," "empowerment," "respect," and "freedom." Feminisms analyze a range of concerns and may take up their perspectives like microscopes or telescopes to examine details or long views of inequities in any realm of human endeavor. Different feminists can converse and act together in common cause, and divergent feminisms ally in specific movements. Alliances are people working together to address problems from multiple angles based on inclusive understanding. By finding what is important to you personally, you can bring your life to feminism and feminism to your life, even if you don't call yourself a feminist. Still, brave souls who claim the name can be numbered among all races and genders. To find out why Dr. Mark Anthony Neal identifies as a "Black male feminist," you can read his book *New Black Man*. To understand how Dr. Stephanie Sellers, a Shawnee/Cherokee/Jewish scholar, made uneasy peace with the feminist movement, you can read *Native America Women's Studies: A Primer* and her story in this book. We now turn to stories from everyday feminists.

Notes

1 Merriam-Webster Twitter, @MerriamWebster, 12/11/2017.

2 "Feminism." *Merriam-Webster*. Dec. 13, 2017, https://www.merriam-webster. com/dictionary/feminism.

3 Frans de Waal. "Moral Behavior in Animals." *TED Talk*. Dec. 14, 2017, https://www.ted.com/talks/frans_de_waal_do_animals_have_morals.

4 "Cooperation, Not Struggle for Survival, Drives Evolution." *National Research Tomsk State University*. May 13, 2016, https://phys.org/news/2016-05-cooperation-struggle-survival-evolution.html.

5 Figures extrapolated from information in https://nwlc.org/resources/the-wage-gap-the-who-how-why-and-what-to-do/.

6 Ruby Bridges, bio.com, http://www.biography.com/people/ruby-bridges-475426; https://www.history.com/topics/black-history/birmingham-church-bombing; Surviving Boko Haram: Kidnapped girls tell their stories, Larisa Epatko, *PBS News Hour*, 10/19/2016 http://www.pbs.org/newshour/updates/surviving-boko-haram-kidnapped-girls-tell-stories/ retrieved 12/8/2016; Malala: the girls who was shot for going to school, Mishal Husain, *BBC News*, 10/07/2013, http://www.bbc.com/news/magazine-24379018, retrieved 12/8/2016.

7 Bill Chappell. "#MeToo movement is person of the year, 'Time' Says." *NPR*. Dec. 6, 2017, https://www.npr.org/sections/thetwo-way/2017/12/06/568773208/-metoo-movement-is-person-of-the-year-time-says.

8 "Transcript: Donald Trump's Taped Comments about Women." *New York Times*. Oct. 8, 2016, https://www.nytimes.com/2016/10/08/us/donald-trump-tape-transcript.html?_r=0.

9 "Person of the Year 2017: The Silence Breakers." *Time*. Dec. 18, 2017, http://time.com/time-person-of-the-year-2017-silence-breakers/.

10 Elizabeth Adetiba. "Tarana Burke Says #MeToo Should Center Marginalized Communities: An Interview with the Woman Who Launched the #MeToo Campaign Over a Decade Ago." *The Nation*. Nov. 17, 2017, https://www.thenation.com/article/tarana-burke-says-metoo-isnt-just-for-white-people/. Also see Tarana Burke on *The Daily Show*, May 30, 2018.

11 Lexi Browning and Lindsey Bever. "'Ape in Heels': W.Va. Mayor Resigns Amid Controversy over Racist Comments about Michelle Obama." *Washington Post*. Nov. 16, 2016, https://www.washingtonpost.com/news/post-nation/wp/2016/11/14/ape-in-heels-w-va-officials-under-fire-after-comments-about-michelle-obama/?utm_term=.bae83af490de.

12 Artemisia Gentileschi, "Judith Slaying Holofernes," 1610, public domain. https://commons.wikimedia.org/wiki/File:Judith_decapitando_Holofernes.jpg.

13 Artemisia Gentileschi, "Judith Slaying Holofernes," 1610, public domain. https://commons.wikimedia.org/wiki/File:Judith_decapitando_Holofernes.jpg.

14 Byron Hurt. "Why I Am a Male Feminist." *ChallengingMaleSupremacy.org*. 2011, http://challengingmalesupremacy.org/wp-content/uploads/2015/04/Why-I-Am-A-Feminist-Byron-Hurt.pdf.

15 Minna Salami. "7 Black Male Feminist Perspectives." *Msafropolitan.com*. Mar. 8, 2012, http://www.msafropolitan.com/2012/03/7-black-male-feminist-perspectives.html.

16 "Trevor Noah Reveals Who Inspired Him to Publicly Identify as a Feminist." *Women in the World*. Sept. 28, 2017, https://womenintheworld.com/2017/09/28/trevor-noah-reveals-who-inspired-him-to-publicly-identify-as-a-feminist/.

17 "Feminism." *Oxford English Dictionary*, 3rd ed. Last modified Mar. 2012, http://www.feminist.com/resources/artspeech/genwom/sojour.htm.

18 Rebecca West. "Mr. Chesterton in Hysterics: A Study in Prejudice." *The Clarion*. Transcribed by Ted Crawford. Nov. 14, 1913, https://www.marxists.org/history/international/social-democracy/clarion/1913/chesterton.htm.

19 Carrie Chapman Catt. "Free Love Charge Held Ridiculous." *New York Times*. Feb. 15, 1914, http://query.nytimes.com/mem/archive-free/pdf?res=9F02E1DD1E39E633A25756C1A9649C946596D6CF.

20 (1) "What I Would Do With Suffragists," 1908, public domain. Wrote to Catherine Palczewski; who wanted $25. Erik says she only owns the high-quality digital image in the archive, not the art itself, so we can use it. https://thesuffragepostcardproject.omeka.net/items/show/333; (2) Polish extremists at 2010 Warsaw International Women's Day march, Creative Commons, https://commons.wikimedia.org/wiki/File:Feminazi_STOP!.jpg

21 "A Man's a Boss, a Woman's Bossy." *Pantene*. 2013, https://www.youtube.com/watch?v=B8gz-jxjCmg.

22 Latinx is now in use to include Latinos (male), Latinas (female), and people of Latin descent who are differently gendered.

23 "Eco-Feminist Appropriations of Indigenous Feminisms and Environmental Violence." Apr. 3, 2015, http://www.thefeministwire.com/2015/04/eco-feminist-appropriations-of-indigenous-feminisms-and-environmental-violence/.

2 Stories

Personal Stories, Bearing Witness, and Testimony: A Feminist Approach

A well-known saying is "history is written by the victor." But any one-sided story is inaccurate. Nigerian writer Chimamanda Adichie describes the "danger of a single story" and explains how it separates us from each other.[1] Partial though they are, single stories are still the preferred way to organize information in standard texts (like dictionaries), scholarship, courts of law, and other venues. All too often, those who have been conquered, exploited, or oppressed are misrepresented, underrepresented, or not represented at all.

Silenced or misrepresented people can assert their truths by telling their personal stories. This is called "bearing witness" or "testifying." But silencing isn't just a personal issue. It's also a collective problem. Individual testimony on its own cannot overcome incomplete knowledge and mischaracterization. Even as women privately tell their stories, they are often excluded from conventional history. Poor people, women of color, differently gendered people, the disabled, elderly, and immigrant peoples' realities are also often omitted.

Because of shared testimonies, feminists have been able to reclaim women's accomplishments and contributions. We've also developed theories about the value of personal stories. Bearing witness can include listening to another's story, sharing one's own personal story, or challenging the authority of official stories. It can enhance our understanding of ourselves and each other. Testimonies serve as bridges between people, places we can meet and learn to respect our differences, reflect on how they affect our interpretations of the world, and discuss our common causes.

You might recall a moment or series of events that led you to be concerned with issues important to feminism, that led you, in fact, to reading this book: We call these entry stories. They can respond to a simple question, like when did you first hear the term feminist, or when did you decide you were, or weren't, a feminist? Other questions are more complicated, such as when did you develop an awareness of sexual inequality or social injustice? Entry stories often contain threshold moments of disruption and awakening that forever alter how we think and feel. For some of us, these moments led us to the F-word, feminism—despite, or even because of, legitimate struggles over what the term means or misinformation spread against it.

Embracing feminism as part of one's identity can include a new sense of self and the world, so entry can take many forms. Some enter quickly, without fanfare or hesitation. Others take longer and struggle or agonize for decades. Some align with feminist values and goals but still don't call themselves feminist. Because our experiences of the world are personal, each journey—and destination—is different. As Adichie says, there's no single story that encompasses us all, and there is no single path that must be walked to advocate the values and goals of feminism. However you get there, we welcome you.

In the spirit of testimony, we offer entry stories. We've placed many here in Chapter 2. Others are interspersed through the book. While reading them, think about where you have been, where you are now, and where you would like to go. Also, look for how stories intersect, overlap, and diverge, find points of similarity and differences, and think about what your own entry story might be.

#WTF: Who's That Feminist?

I. I. "Kathy" Chou

The Ingenuity of the Suppressed Class Can Move Mountains and Part the Sea

Where should I place this mark? My entry story into feminism could have many starts. In the beginning, as barely detectable subconscious streams leaking out of the tiny cracks in this insurmountable dam, a dam that was designed to contain my raging water and slowly forged together over many years into the river that it has become. I traced my fingers over this map. Was it the first time I felt rage about my helplessness and thought the only way out was annihilation, when another force surged within me and mustered up all of my survival instinct which I didn't know I have, the ingenuity of the suppressed class can move mountains and part the sea. Or was it the first time I felt power, electrifying power running through my entire being, when I stamped my feet on the ground chanting until my voice became coarse: "My Body! My Choice! Reproductive Right is a Human Right!" I couldn't admit then as I can now that I wasn't really committed to the cause as others who were deeply immersed in the 90s feminist resurgence, the abortion history and issues, and therefore took it upon their backs to defend Roe vs. Wade. I was drawn to it because it allows me to speak up and hear myself for the first time, my voice as a woman. Or was it, or was it, the list can go on and on and this can easily become a book length essay, the point is, we all start somewhere to be here. You, by picking up this book and turning the first page and staying with it, I, after more than half a lifetime of questioning and searching, was given a chance to examine the way I got here.

I never read any of the feminist classics, and I used to get embarrassed for my lack of classical knowledge about feminist theories, but I came to my own conclusion that feminism is a living organism and can be felt and experienced in many aspects of a woman's life, and feminist theories exist to try to make sense of it. I was born and raised in Taiwan, and feminist writing from the West (where most of today's classics were written) started appearing on the bookstand in Taiwan in the mid-1990s, long after I had already left or more accurately, fled the country in 1987. I only finished a high school education, so I missed the whole "gendering" development on college campuses that started in 1989, and the first and only feminist bookstore in Taiwan called Fembooks was founded in 1994. But feminists were everywhere when I came and settled in New York City between the late 1980s and early 1990s. For two years, I threw my voice and body into the Reproductive Rights Movement with WHAM! (Women's Health Action and Mobilization), and then the Women Caucus in ACT UP (AIDS Coalition To Unleash Power). I hung out with a small overlapping group of mostly radical lesbian activists, wheat pasting and stenciling the sidewalks by nights, planning and participating in Civil Disobedience demonstrations by days. Under their tutelage, I found my purpose and direction; I was remodeled from a helpless runaway housewife with few life skills to a loudmouth, risk-taking, radical activist. But my heart was not in it. I tried desperately to find that inner connection, that spiritual belonging with the women I spent many hours and many days with, my heart was somewhere else, so, I never considered myself a true feminist, but that I had participated in feminist activities for a brief time in my life.

In the next 20 years, I was completely absorbed in raising a family of my own. Becoming a mother was, for me, the final phase of this rite of passage into my own feminism. The whole experience, from pregnancy to childbirth, was a pilgrimage of self-discovery to be taken alone. To enter into this intimate relationship with myself, seeing and feeling the changes in my body, experiencing how the growth of a child gripped and pushed my inside and outside, the fear and uncertainty of how to get this being out of my abdomen cavity, urged me on to an independent study of women's reproductive life and history. On the birthing table, I called out to no one other than my long-deceased grandmother's spirit, who was a midwife, to aid me in passing the ring of fire—the physical sensation of splitting my body apart to let another human being come into the world. Motherhood followed, then warriorhood. For the first time in my life (I thought) there is something I need to protect, and witnessing and guarding the development of a child from infancy gave me a second chance to look at my own history. Motherhood proved that I can be a capable protector and provider, but I was still in an infancy state about protecting myself. Then,

I encountered a turning point when I met an Irish/Native American who found her calling in reviving the long-lost Women's Teaching. She said, and it was incredible why I never heard this from any feminists I know, that every woman should maintain a sacred space for herself. Women tend to give themselves away to everyone else in their circle, husband, children, relatives, neighbors. We are conditioned to give out rather than give inwards. Betty Friedan might have said the same thing, but in that room were women of colors from different continents—Africa, India, Asia, and the Americas—., we were all in tears because no one had ever given us the permission to stop the insanity of giving. Draw a circle around your body, she said, and declare to yourself that no one should be allowed to enter this space if you don't want them to. Easier said than done; as with anything, you get better with practice.

Practicing how to maintain my sacred space took several more years. Then, it became internal, and only then, it became a right. Human right, women's right, the right of every citizen. You can't get there without walking the walk.

So, I am still skeptical about all the isms; nevertheless, I admire those who spent their lifelong career in something good. Feminism is a good thing, that's all you need to know. But finding your way to truly internalize it takes many trials and errors; you'll no doubt make as many friends as enemies because feminism is about tilting the balance of power in the world, and that is always risky; so, practicing feminism also involves taking risks. What helped me decide how much risk I can afford to take, and which battle is worth fighting, is that circle I drew around my body. No battle is too small if it comes near my sacred space.

Patrice LeBron

"Ain't I a woman": My Journey to Divine Feminism

In the summer of 1990, my inner consciousness affirmed—I am a black woman. I cropped my hair in a short natural hairstyle faded on the sides and immediately decided that chemical straighteners were additives from the past. I didn't know at that time that my awareness would be a lifetime journey leading through diverse avenues of testing different selves, which would eventually connect me to my camouflaged feminine self, soul principles, and ethnicity.

Throughout this narrative, I reflect on some of the factors that led to the process of re-constructing my inner consciousness to define my identity and reinforce my aura. I wanted to embody and convey an image of what I consider to be my "Divine Feminine" self to recognize and merge my soul within the tangible world. Hence, for me this translates into what I have named the practice of "Divine Feminism" which incorporates soul principles, racial identity, self-acceptance, and other genders.

"Ain't I a Woman," a sacred vessel that can birth and create everything? I asked myself. I yearned to be balanced in mind and disposition and embody confidence with my gender. I envisioned myself as a receptacle holding an endless flow of water, along with the fervor to perceive, embrace, and demonstrate the attributes of the "Divine Feminine" that encompasses all genders. In the corporeal world, I am a woman. However, in my re-birth, I re-define my womanhood as androgynous. I now employ insight, intuition, and action to discern the wisdom of life's principles.

Prior to cropping my hair, I was a woman who did not affirm her blackness and neither was I confident with my body image and features. Looking in the mirror, I gazed at enormous lips, brown skin, ample breasts, a curvaceous body, medium-length chemically straightened hair. I was not happy or confident with myself—I still wanted something more. It was not the hair cropping and natural style that brought my awareness of who I was, or wanted to be, but the eruption of emotions that occurred when I looked in the mirror and saw someone entirely different from who I thought I was. For the first time in my life I gazed in the mirror and saw my beauty in blackness. I saw a black woman who was beginning to perceive a shift in her emotions about self. I recognized my ethnicity and became comfortable with short hair sans chemical straighteners and no makeup.

My self-esteem about my body image was a result of my upbringing. My mother always implied that I was not good-looking enough. This suggestion meant that according to European beauty standards and *Vogue* magazine, my lips were too big, my body too curvaceous, and my hair was kinky. Therefore, growing up, I was psychologically, physically, and emotionally affected. I was contentious, sensitive, constantly inflamed, forever angry, and I overate all the time. Eventually, I learned that my emotional and psychological states were a result of sexual abuse and molestation. In addition, feeling trapped in an unsatisfactory body culminated in making choices that weren't right for me, such as getting involved with unethical and inappropriate men who I catered to.

As I continued to mature, I also catered to male authority, which supported my belief that things were harder for me because I am a black woman. I deduced that women didn't head households, and men should be the gender in the relationship to have a higher income. To me, I was invisible and unworthy. I had also unconsciously cultivated jealousy of women who appeared to be centered in their lives. Finally, where it concerns relationships, I thought that women were not born to lead. Marriage is an ownership (the man owned me) and not a partnership. Subsequently, I did not have or recognize my voice for many years.

These initial feelings about self began in my youth, around 13 years of age, and lasted until I was in my 30s. I wanted to emulate my mother who has a creamy complexion and weighed 125 pounds. Her hair was always cropped in an elegantly short hot-combed style and she was always chic and constantly attractive to men. I envisioned my mother as being in control of her life. She was divorced, a medical professional, the sole breadwinner, supporting my grandmother, my brother, and myself. She was always financially in control. After living in the US for one year, she was able to purchase a large property in the suburbs of Queens, New York, with all the amenities for family living.

I love and respect my mother; however, with all these attributes, she never taught me about being a confident and self-sufficient woman. Neither did she teach me how to develop and maintain relationships with people of any gender, and I was not encouraged to have and maintain a social life with my peers. I was not allowed to have friends unless they appeared to be middle class, and I spent many days alone or going to the library. Neither did she encourage or support my intellectual abilities. In addition, she did not address the sexual abuse issues I constantly endured.

At the time of my awakening, considering my emotional approach to life, my social influence and social structure, I was not shocked when I gazed at my re-birthed self in the mirror and recognized my womanhood. It was time for a shift, and the cropping of my hair facilitated my newly transformed self. I now celebrated my blackness, life principles of diversity and inclusion, along with my uniqueness in the entire process. Moreover, this was never a solitary journey for me. I have had mentors from all paths through this transformation: spiritual, feminist, academic, and literary. The literary support I got via the work of Audre Lorde, who helped me to address anger and resentment. Finally, my mentors encouraged me to learn and practice new principles through the traditions of Buddhist and Spiritual Psychology and Yoruba Theology.

I am still on the journey of "Divine Feminism" and I do not personally seek traditional feminism. My decision to approach my feminist journey through this type of philosophy is always confirmed by the resolutions I make and the diverse paths that manifest in my life. For instance, while composing a paragraph for this essay about being a "sacred vessel," my doctor called to speak with me regarding my health. After that transient moment of empty space between shock and acceptance, I returned to myself and the practice of my soul principles—incorporating resilience and a balanced consciousness. I am reinforced in my consciousness knowing that no matter what life throws at me, I am unified with the "Divine" force.

Chimine Arfuso

Voice Matters: How Our Stories Impact (or Inspire) Feminist Theory

My name is Chimine. I am the daughter of a Cuban refugee. My family came over from Cuba when my mother was only a few months old and eventually settled in Las Vegas. My mother brought me to California when I was a few years old. When I was a little girl I spent most of my time with my Cuban grandparents. My grandfather, Papi Berti, eventually became a Spanish Professor at the local University and he spent many hours tutoring me on Spanish pronunciation and proper conjugation of verbs. My grandmother, Mami Irma, was an incredible cook and read a divination card deck called the Barajas Españolas. We would spend hours hand grinding ham for croquettas or papa rellenos. And I would watch mesmerized when she would read the cards for herself and others. She would often tell me the story of how the women in our family came to the cards. She said one day a black woman came to my great-great-great-grandmother's house and told her she heard my great-great-great-grandmother read the cards and that is when my ancestors first picked up the Barajas Españolas.

My mother is what they called a Rubio. She has green eyes and light hair. My mom had no interest in our Cuban heritage and raised me in a predominantly white neighborhood. The only semblance of her history was the many trips we would take to Mexico because we lived so close and I would hear her argue in Spanish with the vendors. I had so many identity complexes growing up. My peers would look at my peachy pink skin, courtesy of my French father and would call me white. I look white, but for me it erased my Cuban heritage, so I would retort back, "No, I am Cuban." The second stance I took on my Cuban heritage was to join the ethnic student union's dance team. I always loved to undulate my body in sexy ways, but was always self-conscious of becoming objectified for doing so. Finding dance helped me express part of who I felt I was inside. Even as I got older, I still felt this divide. I would spend summers with my cousins in Miami and they would laughingly call me "gringa." My Spanish was terrible and although Miami was the one place I felt at home, I stood out with my white California girl accent.

It wasn't until I found women's studies that I started to understand why I felt so different and never fit in. My first love was Latina Feminism. While Latina Feminism is predominantly Chicana (Mexican), I felt an affinity from being raised in California close to the border. Mexican culture was the closest everyday experience I had to connect me to my Cuban culture. When I met some other Cuban and Puerto Rican scholars, I learned how I also identified with Black feminism and the experience of the diaspora. My experience growing up and not fitting in had to do with my family being displaced from our home country. The politics of Cuba and US relations further complicated matters; until recently, I was never even legally allowed to visit my homeland. I once took a trip to Puerto Rico because it was the closest I could get, and I fell in love with that country.

Reclaiming my ancestral lineage of reading cards and teaching Zumba are some of the ways that I have learned to recover the severed parts of my history. My grandmother and grandfather have long passed, and it is up to me to leave a trail for my children. Feminism matters because it gives us voice. It also matters because it gives us space to articulate a unique experience to pave the way for other women to have a voice.

Henry Odun LeBron

I Became a Soldier in My Grandmother's Army of Justice for Women

As a child in 1966, I always thought that man would do everything to defend women. Instinctively, I felt that if we as men came from women, it would only be right to protect them. However, another reality was starting to awaken within.

My grandmother assisted me to understand feminism. Grandma was an elder, healer, midwife, and an activist for her family and community. Through her, I learned the struggles that women were having, such as male chauvinism and job inequality; and black women had another strike against them compared to their white or light skin counterparts. I saw the need for women to speak up and at times claim their rights for what was undoubtedly theirs. We had a woman governor and mayor who were very admired by the people of Puerto Rico. I began to see the disproportionate social differences that have been laid out historically between men and women. Grandma was beyond her time. She shared extremely progressive views: for example, equal pay between both genders having equal skills.

I remember the impromptu discussions between her and other women addressing the abuse endured by their husbands. Her words were carefully selected in order to lift their spirits and to help them find the courage to confront their abusers. I became a soldier in my grandmother's army of justice for women.

As I reached maturity, I took upon myself the mission to support women. I could not see a world without compassion, tenderness, and reflection, for these traits are what I foresaw as needed to have a holistic and just world.

In contrast, I saw men destroying, raping, and abusing women for personal pleasure. Men would subdue women by keeping them at home and providing all for them; they had no voice or opinion—a different method of enslavement. This gave women a false sense of security and a lack of self-identity. The men would also sexually force themselves upon the women, although the women rejected their advances. If the women did not heed, they would be beaten or threatened to be thrown out of *his* house if they would not comply. I saw an unbalanced and at times a double standard. Men's salaries were higher than those of women, and yet they performed the same job. Men were expected to have extramarital affairs and were called "*putos*" (players), but women were beaten, at times to a pulp, or humiliated when they had an affair and called "*putas*" (whores). An organ difference between sexes couldn't justify the superiority and entitlement of one over the other. The feminine taught men how to think from the heart. It was a way to balance the male brute force bringing tenderness, understanding, and compassion.

Inequalities still continue—unequal pay, female stereotypes, abuse, and male chauvinism still are prevalent within our societies. Women are still being viewed as sex objects and baby machines. I emerged from a circle of strong, independent, and determined women relying solely on themselves and carrying their own weight, not waiting or asking for men's approval but depending on their senses of self. As a man, dad, grandfather, and uncle, I stand in support of all women and continue to assist in the eradication of these injustices and myopic views of women by men.

Anamaria Iosif Ross

It Was a Rude Awakening

My relationship with feminism began with the struggle of seeking maternity leave in the US, when I learned that I was "not entitled to anything." I had left my native Romania as a 16-year-old, having been raised in a family of creative, independent, and outspoken women with few male figures. The rhetoric of the communist state, at its best, was one of equality between the sexes, which encouraged women into the workforce and taking leadership roles. At its worst, the communist regime had been pro-natalist to the point of making abortions illegal in 1966, which created an enormous wave of births in 1967 and especially 1968, and led to many instances of death and imprisonment. I never felt that I needed to be treated differently or gingerly as a woman. I had been a tomboy as a child. I went to judo lessons, learned to ride, and asked to shoot a rifle and a bow. I enjoyed intellectual debate and mathematics competition. I craved what I now recognize to be male freedoms and privileges.

When I was 16, my mother passed away suddenly. I immigrated to be reunited with my father, who I had not seen since the age of one. I felt broken and powerful. All through college and my graduate school years as an anthropology student, I remained quite oblivious to any discrimination or hardship that women faced. I saw myself as a kind of amazon, a free spirit, while also being an innocent fan of the singer Madonna for her seductive powers. I took Flamenco dance classes, which captured a rough energy that binds the feminine and the masculine.

At the time I became pregnant with my second child, I was a couple of years into a tenure-stream position at a small upstate NY college that demanded a heavy teaching load. When I told my dean that I was expecting, he provided noncommittal reassurance that they would be flexible about my next semester's schedule. I held a notion of academia as an enlightened setting, where bosses and colleagues saw me holistically, as a human being, not merely a worker. As it turns out, the college lacked any formal policy regarding maternity leave in 2007 (and probably still does), letting every woman negotiate for herself the best deal she could wrestle. One fortunate woman had been allowed a whole semester at home, deigning a new course, while others returned in the middle of a semester. The law allowed only six weeks disability leave for birth or eight weeks for C-sections. The luckiest or wisest knew to birth in June.

My baby was due at Thanksgiving, which fortunately allowed me to teach most of the Fall term. I spent most of September, October, and November going back and forth with e-mails about what "we" were going to do about my condition. I advocated for the urgent need to fully breastfeed and nurture my baby. As it turns out, my pregnancy was regarded mainly as a huge inconvenience. I felt strongly that it was a matter of health to have a lot of time with my infant and to nurse exclusively for at least a year. It was November already and I had no answer about the next semester or my maternity leave. A senior colleague was given the charge of researching and reporting what other area colleges our size did for their pregnant women. He made it clear to me that he was much inconvenienced by putting together a giant report and concluded that I did not deserve anything. "The administration is annoyed with you," he said. "You are selfish. You do not care about our college students, only about yourself. The provost decided to give you one course reduction for the Spring semester, so you will teach two online and one in the classroom on Tuesdays-Thursdays. I personally think you should not have special treatment. We all had babies—no need to make a fuss about it. This is not France. I know what it is like . . . my girlfriend is French. This is not Canada, or Romania. If it bothers you, maybe you should consider moving back. . . ."

Needless to say, it was *a rude awakening*. I had been in the US for over 23 years at that point and an American citizen for over 18 years, yet I had not realized that being a woman made my status that different from men. I felt like I had grown another head, not a baby. How could it be that an institution of higher learning had no plan or kind regard for a faculty member bearing a child? What about my emotional and mental well-being? What about the health and well-being of the newborn? I taught until a couple of days before I gave birth and asked for "family and medical" leave to secure 12 weeks instead of the 8 "disability" weeks. That extra time allowed me to recover more fully and bond with the baby before having to leave him with someone else for hours, so I could teach in the classroom twice a week. I realize that I was still very fortunate to have flexibility, to be able to advocate and stand up for myself, and to be able to return to my job. My insistence and persistence strained my relationship with some influential people at that institution. Until that time in my life (age 39), I had barely considered why women may not be able to achieve as much as men nor grasped the full value of maternity leave or job security. I did not realize that being able to nurse and nurture a newborn, a maternal-child health imperative, is seen by some as a privilege not protected by US law. I had never before then felt more deeply vulnerable as a woman, biologically, psychologically, socially, or professionally. It was a humbling and awakening call to action.

Himanee Gupta-Carlson

Preliminary Thoughts on the Non-Becoming of a Feminist

My experiences with feminism are rooted first in the Midwest, where I was born and grew up as the eldest daughter of Indian immigrants; then in the Pacific Northwest, where my career as a newspaper journalist reached its fullest fruition; and finally in Hawai'i, where I experienced academic feminism for the first time.

As a result of these divergent places and experiences, I have never quite thought of feminism as an ethos. I just felt that it was always in me. I was born a girl, always identified heteronormatively, and hence, as my logic went, I always thought of myself as a feminist. I didn't know as a child of the 1960s and teenager of the 1970s in Indiana about the second-wave feminist movement. I didn't realize that when I joined the local swim team, the fact that I could do so was made possible by the Title IX legislation that mandated parity for males and females in such school activities as sports. I also didn't realize that when my mother spoke to me of praying for my future husband and of the arranged marriage system in which she and my father found each other and to which she expected I would want to be a part of that she, too, was invoking a certain kind of feminism, a sense of power that could be found in "women's spaces"—spaces like the home, the university wives club of which she was a part, the parent-teacher associations at our schools, leader of Brownie Scout troops for her children, and so forth. In short, even as I eschewed my mother's path, I never thought of it as a lesser or unequal path. It was just the path that society had carved out for women of my mother's time, and she had found power and strength and authority within it.

My father was a university professor. This meant that education was a high priority in our home, and that it was pretty much a given that my two sisters and I would transition immediately out of high school into college. Still, while we were encouraged to study hard, I do not remember this environment as being restrictive. We were not prohibited from playing outside. There were not limits on our TV watching, up to bedtime, at least. Our wrists were not slapped and we were not grounded for receiving less than perfect grades. The only real restriction that I felt was one that I would call cultural: We were of Asian Indian ancestry living in a predominantly white Midwestern community. We were reminded of this difference daily through the color of our hair and skin, through our parents' accented English, and my mother's wearing of saris (a habit she maintained daily until her 1970s, when the cold winters and difficulties with walking prompted her to follow the lead of many of her female immigrant peers and to start wearing slacks instead). As a result, we were a part of a schoolyard community yet apart from this group. I didn't date— not so much because my parents prohibited me but because social norms of what constituted a normal teen relationship didn't include whites with the brown Indian girl.

I finished my college degree at age 22 and began working as a journalist. At age 25, I began living with a fellow journalist who was about my age and became my partner for the next 13 years. He was of Chilean ancestry, and in the newsrooms of the late 1980s and 1990s where whites were dominant and blacks comprised the major meaning of minority, he and I found each other alone together. He never wanted to get married because he himself saw marriage as a state of inequality. During the years that I was involved with him, I was perpetually conscious of the fact that I was actually in a more dominant position, economically and socially. I earned more money and I had a more prestigious position in the newsroom. I also worked harder. Yet I was also somewhat subtly aware that he could socialize himself more easily into the workplace environment. He could do much more with less effort. I read Gloria Steinem and *Ms.* Magazine, and associated these discrepancies in our relationship somewhat with feminism. But my "equality" vis-à-vis that of males wasn't a particular concern. I was much more interested and attuned to the racial and ethnic differences that had divided me from my peers in childhood and seemed to define workplace and societal power relationships in adulthood.

My interests in race turned academic when I went to the University of Hawaii, initially on a one-year fellowship for mid-career journalists and then in what turned into a long-term pursuit for a master's degree and then a doctoral degree. In courses on India, I learned more about the devastating effects of British colonialism and started to see how the manner in which western imperialist ideas of superiority had "gendered" the brown colonized body as inferior paralleled the workings of race in America. My awareness of these processes angered me and sickened me to the point that I realized I could not return to the newsroom to work. I had to go to graduate school to study these theories more deeply, for therapy perhaps, to work these issues out. In the ensuing years, it never dawned on me—until I read some of the other "coming to feminism" stories in this book—that these realizations had come to me in a course on Gender and Women in Contemporary Asia that was taught by a self-described feminist. So, even as I saw race as the paramount organizing force in American society and as akin to the colonialist conceptions of self-other defined in a hierarchical level of European-Asian, white-brown manner, I was learning to make these associations through the lens of feminism, even if I did not see feminism as such.

In my master's studies, I made many female friends. They saw gender as the primary organizer of social relationships, which really bothered me. I saw race. I was willing to acknowledge that identities intersected and were intertwined, but I didn't see how. I found feminist theory a bit confusing because it seemed like the theorists we were reading were either doing nothing more than fighting with each other or were screaming about the exclusions of women's experiences from virtually all historical and contemporary events. I also felt that gender—which I appreciated as an organizing factor that differed from the perceived biological differences defined by the word "sex"—was forcing me into worlds of universal sisterhood with women whom stereotypically I detested: women who told me not to run alone because being on streets without a buddy was unsafe; women who inadvertently would start stroking my long black silky hair; women who prized motherhood over careers; women who didn't see race as a divisive force among us. I just didn't get it, and while I never stopped seeing myself as a feminist, I rejected feminism as a theory.

I might have stayed in that space if those same female friends had stopped being my friends. Instead, they just loved me anyway, and we grew in our work together. Outside of classes and study groups, we cooked meals together, trained for and ran marathons and other races together, worked on volunteer projects, and organized for Hawaiian sovereignty.

My work in politics was necessarily constrained by the part-time job I had at the Honolulu Advertiser. Still, that didn't stop me from participating in 2000 in the first real, overt political act of my life: Two days after defending my master's thesis, I joined a group of students in spending the night at the Campus Center, sleeping on concrete in protest of the US Supreme Court's *Rice vs Cayetano* decision, which denied the validity of Hawaiian-only participation in the election of trustees to the state's Office of Hawaiian Affairs, as well as a proposal being floated by the university to eliminate tuition waivers to Hawaiian students. My actions might have gone unnoticed if I hadn't given an interview to a television reporter at dawn. My newspaper supervisors hauled me into the executive editor's office and started to play a video documenting the interview. I told them they didn't need to play the video, and when I refused to attribute my actions to a naive act of unwilled ignorance, I was slapped with a heavy reprimand: a strong letter of rebuke that probably still exists in some personnel file to this day and a slash in my hours that resulted in about a 35% cut in my income.

The shock of these consequences might have been even greater if about four other things hadn't happened at the same time: My partner and I of 13 years decided to end our relationship and evolve it into friendship; one of my male thesis advisers told me that my "difficult" personality would make it impossible for me to find a job in academia; I began training for my first marathon; and my female friends pushed me into therapy and started urging me to think about building a different kind of a life.

That moment in time remains pivotal in my memory. Not because I feel that it was the moment that I became a feminist. Rather, because it prompted me to think about what I was doing with my life more holistically. I didn't quite realize it at the time, but I was deploying the methods of feminist inquiry as I considered how to heal my spirit of multiple wounds.

I did complete my PhD. I do have a job as a professor in academia. The male professor who spoke harshly of my difficult personality also supported me in my completion of my degree and in letters of recommendation as I went on the job market. My ex-partner and I have remained friends, and he was the best man for my eventual husband. I completed that first marathon and 11 others. The friends who offered me their arms and their ideas as props during difficult times remain my friends to this day. All of these forces among others have involved a litany of negotiation—with self, with community, with race, with ethnicity, religion, class, and also gender. They have taught me to listen and to look for consensus in a way that seeks to get away from the hierarchization of peoples on the basis of difference and through searches for what exists in common. They have helped me see how hard-headed and unrelentingly aggressive I can be at times, and how warm and generous and caring I can be at others.

In my scholarship and in my teaching, I use what I describe as feminist-inspired methods to draw out differing perspectives, initiate dialogues, and seek to build new knowledge through conversation. It is my understanding—through coursework, I ultimately took in feminist theories and feminist methods—that this is feminism in an academic sense. I still struggle a bit to name this way of thinking as feminist. Yet, if that is what it is, it is what I am.

Katharine Ransom

I Ended Up Desperately Needing Feminism

I come from a lineage of strong and conventionally accomplished women with my mother holding a BA in French and an MBA in Marketing, then teaching high school French for more than 20 years; my maternal grandmother becoming a librarian, then helping my grandfather run the first black-owned grocery store in the Camp Grove neighborhood in Danville, VA; and my paternal grandmother holding a BA and an MA in English, then becoming a professor of literature at the State University of New York at Old Westbury. I was raised to believe I could accomplish anything I wanted without my race or gender holding me back, which I learned was not typical for the location I was raised in; rural South Central Virginia. I believe the first time I associated myself with feminism was in my freshman or sophomore year at Ithaca College (IC) in Ithaca, NY. Although my parents did not use the term when I was growing up, I don't remember them being anti-women's rights or apathetic about the political process; in fact, I remember when my mother went to vote and I watched her in the voting booth.

Coincidentally, my academic advisor at IC, Dr. Shaianne Osterrieich, is a feminist economist, but I was more focused on passing my classes and graduating, although I did address gender issues in several of my papers throughout my studies. Several months after finishing my undergraduate degree, I chose to enter an online MBA program because I had spare time at work and wanted to advance my career. During my MBA program, I did not have the opportunity to ask my most pressing questions about the limits of economic theory and how we expand on those theories. About a year after I started, I knew I wanted to continue to a PhD program, which was something I never thought I could accomplish because I struggled to finish my undergraduate Economics degree, for multiple reasons.

I wanted to pursue women and economics after teaching Economics and Personal Finance at George Washington High School in Danville, VA, during the 2015–2016 school year. I had several students with children and was very concerned that they did not have the proper support to excel in their studies. I saw that the school system was failing students who had problems that could be solved with improved strategies and better communication between local agencies, teachers, and administrators. My topic has shifted focus from attempting to address economics and gender in the school system to a more theoretical approach to gender equity by studying the economics of matrilineal societies through the lens of Marxist feminism. Marxist feminism focuses on investigating and explaining how women are oppressed through systems of capitalism and private property while women's liberation can only be achieved through a radical restructuring of the current capitalist economy.

What has been very apparent during my life is that relationships with men have had the greatest impact on my career and well-being. I didn't have much confidence in my abilities and intellect after my undergraduate experience until I met a man who was 17 years older than me, who was also a student at my graduate school. He helped me to gain a confidence I had never known, yet he manipulated me and consistently lied about his life and who he was. At the time, I thought he was an amazing person, but experience and the work of Silvia Federici taught me men like that use women for their own desires. Federici (1975) states,

> sex is work for us, it is a duty. The duty to please is so built into our sexuality that we have learned to get pleasure out of giving pleasure, out of getting men aroused and excited. . . . Compartmentalization is only one aspect of the mutilation of our sexuality. The subordination of our sexuality to the reproduction of labor power has meant that heterosexuality has been imposed on us as the only acceptable sexual behavior. . . . This has meant the imposition of a true schizophrenic condition upon us, as early in our lives we must learn to draw a line between the people we can love and the people we can just talk to, those to whom we can open our body and those to whom we can only open our 'souls,' our lovers and our friends. The result is that we are bodiless souls for our female friends, and soulless flesh for our male lovers. (pp. 24–25)

I came to these words during a summer class in 2017 after I left a financially, emotionally, psychologically, and sexually abusive relationship and, with the help of my parents, moved to the city where my mother lives.

Silvia Federici is a Marxist feminist and her work finally helped me understand why my relationships have become more destructive as I've become more accomplished in my career and how to break that cycle. I came to feminism because it was a passion of mine, but I ended up desperately needing feminism in a time when I was broken and hopeless. I gained strength through my PhD in Transformative Studies program at the California Institute of Integral Studies and have been allowed the freedom to explore my interests and passions that would not have happened in a traditional PhD in Economics program. I have been able to explore many forms of feminism and womanism to include feminist economics, Marxist feminism, and ecofeminism. As I learn more about feminist and womanist theory and practice, I realize how I can be better in my treatment of others and in helping to create equitable opportunities but also in the treatment of myself.[2]

Lola Rocknrolla

Do Whatever the Fuck You Want to Do

My journey into feminism is not a complicated one. A feminist just thinks that women should have the same power and rights that men have. What a shame that everyone doesn't pound their chest and scream: "Of course I'm a feminist, why aren't YOU!" I grew up gay in a very machismo, homophobic environment. My gigantic Jewish family is from Philly, and we spent every summer on the Jersey Shore. A place where gender was so strict that bikinis were put on toddlers, and speedos with gold-chained medallions were given during bottle-feeding. As I grew older the rights of men versus women were glaring. Men were encouraged to do whatever they wanted (whether they were smart enough or not) and women should be teachers or nurses (even if they were brain surgeons). I never believed any of the nonsense, and once I saw my first John Waters, movie all bets were off. I moved to New York and made *Dragzilla*, a short film about a 50-foot drag queen that crushes New York City. A campier version of *Attack of the 50 foot Woman* . . . if that is even possible. I hooked up with the rocknroll, queer community and never left. The film got into festivals everywhere and most of them just assumed that I was a drag queen. No lesbian would make a film about drag queens, right? I had a few people asking me why I didn't make films about lesbians, which always struck me as funny because my favorite directors didn't have just one subject matter. Hitchcock didn't have to be a murderer to make *Psycho*, George Romero isn't a zombie, and John Waters isn't the friggin' Egg Lady. On the set, there was a lot of sexism as well. I made a musical about a gay alien coming to take over the planet ("Homo the Musical"). When we did it as an Off-Broadway play, I was explaining a scene to a room full of men, and they wouldn't listen to me. I was the writer, it was my play, and these men thought they knew better because they were men. I would make them close their eyes and imagine I was a man, then say the same thing. In the end, they respected me as an equal, but I was actually their boss. Don't be afraid to be labelled a bitch to get what you want. In the end, it's your name on it, and the work is all that matters. The most important thing I can say to any young feminist (which should be everyone) is OWN IT. OWN YOUR POWER. RAISE YOUR VOICE, and do whatever the fuck you want to do. No matter what anyone else says.

Conclusion: The Same and Different

Although social media make us feel we live on a small planet, the world is home to richly diverse ways of understanding life—what we believe, what we value—and uneven experiences due to wide-ranging opportunities and struggles. Still, we are all connected. Audre Lorde said, "I am not free while any woman is unfree, even when her shackles are very different from my own."[3] Understanding feminism is a complex undertaking. Larry Matrious-iban, an Aazhoomog Band of Ojibwe Elder, said that to understand something, you need to stand under it. He referred both to the humility that allows us to open our hearts and minds to something new, and to the wisdom to start learning from the bottom up. In Part One, we undertook both, reconsidering how we think and then listening to stories from the hearts of diverse people.

Notes

1 Chimamanda Adichie. "The Danger of a Single Story." *TED Talk*. July 2009, https://www.ted.com/talks/chimamanda_adichie_the_danger_of_a_single_story?language=en.
2 Silvia Federici. "Why Sexuality is Work." *Revolution at Point Zero: Housework, Reproduction, and Feminist Struggle*. PM Press. 1975, pp. 23–27.
3 Audre Lorde. "The Uses of Anger." *Sister Outsider: Essays and Speeches*. Crossing Press. 2007, pp. 124–133, http://www.blackpast.org/1981-audre-lorde-uses-anger-women-responding-racism.

Part Two

Ways of Thinking

Introduction: Personal, Academic, and Cultural

There are many reasons people do and don't call themselves feminists, but together we share stakes like liberation, equity, empowerment, respect, and freedom. Entry stories help us find shared stakes and bridge differences in thinking to identify alliances. Because alliances are crucial to "organized activity to remedy inequities" (part of the dictionary definition of feminism), we will dig deeper into ways of thinking. A way of thinking is a preferred or habitual approach to ordering information according to beliefs and values. Our way of thinking determines what we notice (or don't notice), how we interpret what we notice, and what concerns us in each story or event we encounter. The more aware we become of what shapes our thinking, the more able we are to perceive different ways of thinking and make informed decisions about how to act in the world.

Ways of thinking are cultural and personal. Everyone responds individually to beliefs and values taught by family, friends, and society. Teaching can be formal or informal, implicit or explicit, and heavily influenced by social media. Academia teaches ways of thinking using specific methods. For example, the natural sciences use material verification to confirm a thesis, social sciences use data to validate points, and historical studies use primary documents to verify or compare stories.

Academic feminists draw from many disciplines. Diverse ways of thinking help us understand movements throughout history and around the world. Comparing and combining concepts and methods from multiple disciplines frees us from the limits of any one perspective. This approach is called **multidisciplinary and/or interdisciplinary studies**. It's the academic answer to the problem of the "single story," a way to balance numerous ways of thinking and get at the amazing complexity of life.

Combining fields helps make sense of different feminisms. For example, an ecofeminist investigation into the relationship between environmental pollution and health may draw on natural sciences (to analyze the physical effects of pollution on the human body) and social sciences (to map data according to race, class, and gender). It might look at populations with water problems, such as lead in Flint, Michigan's water supply, lack of water on the Navajo reservation, and mercury in the water in the St. Regis Mohawk reservation.

Treating each way of thinking in isolation may unintentionally create a narrow sense of human interactions, while combining two or more fields can reveal how different cultures meet, blend, or conflict, offering us a broader sense of human possibilities. Understanding human possibilities helps us make alliances across differences, making WGSS relevant to more members of more communities. To illustrate a feminist multidisciplinary approach to teaching and learning, and to introduce us to cultural differences, this chapter includes a comparative case study about Spanish and Aztec traditions. Rogers's description of Aztec women challenges assumptions that Aztecs were masculinist and helps us take a new look at gender. It reinforces the equalizing role corn has traditionally held in Indigenous cultures in the Americas. The Aztecs were one of many corn cultures, and we weave findings about corn from anthropology, history, natural science, and economics throughout this chapter.

Differences in academic thinking are minor compared to differences in cultural thinking. Academia tends to see power as a subset of human systems, but Lakota philosopher/activist/poet John Trudell sees it differently:

> Power's something that emanates from . . . the human being . . . power is about . . . the relationship to the Earth, to the universe. . . . We live in a time where we have been indoctrinated to believe that authority is power. So when we look externally and we see these ones that would feed off of us, that would control us, they have defined power from the material perception . . . of the human, not . . . the being. . . . [E]conomic systems[,] . . . military systems[,] . . . religious systems, . . . are systems of authority. But we have been programmed into believing that these things are power, and . . . we have really no influence in these things . . . and if we believe they have the power, then it doesn't say much for ourselves. So, power really is about our relationship to life.[1]

Asante culture has a similar perspective. Akyeampong and Obeng describe the importance of "cooperating with nature and the forging of social consensus" for activists; while "authority (political power) [can] be monopolized . . . access to power (. . .'the ability to bring about change') [is] available to anyone . . . Thus, power ha[s] no gender or age delineations."[2]

Because we'll be challenged to think about multiple definitions of power, we'll add to our toolbox first.

3 Cultural Differences

Feminist Toolbox: Measure Twice, Cut Once

Dismantling a system—whether an actual house or the metaphorical master's house—requires structural knowledge. We need to carefully analyze how the house was built before we dismantle or remodel. We'll distinguish between feminist tools (for liberation), master's tools (for domination), and neutral tools that can be used either way. These are not hard and fast distinctions and you may find ways to change a tool's purpose. Those in authority do this all the time. We'll begin by re-visiting the most basic unit: the word. An example of words as a master's tool is the so-called Clean Air Act, which "permits oil, chemical and steel companies dispensing toxic air pollution to kill as many as ten people in one hundred thousand in the neighborhoods surrounding their factories, refineries and mills."[3] While "clean" is associated with safety in daily use, it has quite another meaning in this political context. In contrast, consider the liberating effect of the saying "Black is beautiful," a phrase that captured public attention by challenging centuries of European beauty standards.

Words shape ways of thinking, and different ways of thinking structure personal, social, and political authority differently. How is thinking expressed through language? How does language affect what we believe and value? Can different ways of thinking change our understanding? Let's examine words, beliefs, and values step by step. By taking one step at a time, we can learn some pretty fancy feminist footwork.

Even though words can be misleading, their purpose is to describe reality by indicating that a thing is "this, not that." If we say day, we are not talking about night; if we say rat, we are not talking about cat. That's neutral and useful. "This, not that" indicates that every word is half of a two-part idea—it has synonyms (this = something with the same meaning) and antonyms (that = something with the opposite meaning). An idea based on a two-part opposition is called a binary. Although reality cannot be reduced to opposite extremes, binaries do help us explain the world. Binaries are a necessary part of thinking in words because language's purpose is to differentiate and define. They're useful unless we let them replace reality.

Reality varies like colors in a spectrum with overlapping shades, and a binary is an abstraction that reduces reality to a set of two symbols. Life remains fluid whether or not we classify it into "this" and "that," but as we learn to think in words, we may come to see the world in more fixed ways. When fixity sets in, binaries can lose their neutrality. Binaries simplify communication, but can be misapplied to judge the deep complexity of life. Paying attention to how they are constructed can reveal overlooked or hidden meanings.

Neutral Binaries can be mapped by a line with two opposing poles and describe what a thing is. In US culture, hot/cold is a neutral binary you can say something's "hot" or "cool," and it's all good. We know that there are many possibilities both between and beyond hot/cold temperatures, like torrid, warm, cool, and frigid .

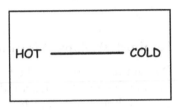

Figure 3.1 Neutral Binary.

Evaluative Binaries attribute positive or negative value to that thing. They occur when a society habitually values one pole above the other. The basic evaluative binary is good/bad (in religious terms, good/evil). It is often hidden behind a neutral binary to create a judgment. Dark/light could be neutral; it could simply refer to the absence or presence of illumination or, in natural terms, day and night. The gradual changes that shift day to night can be understood any number of ways. Myanmar astrologers, who value Day/Sun and Night/Moon equally, measure a day from high noon to midnight. Europeans, who believe light is good and darkness bad, measure a day from dawn to dusk. The hidden evaluator pushes the

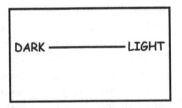

Figure 3.2 Binary with Hidden Evaluator.

binary beyond describing reality and moves it into the realm of beliefs and values. We may believe an evaluative binary represents a natural truth, but that's only if the good/bad evaluation is invisible to us. Since beliefs about good/bad vary from culture to culture, such binaries are cultural, not natural.

Cultural Schemas map beliefs or values. Here, we add the evaluator that was hidden in the previous illustration. It reveals the cultural influence of light/dark corresponding to good/evil. The strength of this Western cultural schema is revealed through language, images, and expressions—you can be

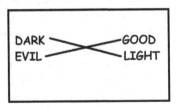

Figure 3.3 Western Cultural Schema with Evaluator.

"kept in the dark" or you can "see the light"—an evil person has a "dark soul" and a good person "brings light." An evaluative binary is always a cultural schema.

Grids of cultural intelligibility organize multiple cultural schemas. Because thinking is cultural, we almost never discuss things as they are. Instead, we discuss what we perceive. How we make sense of things—what is intelligible—determines what we can perceive and therefore what we care about. We can literally create a map or grid of thoughts and beliefs. We can examine these maps to discover the relationship between

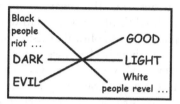

Figure 3.4 Grid of Cultural Intelligibility, Race.

thoughts and social problems. In the film *Black Is Black Ain't*, Marlon Riggs[4] recites Oxford dictionary definitions of black: "deeply stained with dirt," "characterized by tragic or disastrous events; causing despair or pessimism," "full of gloom and misery; very depressed," "full of anger or hatred," "very evil or wicked," "covert." Even clothing is shaped by grids of cultural intelligibility. In the West, black is worn at funerals because it's the color of death, whereas in the East many wear white.

Because grids of cultural intelligibility are expressed in stories and reflected in political decisions, schemas become woven deeply through society and their affects can be hard to perceive and untangle. Most of the time, they're so ingrained that we don't recognize them at all.

European culture's association of darkness with evil becomes a prime example of an intelligibility grid when it's projected onto skin color. Although many of us now condemn racism, this association still permeates the way cultural stories are told. Compare interpretations of images of white youth at sports events with images of Black youth protesting police shooting, similar to Figure 3.5 of Blacks at Ferguson (left) and whites at Pumpkinfest (right). Though similar, whites are reported as

Figure 3.5 Revel vs. Riot.[5]

reveling while Blacks are reported as rioting.[6] Similarly, in New Orleans after Hurricane Katrina, white people "found" food at grocery stores, whereas Black people "looted."[7] Such evaluations can be purposeful or unconscious. But regardless of intent, because they are so embedded in cultural thinking, many fail to see how they shape racial politics, gender politics, and political decisions of all kinds.

As thought becomes more complex, grids connect multiple schemas. In Chapter 1, we said gender is a social construction. Here's how. English language dictionaries say **sex** refers to male/female. It differentiates anatomy, and that's all it does. Differentiations are indicated by he/she, him/her, his/hers. Because the value associated with males and females differs from culture to culture, sex is a cultural schema. **Gender**

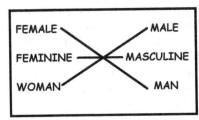

Figure 3.6 Gender Grid with Hidden Evaluator.[8]

refers to behavioral or psychological traits that a given culture associates with each sex. The poles of the gender schema are masculine/feminine. In Western cultures, masculine traits include competition, aggression, rationality, independence, and strength. Feminine traits include cooperation, gentleness, emotionality, dependence, and vulnerability. Gender links these characteristics to male and female, just as morality is linked to dark and light. A person's **social gender identity** is represented by the schema man/woman or boy/girl. When sex and gender are linked as society expects, a person fits one of these social identities. In some cultures, fitting gender identity is necessary for survival.

So, a neutral binary like hot/cold represents a physical range that's not locked to cultural beliefs or values. You can tell it's neutral because it affects all human beings equally—no one wants to freeze in winter. Another neutrality test is that the value of each pole changes according to the situation—a hot stove cooking up dinner: wonderful; a hot fridge: not so great.

Like hot/cold, sex (male/female anatomy) represents a physical range. Each of us has biological traits primarily associated with both poles: regardless of our sex, behavior, or social identity, all humans have varying amounts of estrogen, testosterone, body hair, musculature, and varying shapes/sizes of sexual organs. These are neutral physical facts, but they lose neutrality when linked to a hidden evaluator. Gender is cultural since how men and women are expected to look, dress, and behave varies widely, but if it's unlinked from sex and the hidden evaluator, it could still pass the neutral test; it could be equally fine for a person to be masculine or feminine, no matter their anatomy. In fact, the ideas masculine and feminine as we know them don't exist in some cultures, and in other cultures they're different and more fluid. But since they're linked to sex in Western cultures, males are expected to be masculine and females are expected to be feminine. Your social identity as a boy/girl or man/woman is questioned if you don't meet these expectations; yet there are cultures where sex and gender are never linked in the first place. In that case, social identity relies on different categories altogether.

Western society goes a step further and connects gender to **sexuality**, a separate schema that simply indicates whether a person is attracted to males, females, or both. But it gets entangled with sex and gender. If sex and gender don't match up—if a male is feminine or a female is masculine—some assume the person isn't heterosexual. If heterosexuality is believed to be good, and different kinds of sexual relations are considered evil, then someone who is perceived as non-heterosexual may be threatened or injured.

These four binaries—sex, gender, social identity, and sexuality—demonstrate how grids of cultural intelligibility composed of interlocking schemas shape our thinking and actions in the most personal arena. How would you describe the hidden evaluator that interlocks this grid?

In a study of feminist thought like this book, we must address the fact that there have always been very different approaches to these schemas—is there gender, and if so, what is it—from culture to culture, and from era to era within cultures. As an example, we'll compare Western and Indigenous cultures. As mentioned in Chapter 1, patriarchal concepts didn't exist in many Native American matriarchal and gender-balanced cultures until contact with Westerners. Because of the hidden binary that limits Western thinking to the gendered grid of intelligibility, some assume matriarchy is patriarchy in reverse. But the Indigenous practice that Westerners call **matriarchy** does not place women above men; instead, it traces lineage along female lines and accords women certain responsibilities. Many matriarchal societies are matrilocal: the mother's home is the locale of the family; a husband moves to his wife's family home. In cultures that rely on corn, such as the Haudenosaunee and Hopi, women distribute the crop with the ideal of feeding everyone equally. This responsibility assures them economic and political respect. Men fill equally respected economic roles as hunters and political roles as diplomats. **Gender-balance** means males and females have equal roles. Some gender-balanced cultures are matrilocal, some patrilocal, some both. At least, that's how it's described from the outside, but clearly, when both appear together, something besides gender is going on. This alerts us that the very idea of gender is only a way of thinking about people, not a universal human truth.

Humans around the world have built varied cultures based on different ways of thinking. To bridge differences, we need to consider how enculturation—how we learn to be a member of a particular culture—affects our understanding. At its best, enculturation includes life-saving membership in a group. Groups are life-saving because humans are not intrinsically solo; we are cooperative creatures. There are logical reasons to value difference—groups that encourage the development of diverse individual strengths and skills maximize survival. A group that makes full use of everyone's talents can engage the world in creative and productive ways, and studies show that socially diverse groups are more innovative than homogenous ones.[9] In our contemporary global society, it's especially important to recognize that if we don't respect differences, we can devolve into endless conflict. Nowadays, technological prowess means that conflict could instantly end the world as we know it.

Reflexivity: A Personal Feminist Tool

Audre Lorde wrote, "It is not our differences that divide us. It is our inability to recognize, accept, and celebrate those differences."[10] The first step to celebrating differences is to understand your own system, whatever it may be, as one of many. Instead of taking our belief systems for granted, we should scrutinize them in historical and cultural context. We must unearth how **assumptions** affect what we think and feel. An assumption is a belief that's so invisible to us that it seems like a natural truth. It's often a cultural schema.

Before we compare Western and Indigenous ways of thinking, we offer a tool called reflexivity. However much we examine cultural schemas, they continue to operate. Since we are social beings, they will always matter. However you were raised and whatever you personally feel or think, you're in alignment with cultural expectations, in opposition to them, or tangled in between. But it's possible to uncover our assumptions, set them aside, and consider other ways of thinking with a fair amount of clarity. That's reflexivity's job.

Reflexivity begins with reflection on one's thoughts and feelings. It advances through unveiling and carefully mapping cultural grids of our assumptions, beliefs, and values. We can gauge how they shape us and how we've personally adapted them and/or challenged them to support our individual stakes in society. We can begin to perceive how those stakes affect our understanding of other cultures.

Each of us must personalize reflexivity in order to activate it. Nancy Babbitt describes how a reflexivity exercise offered in a course on Native American women's studies changed her perspective. Following cultural norms, her original

> purpose in life was to get married, be a "helpmeet" to my husband, and to raise our children. . . . I never asked myself "Why [am I] always a damsel in distress in [my] stories?" . . . Native American women authors, in particular, have shown me that I no longer need to . . . [wait] for my hero . . . to save me . . . I can . . . become a mature human being doing . . . what is healthy for me and my family, as well as others.

Like Babbitt, you can begin with examining your own personal and emotional relationship to cultural schemas we take for granted as natural. As you examine, map how they are constructed. Understanding how she had naturalized Western gender norms helped Babbitt better perceive Native gender norms.

We already began this work by looking at schemas of race and gender common in Western societies. Your personal task is to dig deeper and map in more detail. This takes honesty and courage, and it can be complicated. For example, as a woman, you may state you're equal to a man. But having watched your mother put your father first and seen this pattern countless times in media, you might unconsciously put men first too—giving them the last word, adapting your style or behavior, holding their opinions above your own or those of other women, or staying silent when someone else does this. This self-undermining is called **internalized oppression**. It happens when we absorb society's negative judgments about our sex, race, or other category without even realizing it. Or, as a man, you may say women are equal, but still unquestioningly benefit from patriarchy every day in small or big ways, such as higher wages. This is **unconscious oppression**. You may not mean anyone harm, but you may benefit from the harm society does them.

Reflexivity requires that you identify and set aside assumptions, including those you might not yet know about. Some are tied to painful personal experiences, some to desired results like higher wages. This process can radically change how you think (like Babbitt) or not at all. You may not want to change your beliefs or values, and you don't have to. Just map them so you can set them aside as needed. Think of it as taking off a pair of sunglasses. You still own them and can put them back on any time. But you can remember what you saw without them and better perceive other people or cultures without your accustomed lenses. Here's an exercise to help you do it.

1   Identify a belief, value, or assumption that affects your perception. The clue to locating them is your emotions. Read a story or watch a film that moved you in the past, and take note of when feelings such as fear, confusion, repugnance, or anger arise (excitement, enthusiasm, admiration work too, but not as easily). Look for emotions that seem out-of-proportion to the simple, non-threatening circumstance of reading or watching entertainment.
2   Identify another belief, value, or assumption that's related to the first.
3   Using these two to begin your mapping project, consider your habits and patterns of thinking as an organizational grid that explains your world.
4   When you've identified enough to begin to see a pattern, imagine the pattern on a carpet spread below your feet as a "ground of being." Now, roll up the carpet, put it in the corner, and give that original disturbing story the floor. What does it say when it speaks for itself directly instead of through your filtering pattern?

Can we completely do that? No, not usually, and not easily. That's why the term reflexive works between reflecting (mirroring yourself) and reflexes (knee-jerk reactions). But you can learn to take a step back whenever you have a strong reaction, hold up a mirror, and better understand what your cultural schemas might be so that you can listen more clearly. In feminist terms, this means that you can better hear testimony. You still own that carpet, and you can always lay it out again. You can stay true to your beliefs and learn to understand the world in a new way. Hopefully, we are all open to change and learning.

To further prepare for our comparative study, we'll analyze assumptions that most European American societies deem natural truths. One is that Indigenous cultures are simple and local: that Indigenous people have "stayed still," lack exposure that could inspire development, and therefore "stayed primitive." The other side of this assumption is that European travels, whether praised or criticized, have produced sophisticated global civilizations. But many sophisticated civilizations pre-date Europe's, and history has always been global. Researching the accomplishments of ancient civilizations (e.g., surgical and medicinal techniques practiced in ancient Egypt or Inca pre-Columbian water technologies[11]) is a worthwhile project. For now, we'll talk about human travel and the globalization of foods.

Humans have always migrated, and though it once took longer to travel than it does today, we've always traded and engaged in cultural exchange. Corn, a food that now feeds much of the world, is a testament to horticultural genius, travel, and exchange. Developed in southern Mexico by Indigenous farmers from a wild grass called teosinte, it has long been grown throughout the Americas. Each Native American nation holds a story of how corn arrived in their homeland.

You might also know about the ancient mounds or pyramids spread throughout the Americas, some of which contain artifacts that span the continent: in the Cahokia mounds near St. Louis, Missouri, archaeologists found seashells from the northern and southern Atlantic and Pacific oceans, and copper from the Great Lakes area. As scientists develop new techniques, they recognize evidence that confirms oral histories. Recent findings show that Native Americans visited Polynesia[12] in the 13th century, evidenced by both DNA and that American root, the sweet potato.

To imagine early travels, European Americans have to challenge assumptions about Native Americans learned from media and Eurocentric history books. Eurocentric means these books were written by and for Europeans and convey interpretations of events that support belief in the superiority of their own cultural group, despite what reality may be. Eurocentric interpretations are not always intentionally conspiratorial, but a way of thinking that runs deep.

A **cultural group** may be defined by ethnicity, shared language, cuisine, history, and so on—in many cities you can find a "Little Italy" or a "Chinatown"—or it can be defined by shared beliefs and values, such as religion. A person can belong to several overlapping cultural groups. Whiteness includes numerous ethnicities whose importance may fade in the US when compared to shared skin color. Cultural groups may share a basic belief, but vary in other ways, like sects of Christianity. We'll apply our tools to two broad sets of cultural groups: those with European Christian roots and those with Indigenous roots. While there are certainly diverse sub-groups within both categories, this distinction helps us hone in on ways of thinking.

Master's Tools: Western Systems of Authority

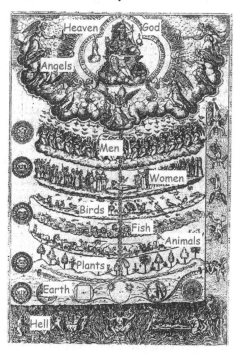

We return to Galileo, the "father" of modern science associated with Western patriarchal values. The belief that the Sun circles the Earth was based on Biblical interpretations that place Man at the peak and center of God's creation. Derived from Plato, **The Great Chain of Being** (sometimes called Scala Natura or Ladder of Being) was developed by medieval Christians to illustrate Genesis. It shows a universe ordered by rank: equality is inconceivable, each entity has more or less authority, is more or less valuable, and more or less important than another. Using our tools, we can observe how evaluative binaries order this particular grid of cultural intelligibility.

Figure 3.7 Great Chain of Being.[13]

- The first binary is God (in heaven)/Creation (on earth). God is above and separate from "His" creation. This is something many of us take for granted, although there are other ways to think about it.
- The second binary is God/angels; God is omnipotent, angels are not.
- The third binary is angels/humans; angels are pure, humans are not.
- The fourth binary is humans: we are spirit (can be purified) and matter (always impure).
- The fifth binary divides humanity. Humans were originally ranked according to sex and later in history, race (male above female, white people above brown people), and that got complicated.
- Humans are ranked above "everything else." Animals are next (beginning with birds and devolving to insects), then plants. At the bottom are rocks, water, and soil.

- All plants depend on rocks, water, and soil, all animals depend on plants or animals who eat plants, and humans depend on plants, animals, soil, and water for life itself. But our dependence does not give them status. Instead, belief in human superiority re-interprets dependency as "dominion over" everything else. This grid of intelligibility tightly links to instruct people as to what they should value and therefore how they should feel, think, act, and legislate.

- Belief in human superiority has become widespread, but not everyone holds it to be true. Many Indigenous cultures respect animals as Elders. But because Europeans followed medieval church doctrine, they believed white men were higher beings with the right to dominate everyone else. They set out to conquer the world, to gain colonies, build empires. Conquest entails not only physical battles but also a clash between Western and Indigenous ways of thinking. The Great Chain of Being was a major weapon in these clashes. The experience of the Aztec is one example.

Feminism, Patriarchy, and the Aztec Empire: Spanish Traditions by Rhianna Rogers[14]

The Spanish believed it was their Christian duty to destroy heathen nations. Fray Diego Durán's book *Historia*, written in the 1580s, illustrates how Cortés erased the role of armaments from the conquest of Tenochtitlan. Instead, he asserted that the appearance of sacred Christian figures proved that domination of Mexico was God-ordained and justified confiscation of wealth and power from natives:

> The valorous Cortés conquered Mexico on the feast of Saint Hippolytus, three days before the Assumption of the Most Blessed Virgin, Our Lady. It is said that the latter appeared during the conquest in order to aid the Spaniards. [. . .] At that moment the glorious Saint James appeared, frightening away the Indians and favoring the Spaniards through divine permission [to seize Tenochtitlan].[15]

Imposing Christianity to annihilate Aztec religious customs, the Spanish promoted fear, obedience, and subservience to satisfy their own social, religious, and economic agendas. Feminist scholar Nalia Kabeer argues that patriarchy is not biologically innate, but an ideology of male superiority.[16] Spanish priests and officials believed it was a God-given mandate. They interpreted the Biblical story of Adam and Eve to assert women had originated sin and should strive to make amends through wifely virtues as caretakers, mothers, and child bearers.

Because they believed women were weak in nature and had a natural propensity toward sin, they could have no role in the public domain, where they would only cause problems and chaos.[17] Therefore, the Spaniards transferred all Aztec women's leadership roles in economics, religion, and politics to Aztec men, destroying her status in the public domain. Even within their own households, Aztec women were limited to activities the Spanish deemed feminine. Transferring authority in the household from the Aztec female to the male reduced a woman's ability to maintain her status in the private domain.

This invasion took place in the 15th century, when Portuguese and Spanish, and later French, English, Dutch, and others, claimed lands in the Americas, Africa, the Middle East, India, and East Asia. Using words to claim authority, they re-named conquest, calling this era the "Age of Discovery." Europeans didn't actually discover anything since people had already been living in these places for millennia. Ignoring that the Aztecs (among others) boasted magnificent cities, Europeans claimed they had discovered unsettled land populated by inferior beings.

The Doctrine of Discovery and **Manifest Destiny**, patterned on the Great Chain of Being, are master's tools that constructed the laws of nations such as the US and Canada. In 1452 a papal decree stated European Christians were entitled to own any lands they "discovered" because primitive people didn't know how to properly "use" them. This formalized the Doctrine of Discovery as religious policy. They felt it was their Manifest Destiny to civilize the wilderness and "tame" the "savage." They believed non-white people around the world, including Africans and Native Americans, were in-between human and animal on the Chain, and that this gave them the right to the land, resources, and labor of Indigenous peoples. This justified slavery: they were entitled to own these people just as they were entitled to dominion over plants and animals. Some clerics believed Africans and Indigenous Americans could "be civilized" if they were controlled and Christianized, and that, slavery was good for them.

The US Supreme Court confirmed the Discovery Doctrine as US law in 1823. Both Doctrine and Destiny were embedded in the original US Constitution, which referred to Indians as savages and Africans as three/fifths of a person, formalizing racism that we still endure today. Although the Constitution has been amended, the Chain was an acknowledged basis for Western thought from medieval times through the middle of the 20th century and has returned in the 21st century.

Because beliefs and values are complex, ever-changing systems, a belief discredited in one part of a system can remain alive in another. As schemas or grids change, we hold onto some parts and let other parts go. The parts we hold onto are the things we believe allow us to fit in a group and survive or thrive. They are called norms.

Norms enforce the investment societies have in their own belief and value systems. Norms are its lifeblood, the foundation of its identity, the creator of its shape as a distinct entity. They drive a culture's sense of the actions they believe are justifiable to insure survival. Whoever fits the norms of a group is a member of that group, and whoever doesn't is a **cultural other**.

From a binary perspective, a person is either "me" *or* "you" and a group of people is either "us" *or* "them." Although it's possible for both poles of this binary to be equal, in Western culture, the norm is the pole of the binary that's evaluated as superior, while the opposite pole is devalued. *Devalued* doesn't mean there is no actual value, but that value is unrecognized, unrewarded, or poorly rewarded, as we saw in Wages for Work in Chapter 1. Those who don't fit a norm disrupt a grid of cultural intelligibility. Individuals may agree or disagree with any one schema or even an entire grid, but it can continue to shape society and determine the degree and nature of cultural membership. Though we can change them, several core schemas typical of Western cultures seem locked in place by evaluative binaries.

Table 3.1 Western Norms: Cultural Schemas with Hidden Evaluative Binaries.[18]

Valued Pole	*Devalued Pole*	*Rationalization of Evaluation*
Male/masculine/ man	Female/feminine/ woman	Anatomy compels behavior and social worth.
White	Person of color	White rhymes with "might makes right": superiority is evidenced by conquest.
Wealthy	Poor	Wealth is deserved and means one is a better person.
Heterosexual	LGBQT+	LGBQT+ may be considered an illness.
Citizen	Immigrant	Borders must be enforced to maintain us/them.
Able body/mind	Disabled/differently Abled	Disabled are pitied and looked down upon.
Youthful	Elderly	Old age is shameful and the aged are a burden.
"Attractive" looking	"Different" looking	Beauty norms reflect other schemas (sex, race, age).
Christianity	Other religions	Islam and Judaism are suspect; Indigenous are primitive.
Second generation white citizen	Second generation citizen of color	In the US and some European countries, descendants of white immigrants are not identified as foreign, but descendants of immigrants of color remain foreign.

Norms are enforced through laws or cultural pressures. Some have long been part of Western civilizations; others are more recent. Plato believed Greek men were born to a public role, either gold, silver, bronze, or iron, and woman's only role was to support him in the private domain. This description of gender, class, and citizenship is about 3000 years old. Scientific racism, a theory about dark-skinned people, originated in the 17th century, was added to the Great Chain, and systematized in the 19th century; it's only about 400 years old. Some norms are fluid while others are extremely limited and inflexible: to be valued by white supremacists, you must be a white heterosexual Christian. Extreme norms lead to extreme actions because a sense of superiority relies on devaluing the other pole of the binary.

Assumptions arise when the cultural schemas and grids that shape norms remain unexamined. Like girders in a house, they're hidden by siding on the outside and sheetrock, paint, and maybe some pretty wallpaper on the inside. Our work as feminists is to expose the structural components below surfaces. In the case of Galileo, the surface was a belief that the Sun circles the Earth; for Artemisia, the surface was the belief that women can't be great artists; the supporting structure for both was valuing Man as the most important being in creation. Galileo objected because it didn't match his observations, and Artemisia objected because it cramped her talents. Questioning norms can be liberating.

Living on the devalued side of a norm can be cramped, tortured, or even obliterating. If we're uncomfortable in the master's house—either with our own cramped quarters or because we're distressed that fellow dwellers are oppressed—we'll want to alter it. To do this, we need to reveal which structural elements cannot support equity, take them apart, and build differently. The stakes? Our survival on Earth.

But why is the Earth at risk? To understand this, we need to consider how Western beliefs and value systems led to current crises such as pollution and climate change. A comparison of Western and Indigenous beliefs can help us do that. But living in the master's house can make this difficult, so we suggest you examine your personal relationship to Western cultural schemas and evaluative binaries first. Where do you fit in the norms table, and how does it affect your thinking? You can use the reflexivity exercise to consider this before you read on or any time throughout the book.

All My Relations: Indigenous Systems of Equity

Europe is home to diverse languages and cultures. Each nation has its own Indigenous people, its own history of wars, conquests, and cultural exchanges. Likewise, there are thousands of non-European Indigenous cultures. Indigenous refers to cultures that are native to a particular place. How long a history, exactly, makes a culture Indigenous is subject to debate, but we'll

Figure 3.8 Circle of Life, All My Relations.[19]

look at peoples who have been associated with a region for at least 10,000 years. We need reflexivity to put aside schemas that became norms over several hundred years (race) or several thousand years (gender), so we can look at Indigenous beliefs that have been prevalent for millennia and remain active today.

We'll specify through three groups: the Yoruba of West Africa and two North American groups—the Anishinaabe Council of Three Fires (Ojibwe, Ottawa, Potawatomi) and the Haudenosaunee Confederacy (Mohawk, Onondaga, Oneida, Cayuga, Seneca, Tuscarora). The Yoruba are native to Nigeria, Togo, and Benin. Anishinaabe peoples are native to the northern US and Canada, from the east coast to about half way across the continent. Separated by a newish border between two settler groups, when combined they are the largest Indigenous group in North America. Haudenosaunee are also native to the northeast on both sides of the border. There are core similarities between these West African and North American ways of thinking that may indicate something about the nature of Indigenous thought, also called Indigenous Knowledge.

Indigenous Knowledge challenges the Great Chain of Being and highlights how words convey culture. English translations of the Bible say God created Man in *His* image. But there are no words for he, she, or it in Anishinaabe or Yoruba languages—there is just one gender-neutral pronoun to indicate all beings. Translating a Yoruba or Anishinaabe creation story to English is difficult; since God has no gender, we can't say He. Substituting explanations for pronouns can be clumsy because we're forcing words in a gender-driven language to convey an utterly different way of thinking.

Yoruba language demonstrates minimal gender impact since there is one word for child and no single words for son or daughter. There are words for man and woman, so adults can discuss marriage and procreation. Some scholars say "masculine" and "feminine" behavior don't define a Yoruba child's world, and the words man and woman don't define gender behavior in the Western sense.[20]

In Yoruba and Anishinaabe cultures, the binary of anatomical sex is neutral. Neither male nor female is superior or inferior to the other. Sex doesn't interlock with the gender binary; character and behavior aren't tied to genitalia. Therefore, gender identity doesn't prohibit a full range of personal characteristics. This isn't to say there are no male or female roles. For example, Yoruba men generally weave while women dye cloth; men cultivate crops and women prepare and sell them in the marketplace. But neither status is superior to the other. Also, if a girl feels drawn to weaving, she can do that. Character, behavior, and roles are not locked to anatomical sex and thus not gendered. Likewise, Anishinaabe men and women have roles, but both learn all activities. Men traditionally go on longer hunts for bigger game and women snare rabbits, but when the situation calls for it, both can do either. Most importantly, biology doesn't convey social status and both cultures value how individual differences contribute to the group and expect roles to be adapted accordingly.

While traditions vary by culture, the majority of Indigenous cultures are gender-balanced. Returning to our earlier example, let's look at Aztec women's roles when the Spanish arrived in 1519.

Feminism, Patriarchy, and the Aztec Empire: Aztec Traditions by Rhianna Rogers[21]

The traditional Aztec social system was based on ideologies of cosmic dualism and parallel gender relations.[22] These created positive roles for women and complimentary relations between genders. As native feminist scholar Enriqueta Longeaux Vasquez states:

> [The position of Pre-Columbian Aztec women] in society was not only free [from patriarchal restraints], but honorable . . . Aztec women held a degree of political influence never equaled by any [European nation], and Mexican women's positions were far superior to that of Spanish women in Spain, then and now.[23]

Since males were primarily occupied with military affairs, often leaving the empire to take part in battles, women controlled the activities that males left behind, that is, government, trades, and crafts. In the religious district, women could act as priestesses, *ixiptlas* (God-like representations, either male or female, which danced, took on the role of individual gods, and sometimes died at Aztec religious festivals) leaders of festivals and rituals, and possessors of the sacred. Within the political world, women had the ability to govern individual *calpoltin*, inherit hereditary positions of power, and participate in selected branches of government. In the socioeconomic marketplace, elite women acted as administrators, buyers, traders, organizers, and merchants, which involved regulating and governing activities important to Aztec society.

Considered the cultural center for life and society in the pre-Hispanic era, the Aztec marketplace was primarily run by females and encompassed an enormous amount of social status and political power. Women could enhance their social positions based on affiliations with traders, merchants, and other vendors. Utilizing effective management skills acquired in the market, women governed with ease in men's absence. Overall, women influenced all aspects of the Aztec world.

While all cultures today are affected by Western values, many retain older egalitarian roots, stories, memories, languages, and practices. To discuss these cultures, we need a new norm table. We've removed white/ person of color and citizen/immigrant. Skin color was not traditionally relevant (there were no characteristics or behavior associated with it until the European invention of racism), and migration and membership were understood completely differently than they are now. For example, when the US divided Ojibwe from Dakota territory, they ignored close relationships between the two nations. In response, Dakota living on the Ojibwe side of the new line were adopted as Ojibwe and became the Wolf Doodem (totem or clan). Similarly, the Dakota adopted the Ojibwe people living in their designated territory.

Table 3.2 Indigenous Cultural Schemas[24]

Pole 1	Pole 2	Indigenous Evaluation
Male	Female	Neutral: no gendered pronouns in many languages. Little or no association with masculine/feminine or man/woman social roles, women warriors, and more.
Poor	Wealthy	Opposite: generosity and equity are valued; wealth is considered greed.
Heterosexual	LGBQT+	Neutral or opposite: fluid understanding of sexuality and in some cases, multiple designations; some consider LGBQT+ people sacred.
Able	Disabled	Opposite: different abilities are appreciated; each person is unique.
Youthful	Elderly	Opposite: Elders are revered for experience, knowledge, and wisdom.
Attractive	Different	Neutral or varied: attraction isn't necessarily based on appearance, and is therefore more personalized, although in some cultures, norms may exist.
Christianity	Other religion	Opposite: Original Instructions are valued over the Great Chain of Being.

Indigenous schemas tend to be neutral. Neither pole is better than the other, each has its own inherent value; they are not predictably evaluative and often oppose Western norms.

When we unlink anatomy and gender, what we call masculinity or femininity isn't required to be a socially respected man or woman. The entire grid of cultural intelligibility that maps the social construction of gender in Western culture doesn't apply, not only because anatomy, behavior, and social roles are not interlocked, but also because both poles of these components are equally valued. Other gender-balanced societies in the Americas include the Apache and various eastern Woodlands tribes.

The Haudenosaunee Confederacy is a matriarchal culture. Clan Mothers form a Council of Matrons, an executive branch that assigns other roles and determines general policy and equitable distribution of corn. Village, tribal, and confederacy councils have legislative branches and implement policies. A joint Matrons' Council and Men's Council oversees the judicial branch of governance. Their Constitution was admired by

Benjamin Franklin, among others, and influenced the formation of the US Constitution by Englishmen with no previous experience of democracy. Other matriarchal Indigenous cultures in the Americas include the Hopi, Lenape, and Chickasaw.

Many Native American societies recognize sexuality in different ways too. Anatomical males may become wives, females may become husbands. There are various understandings of this phenomena, from natural and not worthy of comment, to special and worthy of praise. Homophobia was not part of such traditions. Similarly, those with different abilities are just that: different.

When Indigenous schemas *are* evaluative, they're often the opposite of Western values. For example, in most gender-balanced and matriarchal cultures, because sharing is valued above accumulation, wealth is unacceptable. Because generosity is valued, there are positive representations of "poor," as in the Yoruba praise poem, "Obatala has many cloths, but he wears rags; he has oil and salt, but he eats his food plain."[25] Well-respected, Obatala was showered with gifts but lived simply. By giving to those in need, he earned praise. The exceptional accomplishments of an individual should never undermine equity which is the foundation of community well-being: this is called **communal values**. Some mistakenly oppose it to individuality, but for such cultures, individual/community isn't an opposition. People are encouraged to develop their *individual* talents to contribute *to* community.

Some cultures clearly articulate the **positive value of difference**. In Yoruba, *Ori*, the spark of the Creator's divine consciousness, is a foundational principle. Because everyone and everything has *Ori*, humans are not intrinsically superior to any other being. It is understood that multiple, varying, and sometimes contradictory expressions of *Ori* are necessary for the well-being of a society or an ecosystem as a whole. Beauty is a matter of the distinct nature of individual character; *iwa l'ewa* means character is beauty. In almost every traditional culture, elders are respected and revered. In Anishinaabe, they are called *gichi aya'aa*, literally, great being. In Yoruba, they are considered wise, and elderly women are considered especially powerful.[26]

Just as the Ten Commandments layout principles of behavior in the Judeo-Christian-Islamic lineage, all cultures have guidelines for living. In Yoruba, behavior is measured against the standard *iwa pele*, sometimes translated as good or gentle character. This phrase is elision of the longer phrase *i wa ope ile*, which means "I come to greet the earth."[27] We come to earth through a mother, and longevity on earth cultivates wisdom. Therefore, respect of women and elders is part of *iwa pele*. Yoruba principles are recorded in *Ifa*, an oral text with 256 chapters and innumerable verses. The chapter called *Ika Ofun* includes advice such as don't say what you don't know; don't disorient people nor make them take false roads; never cheat people; don't pretend to be wise; be humble; don't be false; respect the weakest; respect moral laws; respect elders.

Many American Indigenous nations refer to **Original Instructions** on living in accord with Natural Law. The basic principles are evoked by phrases like Circle of Life or All My Relations, similar to *igba iwa* or Calabash of Existence in Yoruba. In both Yoruba and Native American cultures, the sacred spirit of life is recognized in all beings.

We've seen how gentle care for the Earth and her many and diverse children, each with their own *Ori*, is intrinsic to Yoruba thought. Anishinaabe thought identifies four levels of life: Earth (minerals and water), plant, animal, humans. Opposite the Great Chain of Being, humans are not superior but, rather, completely dependent. Humans, the youngest beings on Earth, learned everything about life from plant and animal Elders. For example, we learned to prepare for winter from observing squirrels. Each level is one step removed from the self-sufficiency of minerals and waters. Water, blood of the Earth, moves through seepage, evaporation, and air currents. Water circulation is global and knows no borders. Mother Earth who birthed us is generous and abundant. As long as we respect our Relations and Elders and follow the Original Instructions, She will provide care. For this reason, Indigenous people today are often on the forefront of movements for ecological protection and justice, and women activists generated the phrase "Water is life."

The Original Instructions begin with basic guidelines that developed over time from nation to nation. The Anishinaabe Grandfather Teachings[28] describe how a person should live. They are respect, love, truth, courage, wisdom, generosity, and humility. The Haudenosaunee, after long wars, developed the Great Law of Peace. Its main points[29] are peace, equity and justice, and the power of good minds.[30]

Because humans are biologically wired for cooperation *and* competition, there are guidelines, concepts, and stories for assuring a healthy balance between these two drives. For example, the first of the Anishinaabe Seven Gifts, *minwaadendamowin* (respect), instructs, "place others before yourself in your life, don't look down on anyone. . . . Respect your fellow living beings." *Zaagidiwin* (love) instructs, "I have to love myself before I can love anyone different." The word for humility literally means "He or she does not think that s/he is more important than our relatives, all of the beings that feed, that clothe, that shelter, that heal us . . . we're equal with everyone with whom we have a relationship."[31] Wisdom includes the ability to listen to others' perspectives. As the instructions continue, they maintain balance in various aspects of living.

Indigenous cultures warn what happens if you violate Instructions. Anishinaabe stories tell of the *Wiindigo*, a cannibal who's never satisfied: the more s/he eats, the more s/he wants. S/he's so hungry that s/he chews her/his own lips, and her/his face drips with blood. The only way to cure a *Wiindigo* is to feed him/her boiling hot soup to thaw her/his icy heart. In Yoruba, it's understood that "there can be no personal growth at the expense of others." Conversely, a Yoruba proverb states, "if your life gets better, my life gets better." Reflective practices help a person "identify self-destructive tendencies before others in the community are damaged."[32] If individual imbalances aren't identified and changed, they become communal problems. Communal problems create *elenini*. *Elenini* have no *Ori* of their own (they are not a direct creation of God) but come into existence when greed, anger, fear, and related feelings are fed by multiple individuals in a community.[33]

Western and Indigenous ways of thinking oppose each other in many ways, but people enculturated in different systems are not different kinds of beings—we're all human. Many history texts and much media romanticize Western values and demonize Africans, and demonize or romanticize Native Americans, but this isn't useful to anyone. Terms like *wiindigo* and *elenini* demonstrate that feelings like fear, greed, jealousy, and anger arise, and things do indeed go wrong in Indigenous cultures too. All humans have both impulses, but according to the Indigenous Original Instructions, empathy/cooperation is for daily life, and fight/flight/freeze is for emergencies. Western culture promotes fight/flight/freeze because constant fear maintains ranking. From an Indigenous perspective, a culture that believes bossing others around and having more than others makes you a winner or that greed for authority or goods is something to celebrate is in serious trouble and will get everyone else in trouble, including Earth Herself.

While beliefs separated by space, time, or identity seem wrong to some, members of each group may hold them as inalienable truth. Just as the "truth" that the Sun circles the Earth was revealed as belief, some of what you or I consider to be inalienable truth may be revealed over time as belief.

Cultural Change, Exchange, and Comparison

There are differences between and within cultures, and at any time or place, there are multiple sets of beliefs and values. If this was true in Galileo's time, it's even more true today.

We saw how changing values transformed Galileo from scholar to felon to scientist. But changes to beliefs are typically slow, uneven, and take some doing. Popularized after Galileo's death, the belief that the Earth revolves around the Sun persists. Contemporary physicists, however, show that neither the Earth nor the Sun is immobile. Both are part of a continually shifting galaxy among galaxies. The two bodies rotate *around* each other at radically different speeds. Today's science teachers choose to teach one view or the other.

Sometimes beliefs appear to have changed but are instead relocated. Although it was considered an unshakeable religious truth, the belief *behind* the belief (underlying premise) that the Sun circles the Earth was that man is the center of the universe. Today, a branch of human knowledge, natural science, is considered a source of unshakeable truth. But science is always a work in progress, and we can be sure that what is believed today will be revised or overturned by new knowledge tomorrow. Astrophysicists like Dr. Chandra Prescod-Weinstein, "the 69th Black American woman to get a PhD in physics," study "dark matter, and . . . what happened in the universe during the first second after whatever came before."[34] Such studies center neither the Sun nor the Earth, nor even their relationship. They position dark as something alive and vital, not merely the absence of light and certainly not evil.

Most people now believe the Earth circles the Sun, but some still believe the Sun circles the Earth,[35] which demonstrates how beliefs continue to structure culture long after being challenged. We don't easily shift gears with new information because there are always stakes involved. The stakes of Earth-centric versus Sun-centric incited battles between religious leaders and scientists. What are the stakes of battles between religion and science today? What is the language of these battles?

Facts, it turns out, are often less meaningful to people than stories about them. For example, the Civil Rights movement gave African Americans voting rights, and many Euro-Americans no longer officially believe in ranking human beings according to race. Still, many do believe in white supremacy. This can hide below consciousness in people who think they're unbiased. This was evident when a young #BlackLivesMatter activist confronted Hillary Clinton, a woman who prides herself on "lifting up . . . African American communities," for having referred to some Black children as "super predators," a term that implies they are animalistic.[36] Clinton had to explain that she had been unaware of her bias and had educated herself since she made that statement. This demonstrates that admitting error and changing is valuable to feminist thinking. It also shows that the heritage of the Great Chain of Being still lives in sexism, racism, and other modes of social ranking, even among those who consider themselves feminists. Whether consciously or not, many people still believe that some cultural groups are inherently superior to others. What are the stakes of belief in white supremacy?

Cultures continually change and exchange. Shifting knowledge produces struggle, similar to that endured by Galileo in 16th-century Italy or the Freedom Riders who pursued racial equality in 20th-century US. One battlefield today is climate change. Most Western thinking still holds humans as more important than plants, dirt, water, or animals. Belief in the superiority of wealth, belief that the wealthy deserve whatever they can take from nature, leads to a consumer lifestyle. A consumer lifestyle relies on scientific innovation to produce the latest technological advancements, which rely on mining, drilling, and manufacturing that damage the environment. This set of beliefs forms a self-contradictory grid since the science that produces wealth warns us sharply about this damage. What are the beliefs and values that cause people to deny or affirm climate change? What are the beliefs and values that cause people to ignore the damage that pollution does to some groups? What are the stakes? In the long run, whether you understand nature through resolving contradictions in science and/or through Indigenous knowledge, it's the beliefs in accord with nature that will allow us to thrive on Earth.

Like race and the environment, gender schemas carry stakes too. Sexuality has been perceived radically differently through time and space. In our own lives, we've seen an enormous shift from several hundred years of maligning homosexuality to the Supreme Court's support of same-sex marriage rights, yet hate crimes persist. Although women are no longer officially prevented from studying or producing art, sexism still affects who buys what, influencing modern art just as it did early flower painting trends. The Guerrilla Girls, a group of feminist activist artists, famously noted that "women have to be naked to get into the Met" because "less than 5% of artists in the Modern Art section are women, but 85% of the nudes are female." [37]

Figure 3.9 Guerrilla Girls.
Copyright © Guerrilla Girls, courtesy guerrillagirls.com.

We may assume gender norms to be natural truths because they're present everywhere. In Western cultures, differentiation between males and females begins at birth (pink/blue clothes) and is associated with behavioral characteristics (nurturing/aggressive). As we read in Chapter 1 about Tulik, ideas of how males and females should act to be respected as men and women vary across culture. In some cultures, roles are ranked by gender; in others, they are egalitarian. For example, in North America and Canada, Anishinaabe men are Fire Keepers, and women are Water Keepers. Fire and water are equally essential to life.

European settlers coming to the eastern Americas experienced these crucial differences firsthand. When they arrived in what is now Virginia in 1585, they encountered people who dwelled in well-kept woodlands that seemed park-like, with abundant game and gardens. When the next colony was settled in 1607, those same woodlands were overgrown and wild. The second wave of settlers was unaware that the first wave had decimated Native populations with European diseases. Because Woodlands Indians, as the colonists called them, built portable and biodegradable dwellings, once the land was overgrown there was no sign they had long been settled there. A third group, the Pilgrims, was able to observe thriving northeastern Native cultures, and famously survived because the "Indians" gave them corn and showed them how to live on the land. But their beliefs about these generous people were distorted by the Great Chain of Being, the Doctrine of Discovery, and Manifest Destiny. Primary documents written by Pilgrim patriarchs voice their shock to find that Native women held enormous social value because they managed corn, the heart of the economy. Perhaps they therefore held the men in contempt as Tulik experienced in *Solar Storms*. Understanding these kinds of encounters can help us toward a historically accurate understanding of gender and can alter how we proceed together to renew equitable, sustainable societies.

An enormous number of widely divergent cultures have come in direct contact over the past 500 years, and today we're in constant indirect contact via globalized media. Over those 500 years, border changes led to changes in the citizenship/immigrant schema: in the US, members of the same Indigenous family suddenly found themselves unable to visit when the US/Mexican border changed or when the Canadian/US border was established. Borders drawn by Europeans over the centuries around the world have led to problems that generate confusing or embattled assumptions about who belongs where. These issues continue to trouble Africa and the Middle East. But though the West became economically dominant, cultural influence has always been a two-way street. Indigenous American cultures had a powerful effect on US women's rights[38]; they are the foundation of all our rights due to their influence on the US Constitution, African arts are the roots of many US arts, and so on. Driving forces behind Indigenous Feminisms include remedying injustices rendered during change and inequity resulting from forced exchange and restoration of gender-balanced traditions.

Notes

1 John Trudell. *Trudell*. Dir. Heather Rae. Appaloosa Pictures. 2005.
2 Emmanuel Akyeampong and Pashington Obeng. "Spirituality, Gender, and Power in Asante History." *African Gender Studies: A Reader*. Ed. Oyeronk Oyewumi. Palgrave. 2005.
3 William Greider. *Who Will Tell the People: The Betrayal of American Democracy*. Simon & Schuster. 1992.
4 Marlon Riggs. *Black Is Black Ain't*. California Newsreel. 1995.
5 Matt Weinecke Twitter, 10/14/2019, @MattTW, public domain, https://twitter.com/matttw/status/523833164758675456?lang=en.
6 Derrick Clifton. "11 Stunning Images Highlight the Double Standard of Reactions to Riots Like Baltimore." *Mic.com*. Apr. 27, 2015, https://mic.com/

articles/116680/11-stunning-images-highlight-the-double-standard-of-reactions-to-riots-like-baltimore#.DT3BDG0ma.

7 Chloe Cockburn. "Black People 'Loot;' White People 'Find.'" *ACLU*. Jan. 22. 2010, https://www.aclu.org/blog/speakeasy/black-people-loot-white-people-find.

8 By Menoukha Robin Case.

9 According to Katherine W. Phillips, in her October 1, 2014, *Scientific American*, "How Diversity Makes us Smarter," decades of research by organizational scientists, psychologists, sociologists, economists, and demographers show that socially diverse groups (i.e., those with a diversity of race, ethnicity, gender, and sexual orientation) are more innovative than homogeneous groups. https://www.scientificamerican.com/article/how-diversity-makes-us-smarter/.

10 Audre Lorde. *Our Dead Behind Us*. Norton. 1994.

11 Larry Mays. "Water Technologies in the Pre-Columbian Americas: The Inca." *Ancient Water Technologies*. Jul. 10, 2013, https://ancientwatertechnologies.com/2013/07/10/water-technologies-in-the-pre-columbian-americas/.

12 Andrew Lawler. "Epic Pre-Columbian Voyage suggested by Genes." *Science*. Vol. 346, No. 6208, Oct. 24, 2014, p. 406.

13 Drawing of the Great Chain of Being from Didacus Valades in 1579, *Rhetorica Christiana* public domain, with notations by Menoukha Robin Case, https://commons.wikimedia.org/wiki/File:Great_Chain_of_Being_2_(lighter).png

14 Excerpt adapted with permission by Menoukha Robin Case from "The Spider Woman Rules No More? The Transformation and Resilience of Aztec Female Roles." Rhianna Rogers MA Thesis. Florida Atlantic University, 2004.

15 Fray Diego Durán. *Aztecs: The History of the Indies of New Spain*. Trans. and ed. Doris Heyden and Fernando Horcasitas. Orion Press. 1964, pp. 316–324.

16 Nalia Kabeer. *Reversed Realities: Gender Hierarchies in Development Thought*. Verso. 2003.

17 Juan Luis Vives. *The Life of Juan Luis Vives*. Institutio Feminae Christianae. 1524.

18 By Menoukha Robin Case.

19 Ojibwe Beadwork, Missouri History Museum, Public Domain. https://commons.wikimedia.org/wiki/File:Native_American_beaded_bandolier_bag.jpg

20 Oyeronke Oyewumi. *The Invention of Women: Making an African Sense of Western Gender Discourses*. U Minnesota. 1997; "Conceptualizing Gender: The Eurocentric Foundations of Feminist Concepts and the Challenge of African Epistemologies." *Jenda: A Journal of Culture and African Women Studies*. Vol. 2, No. 1, 2002, https://www.africaknowledgeproject.org/index.php/jenda/article/view/68.

21 Excerpt adapted with permission by Menoukha Robin Case from "The Spider Woman Rules No More? The Transformation and Resilience of Aztec Female Roles." Rhianna Rogers MA Thesis, Florida Atlantic University. 2004.

22 Cosmic dualism is the idea that for society to work harmoniously, both males' and females' existences were complementary, both feeding off each other's reciprocity and paralleling values.

23 Enriqueta Longeaux Vasquez. "Despierten Hermanas! The Women of La Raza—Part II." *Chicana Feminist Thought: The Basic Historical Understandings*. Ed. Alma M. García. Routledge. 1997, p. 111.

24 By Menoukha Robin Case.

25 Ifayemi Elebuibon. *Obatala in Praise*. Hardcore Media. 2000.

26 Teresa N. Washington. *Our Mothers, Our Powers, Our Texts: Manifestations of Àjẹ́ in Africana Literature*. Oya's Tornado. 2018; *The Architects of Existence: Àjẹ́ in Yoruba Cosmology, Ontology, and Orature*. Oya's Tornado. 2014.

27 Falokun Fatunmbi. Personal Conversation with Menoukha Case. 2005.

28 "Anishinaabe Values and Teachings." *White Earth Tribal & Community College.* 2017, http://www.wetcc.edu/mission-vision-and-values.html.

29 Oren Lyons and John Mohawk interviewed by Carol Boss. "Peacekeeping Traditions of the Iroquois Confederacy." *PRX Radio.* Nov. 22, 2005, https://beta.prx.org/stories/7335.

30 Ibid.

31 James Vukelich. "Gichi-aya'aa." *Facebook.* 2018, https://www.facebook.com/james.vukelich.7/videos/10214624727907517/.

32 Falokun Fatunmbi. Personal Conversation with Menoukha Case. 2005.

33 Ibid.

34 Nico Pitney. "Meet the 63rd Black Woman in American History with a Physics PhD." *HuffPost.* June 24, 2015, Updated Dec. 6, 2017, http://www.huffingtonpost.com/2015/06/24/chanda-prescod-weinstein_n_7574020.html.

35 Samantha Grossman. "1 in 4 Americans Apparently Unaware the Earth Orbits the Sun." *Time.* Feb. 16, 2014, http://time.com/7809/1-in-4-americans-thinks-sun-orbits-earth/.

36 Anne Gearon and Abby Phillip. "Clinton Regrets 1996 Remark on 'Super Predators' after Encounter with Activist." *Washington Post.* Feb. 25, 2016, https://www.washingtonpost.com/news/post-politics/wp/2016/02/25/clinton-heckled-by-black-lives-matter-activist/.

37 Guerilla Girls. Last updated 2018, https://www.guerrillagirls.com/.

38 Paula Gunn Allen. "Who is Your Mother? Red Roots of White Feminism." *The Sacred Hoop: Recovering the Sacred in American Indian Traditions.* Beacon. 1992.

4 Indigenous Feminisms

Case Study: Agriculture and Gender Disparity

We've briefly reviewed several feminisms. We'll add to these and explore a few in more depth as we continue. We'll begin a discussion of Indigenous feminism with a case study of corn, a plant heavily affected by relations between Western and Indigenous peoples. Because corn is a Native American plant that became a major global food and was industrialized, it's an excellent example of the dynamics of cultural change, exchange, and comparison.

Gender norms in today's world vary widely. On one side of the spectrum, there are languages that don't include gendered pronouns, like Yoruba, Ojibwe, Malay, and Tagalog, and matrilineal societies, like the Asante of Ghana and the Indonesian Minangkabau. On the other end of the spectrum, women's behavior is strictly regulated, like in Saudi Arabia, where women have only recently been granted the right to drive a car[1] and are prohibited from traveling without male permission.[2] But the global gender landscape is far less varied when it comes to food systems, and women's and men's participation in agriculture is predominantly hierarchical. This is because agribusiness, a form of economic conquest, has affected traditionally gender-balanced and matriarchal communities. Once associated with gender equity, corn has become a global commodity that reveals how gender inequities have spread.

Native American cultures traditionally shared and distributed corn in ways that figuratively and literally cultivated gender equity. Women were responsible for safeguarding corn seeds from one season to another and, during the planting season, for distributing work evenly among tribal members. The community's survival depended on a successful harvest, so each member of the tribe was expected to contribute. Sustainability came through crop rotation, a practice used all over the world by many cultures. It can be as simple as moving where corn is planted each year to preserve the nutrients in the soil, to rotating different kinds of crops in one location. It has been displaced by monoculture—single crops produced in the same soil over and over.

Indigenous agricultural models were largely replaced by Western models, which operated as a kind of agricultural Manifest Destiny. Today, a few multinational corporations own the majority of the world's corn crop and dominate international farmers and farm markets through genome "ownership."[3] The corn we eat today is easier to grow but far less nutritious than its predecessor. And because, as the UN reports, the "main causes of marginalization of indigenous peoples derive from the violation of their right to their traditional land and territories," gender disparity has a great impact on Indigenous women around the world.[4]

This global transformation has historical roots. In England, the law of coverture gave husbands ownership of their wives' property. Well into the 19th century, coverture meant a wife *was* her husband's property. The US followed this legacy directly and indirectly. One direct way was the "Head and Master" law, which said that upon marriage, a woman's property became the property of her husband. The last "Head and Master" law wasn't eliminated until a Supreme Court decision in 1981.[5] An indirect example is the 1887 Dawes Act, which eliminated Native American women's administrative rights to communal land, dividing it into individual parcels owned by "male members of said tribe."[6] Social practice and force of law combined to transform traditionally matriarchal or gender-balanced family structures into patriarchal ones, where men were "heads of household." And though the details of legal and social gender policies differ across culture and geographical region, they consistently disadvantage women. International organizations note, "Women in many of the poorest regions of the world are denied equal rights to access, use, inherit, control, and own land, though they make up an estimated 43 percent of the agricultural labor force."[7]

Because of the way gender is built into agricultural systems, the food we eat every day reflects and reinforces gender hierarchies:

> Women in most societies today continue to carry the responsibility for mental and manual labor of food provision—the most basic labor of care. [...] Women perform the majority of food-related work, but they control few resources and hold little decision-making power in the food industry and food policy.[8]

Participation in agribusiness depends on many variables, including the types of crops that can be grown in a location, how crops are sold and to whom, and expected gender roles. Although women may work more than men, their "contributions are often invisible and unpaid."[9] Women are primary caretakers of children and the home, often referred to as the "second shift," yet are paid less and receive fewer benefits than their male counterparts for the same farmwork (women are often the "preferred" employees for these reasons[10]). Women farmers are obstructed by little or no access to formal education, and agribusinesses almost exclusively award contracts to male farmers.[11]

Because of these persistent inequities, women are on the front lines of changing how food is manufactured, processed, and distributed. Women like Dolores Huerta, co-founder of the United Farm Workers Association, have been instrumental in organizing efforts for better wages and working conditions for all farm laborers, and women continue to be crucial to innovation and progress. There is broad global consensus that gender disparity in agriculture must be evened out. According to the UN, "[i]f women had the same access to productive resources as men, they could increase yields on their farms by 20–30 percent," which could "raise total agricultural output in developing countries by 2.5–4 percent, and in turn reduce the number of hungry people in the world by 12–17 percent."[12] From battling climate change in Zimbabwe[13] to permaculture training sessions in Uganda[14] to vastly increasing numbers of women farmers in India,[15] women are changing the agricultural landscape.

#WTF: What's That Feminism?

Indigenous feminists around the world—like Vandana Shiva in India and Winona LaDuke in the US—are working to restore food equity. We'll begin with the US now and look at Indigenous women's feminisms elsewhere on the globe in Part Three.

Indigenous Feminism by Stephanie A. Sellers[16]

Native American, also called Indigenous, nations had no need for feminism until the European settlers arrived in North America over 500 years ago. The reasons for this include some key differences between Native American nations' cultural values and the values of Western culture that the Europeans brought with them. First, and most importantly, almost all Indigenous nations of the Americas have a female deity in their creation story. Creation stories set up the foundational belief systems of all cultures. Second, many Native nations are woman–centric, mother-right peoples, which means women have key leadership roles in the government and socioeconomic systems and are highly revered. In addition to these fundamental aspects of their cultures, most Native American nations are strongly gendered, with all the sexes (females, males, and transgender) having important, equally valued, roles in the society. Women have their duties and men have theirs. Transgender people decide where they want to belong in this framework. Keep in mind, though, that there are hundreds of Native American nations in the Americas and they all have their unique languages and cultures. In some of those nations, women did not have the centrality or power of mother-right nations, but very few had the types of oppression women experience in Western cultures.

Tragically, after the European settlers arrived, these Native American cultures were brutally challenged and damaged, though most Indigenous nations today still function by their original cultural values that are based in communal ethics. To understand Indigenous Feminism, one must understand communal ethics, which is a cultural belief in the value of everyone in the nation that ensures everyone's needs are met. The community includes not only people but also responsibility to the entire biosphere. Trees, waterways, animals, and the elements are all considered relatives to Native Americans. So, when Indigenous feminists are fighting for rights, they are not fighting only for themselves as women, but for their men relatives, their nations, and for Mother Earth herself. At its core, Indigenous Feminism is about cultural preservation and Indigenous sovereignty. Indigenous Feminism is about fighting the ongoing effects of colonization.

At the time of European colonization, the European Common Law, social practices, and Christian beliefs that the Pilgrims brought with them across the Atlantic Ocean understood women to be less than men: Husbands legally controlled wives and women could not speak in most churches, own property, or vote in elections. Men had the legal and religious right to "discipline" their wives with violence, and women could not divorce such a husband if she wished. Children belonged to fathers, not mothers. These beliefs and practices about women were promulgated throughout North America as the European settlers gradually took over the land and pushed Native American nations further westward, killing and starving them out as they went.

Now that the European colonizers have taken over much of what was once all lands of Native Americans, violence against women, poverty, and cultural-alienation in their communities is rampant. Because of the legacy of colonization, Indigenous women now implement a brand of Indigenous Feminism that focuses far more on rebuilding their communities and traditions rather than elevating women alone. This is how Indigenous Feminisms differ from mainstream American feminisms that focus primarily on ending *women's* oppression. Since Indigenous women are the hearts and culture-keepers of their nations, their survival is critical to the survival of their nations. This is what being an Indigenous feminist means: closely aligning one's self to the traditions of one's people to fight the legacy of European colonization and heal Native American nations.

#WTF: Who's That Feminist?

Nancy Babbitt

A Fortuitous Feminist

I was not raised to be a feminist; I came to embrace feminism later in life. Here is my story.

I grew up in the 1960s and 1970s as a white-skinned girl in a white-skinned, working-class "traditional nuclear family" consisting of a mother, a father, and three children living in a white-skinned upstate New York neighborhood, Whitestown, and educated in the Whitesboro school district. In my early childhood, as was often the case at that time, my father was the wage earner while my mother stayed home raising us children. However, Mother did eventually seek employment due to economic hardships. Her jobs were those typically associated with women, including, first, cleaning hotel rooms; then dishwashing at a childcare facility; and finally acting as a file clerk at an insurance agency, where she was able to "move up" and from where she eventually retired. Of course, these were all low-paying jobs that "supplemented" my father's income. To me, this difference and mental framing were normal, and when I entered adulthood, I did not expect (or desire) anything different in my own life circumstances. To my way of thinking at that time, my purpose in life was to get married, be a "helpmeet" to my husband, and to raise our children. Looking back at my life now (at 50-something years old), I can see how I strove to live out a pre-determined path that was set before me.

I also grew up in a family suffering from addictions, and what I now understand as historical traumas and associated generational cycles of violence. My response to that upbringing is that I was determined to create a life for myself and my children that was different from my early years. I wanted for us a normal, peaceful, and joyous life. I married my knight in shining armor, so to speak. He literally rescued me from a beating by my intoxicated father. I thought that we were going to live happily ever after.

During the next decade of my life, for the most part, I felt safe, as though I was living in a protective cocoon. However, underneath that semblance of protection, there was ongoing turmoil. There was disagreement with in-laws who dealt dishonestly in our shared business and requests from my husband at that time to "keep the peace," which meant that I should submit to the wishes of his parents. Eventually, I left that marriage and joined with another man, who for me, was (again) acting in the role of savior. Since my entry into adulthood, I tended to think of myself as a good submissive wife and later as a good submissive wife and supportive mother. I married, the first time, a man who I believed would be a good protector: strong and gallant. When that marriage failed, I married, the second time, a man who I believed would be a good protector: confident, generous, and wise. It never occurred to me that my life was a sort of Disney fairy tale, and I never asked myself, "Why is there always a damsel in distress in those (my) stories?"

Anyhow, after many more years, I began to ask important questions and search out answers. In particular, and after an unusually tough day at work (one in which I was not able to successfully resolve a conflict), I decided that I needed to go to college to earn what I envisioned as a degree in Peace Studies. My studies began with classes related to conflict resolution. I added those that would help me in understanding people's attitudes and actions, that is, introductory classes in each of the social sciences. Yet I signed up for nothing related to feminism beyond a course dealing with the intersecting social inequalities that we call race, class, and gender. I was still content in my role as submissive wife and supportive mother living her life for the benefit of her husband and sons. However, in many ways, I felt helpless and I knew something was terribly wrong. I was increasingly determined to understand the underpinnings of conflict and social unrest.

Therefore, I signed up for courses related to social inequality, power, and privilege as well those dealing with peace and social change, while I furthered my inquiry of human behavior with more advanced courses in the social sciences. My questions increased. Who were the people who built US wealth, and what were their lives like? Why does our educational system label Native American studies as "Other World Civilizations" and US History as the equally inaccurate and ethnocentric "American History"? America, composed of two continents and many nations, encompasses more than the US and definitively includes Native America. Why, in Western history, was there so much violence toward women? Why, in Western history, have women's voices been too often silenced? My professors guided me with a growing understanding of social inequities and change as well as the fact that we imperfect human beings, because of various cognitive biases, have problems with perception. That is, I began to realize that perhaps the world as I see it is not all there is to see.

For this reason, I began to delve into searching out other ways of knowing and understanding our world. A class titled *Indigenous Knowledge and Ways of Knowing* turned out, to my surprise, to be a social science methodology class, one that focused on methods that differ from those in the Western academy. This is also the time I came across courses with an interesting word in their title: survivance. That term survivance resonated with me and roused my interest in courses that I otherwise would not have considered in my degree plan. So, I added *Native American Plants: Pathways, Prophesies, and Survivance* as well as *Native American Women: Cultural Transformation and Survivance*. These three courses, in particular, helped me to see the world through new eyes and this is the point when I could begin to relate to feminism.

That is to say, prior to the concepts learned in classes focused on indigenous ways of knowing, I thought of feminism in a rather constrained fashion. Perhaps my ideas were shaped by advertising, Virginia Slim cigarettes advertising, in particular. According to their ads, I, as a woman, could earn the bacon, fry it up in a pan, and never ever let him forget he's a man—but did I want that sort of life? I did not see the benefits of taking on the traditional male role of wage earner while still maintaining all of the traditional roles expected of women—cooking, cleaning, and childrearing. That was a feminism to which I did not relate. Nor did I, after years of conditioning to be caring and nurturing, relate to a feminism that dictated women competing to rise on the corporate ladder, which to me involves leaving others behind. In essence, I did not find comfort in a feminism that continued to benefit males disproportionately in their favor, nor did I find comfort in a feminism that was contrary to deeply held values that I associated with womanhood and motherhood, and importantly, I had the privilege to choose otherwise.

Thus, the notion of survivance was an awakening for me. Rather than waiting for the powers that be to shape greater social justice, survivance, as Anishinaabe writer and scholar Gerald Vizenor explains, involves (in part) people standing against domination by making oppression-free spaces for creating and maintaining healthy (healthy means power balanced and reciprocal) relationships and more just and peaceful societies. Survivance, then, is the expression of empowerment in action, but not the sort of power that involves moving up a hierarchy, but rather a power that dismantles the hierarchy by creating a balance where power imbalances exist. That sort of power can be, as explained by Haudenosaunee authors such as Barbara Alice Mann, Patricia A. Monture, and Lina Sunseri, enacted by women as they strive to "Mother their Nations." Survivance is a sort of feminism that I can understand and to which I can readily relate and adopt in my own life circumstances.

That is, I, as a white-skinned woman married to a white-skinned man and having two white-skinned sons, can enter into conflict in my family relationships as I attempt to dismantle the patriarchy. Specifically, I recognize that my husband and sons enjoy white male privilege and it is this very privilege that helps them provide for and keep their family (including me) well and safe. My striving to dismantle the patriarchy can make them feel vulnerable as they become diminished in their positions of power. I can, if I so choose, ignore social inequalities that do not personally affect me and enjoy the privileges bestowed on me by society through my relationship with the white-skinned male power holders. However, approaching issues of inequities and social injustice in the context of creating and maintaining power-balanced and reciprocal relationships helps all parties to feel safe while working to shape change, and that more healthy way of being is as good for the males in my life as it is for me.

In sum, I did not always associate myself with the term feminist. In fact, for much of my life, I was more anti-feminist than feminist. I came to relate to the term feminist quite unintentionally. Looking back, I perceive that, to me, becoming feminist is much like rising up out of a fog—white fog. Native American women authors, in particular, have shown me that I no longer need to play out the female role prescribed in fairytales of European origin, of damsel in distress waiting for my hero, my knight in shining armor, or prince charming to save me so that we can live happily ever after. I can instead rise up and become a mature human being doing feminism by doing what is healthy for me and my family as well as others. Creating greater health and well-being in this way is accomplished by building equity through the establishment and maintenance of healthy power-balanced and reciprocal relationships that, in turn, shape greater social justice, which leads to forming more peaceful societies.

Roberto Múkaro Borrero

A Taíno Perspective on Feminism

Thinking on the subject, I can honestly say that I did not have a positive image of feminism growing up in the US. My perspective has changed over time, and today, I stand in solidarity because for me, feminism is fundamentally concerned with upholding and implementing human rights as well as basic respect and equity. Recalling conversations of my youth, however, when the topic of feminism arose, the dialogue seemed to always quickly digress into how those women, "the feminists," wanted to control, rule over, or even be men. As outrageous and uneducated as that may sound, unfortunately there are those who still believe this rhetoric. For these people, there is a certain underlying notion that links feminism with a threat to what some consider the traditional American societal norm, which is based on patriarchy. Like many people these days, I link these abhorrent and discriminatory anti-feminist viewpoints to male chauvinism and sexism.

With this understanding, coming from a family whose roots are in what is now considered the Latin American Caribbean, I am fully aware that discriminatory, anti-feminist views are not limited to the US alone. Unfortunately, this is a global phenomenon. For instance, the tendency for anti-feminism can also be considered a traditional viewpoint of a significant portion of the general populace throughout the Latin American and the Caribbean. From my understanding of history, the insular area of the region was the Western Hemisphere's first breeding ground for the export of the cultural phenomenon called *machismo* following the arrival of Columbus in the so-called New World. Analogous to patriarchy, machismo has similar connotations in English, Spanish, and Portuguese, being, as Webster's Dictionary describes, a "strong sense of masculine pride" or an "exaggerated masculinity."[17] At its core, machismo is an inflated sense of male power, manliness, and virility, but it does not stop there. In my view, the promotion of machismo, and its assumption that masculinity is superior to femininity, has generationally institutionalized hyper-masculinity and gender imbalance in ways that affect virtually every aspect of life in the region in tandem with "isms" like racism and colonialism.

Evidence gleaned from the period soon after the arrival of Columbus is clear that the views on gender equality from a then emerging Europe clashed with the views of my indigenous Taíno ancestors, whose society, by all accounts, held women in a much higher esteem. Firsthand statements from Spaniards along with archeological evidence should affirm for those outside Taíno communities that women significantly, if not equally, participated in and contributed to Taíno society.[18] Further, the cultural collision between the "Old and New Worlds" was not only a secular clash but also a spiritual one as generations of indigenous islanders previously saw the very creation of all life emerging first from the sacred feminine energy. In Taíno cosmovision, it is *Atabeira* who gave birth to *Iukahu Bagua Maorokoti*, the solar spirit of the *iuka* (yuca/manioc) and the sea, who was without a male ancestor. It is *Guabonito*, the sacred matriarch, who first brought the healing arts and presented the symbols of leadership to the people. It is *Guabanseh* who is the ultimate manifestation of one of the most powerful elemental forces the people knew—she is the winds and the rains of the hurricane. This indigenous, foundational relationship with feminine divinity was in great contrast to the views of the Spanish colonizers whose higher power was a male entity, who transferred authoritative leadership to human males, and who, in turn, exercised dominion over women in the same way they exercised dominion over the land and all manner of life.

Following the arrival of Columbus, the horrors of the Western Hemisphere's brutally sadistic conquest period and its devastating, multi-generational effects on Indigenous Peoples, especially Indigenous women, are well documented. For over 500 years, local, national, and regional manifestations of dominion accompanied by racism, chauvinism, misogyny, and sexism continue to entrench themselves wherever they can, at times shape-shifting in attempts to normalize their continuous efforts to propagate and perpetuate. The struggle is real, but there are signs of progress as visibility continues to be raised, and the resistance gains ground. While keeping in mind the complexities and particularities of each case, in the Latin American and Caribbean region, for example, 11 women have attained the position of head of state since 1974.[19] We are yet to see this type of shift in the US or Canada.

Even with these signs of political progress, there is still a long way to go as the region lags behind globally. Throughout Latin America and the Caribbean, gender equity and the full exercise of women's rights is linked to political parties, parliaments and governing bodies adapting their legal frameworks, rules, ethics, altitudes, and behaviors to ensure the equitable treatment and representation of women.[20] With this backdrop, it seems that quota or parity legislation is an essential strategy as it has proven to be effective in several countries in the region.[21] Still, women striving for or in political positions long held by men only face especially high degrees of scrutiny as deeply rooted machismo attitudes continues to systematically perpetuate patriarchy. Beyond the notable achievements in the political realm, however, general progress toward gender-balance and equity in the Latin American and Caribbean region in most social spheres is alarmingly limited.

According to the UN, for instance, just in the last decade the numbers of women entering in the region's workforce has dramatically increased. While this seems positive, wage gap data reveals that women earn between 60 percent and 90 percent of men's average income.[22] While this example of inequality is distressing, and economic status varies among countries, the UN also affirms significant inequities between women themselves. Variables include ethnic or indigenous identity, age, and citizenship, among others.[23] Similar gaps and inequalities among women in the region are just as disconcerting when the focus turns to poverty, health care, education, and violence against women, which the international community identifies as a public health problem, a violation of human rights, and a barrier to economic development.[24]

These more specific circumstances of inequity between women underscore why many indigenous and other women of color are often concerned and vocal when they are overlooked in mainstream feminism activism. Furthermore, for many indigenous women in Latin America and the Caribbean, in particular, feminism as a movement cannot ignore and needs to intersect directly with other issues such as racism and colonialism.[25] For these women, equality moves beyond social exclusion and gender issues to an issue of balance between people and nature. As a Taíno man and a human rights advocate, I fully support these holistic views expressed by my sisters as they acknowledge that the empowerment of and equity for Indigenous Peoples, and especially Indigenous women, is not only a secular clash of ideas. It is also a moral and spiritual battle that links directly to the fate of all life on this planet.

It is within this context that I stand in solidarity with the feminist movement and why we should fully support systematic change that empowers all women within and beyond their communities at the national, regional, and international level. The empowerment and contributions of women are critical not only for reaching vital global sustainable development and climate action goals, but also to renew the sacred relationship between humans and the natural world.

Many Indigenous women recall gender equity as fundamental to their cultures and can recount how it was lost. Ojibwe Elder Mary Moose explained that "everything men had, they had received from women, and women had played equal roles in polity . . . Europeans, used to dominating their own women and wanting to maintain that ascendency at all costs, kidnapped, enslaved, raped, tortured, and harmed Anishinaabe women. In response, the men hid the women to protect them. This disrupted bilateral power within tribes as women lost the ability to participate in the political and ceremonial realms. European norms were internalized and still affect women today."[26]

In response, Indigenous women offer a unique approach to gender inequity.

Paula Gunn Allen by Stephanie A. Sellers

Paula Gunn Allen (1939–2008) was a Laguna Pueblo Native American poet and scholar who was one of the primary founders of Native American Women's Studies. Her seminal work *The Sacred Hoop: Recovering the Feminine in American Indian Traditions* (Beacon Press 1986) was a landmark book that helped establish the Native American Studies discipline overall and launch her career that made her an international icon. A professor at University of California at Berkeley and later Los Angeles (1986–1999),

Figure 4.1 Paula Gunn Allen.[27]

her poetry and scholarship have earned prestigious recognition that includes a nomination for a Pulitzer Prize and the Hubbell Medal for Lifetime Achievement in American Literature, among others. A lesbian and outspoken advocate for women and Native American rights, Allen inspired generations of students and writers during her lifetime and continues to reach out through the legacy of her works. As she often said, "She who tells the story rules the world." The story of Dr. Gunn Allen's life was to create a body of knowledge that demonstrated how Indigenous women and the divine creatrix have always been centralized in Native American traditions and to bring that cultural reality into the academy, despite colonial opposition from the power-brokers in the Ivory Tower. She discredited the stories about Indians promulgated by ethnocentric anthropologists and historians who set the prevailing beliefs about the First Americans in the academy. Her contemporaries describe her as a sharp-witted, compassionate genius who unrelentingly fought the effects of colonization on Native communities and oppression in all its guises. Allen hinted at her reputation as a fighter by cautioning audiences at her hundreds of speaking venues from UCLA to Harvard with an impish twinkle in her eye, "Remember, there's a gun in my name."

Gunn Allen's essay "'Who Is Your Mother?' Red Roots of White Feminism"[28] explains how the US itself entered feminism through contact with Native peoples. You can read this essay online. Early interactions with matriarchal native nations shocked and surprised colonists and changed European women's thinking. It's no coincidence that the 1848 first women's rights convention in the US was held in Seneca Falls, home to the matriarchal Seneca people. Many Native Americans will tell you that they don't need the F-word: They just need colonialism to get out of the way of their traditionally egalitarian, gender-balanced, or matriarchal cultures. Roberto Múkaro Borrero described this from the perspective of the Taíno, the first people encountered by Columbus. Borrero is a Cacique of the Taíno tribe and active in the UN, so he often includes his point of view in international venues.[29] They demonstrate that personal entry stories like Babbitt's and Borrero's are part of collective stories. Collectives that share a narrative are the roots of movements.

#IdleNoMore is a North American Indigenous movement that has gone global. It was started by **Nina Wilson** (*Nakota and Plains Cree*, Kahkewistahaw First Nation), **Sylvia McAdam** (Cree, nêhiyaw Nation), **Jessica Gordon** (*Pasqua Treaty 4 Territory)*, and **Sheelah McLean** (*Scottish and Scandinavian*) to protest the 2011 Canadian Bill C-45 which deregulated waterways so tar sands pipelines could cross First Nations' lands; 99 percent of Canadian waterways lost protection. In Anishinaabe culture, women, as Water Keepers, work to maintain or restore the health of bodies of water through activism and prayer.[31] Some women, following **Josephine Mandamin**, circumambulated the Great Lakes and walked the traditional Anishinaabe Migration Route followed from 1000 to 1500 CE, performing traditional Water ceremonies each step of the way and raising awareness of abuses of Water.[32] **Chief Theresa Spence** of the Attawapiskat First Nation went on a six-week hunger strike on behalf of the waters as well as the women

Figure 4.2 #IdleNoMore.[30]

who defend them, including protest about the murders and disappearances of Native women.[33] Other Anishinaabe women, such as **Winona LaDuke** (previous Green Party vice presidential candidate), are working to prevent mining, pipelines, and fracking from occurring on sovereign Native lands.

Native activist/feminists like **Rene Ann Goodrich** ally with other feminists, such as ecofeminists

Figure 4.3 #NativeLivesMatter and #BlackLivesMatter Coalition Minneapolis, MN, Formed by Rene Ann Goodrich (see Chapter 10).[34]

and Black feminists. There has been controversy about hashtags like #BlackLivesMatter and **#NativeLivesMatter**, with some people insisting that all lives matter. Certainly, from the perspective of Natural Law, all life does matter, but the "all lives matter" hashtag is only designed to detract from social justice movements that call attention to inequity.

While the justice system works quite well to protect white American lives, it fails miserably when it comes to people of color, as demonstrated by racial profiling, police shootings, uneven sentencing, false imprisonments, and much higher incidents of rape among women of color (especially Native women raped by white men), yet much lower rates of indictment and imprisonment of perpetrators. Since they are concerned with the bodily safety of all people of color,

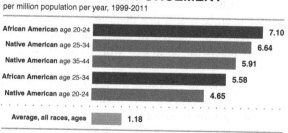

TOP 5 GROUPS MOST LIKELY TO BE KILLED BY LAW ENFORCEMENT
per million population per year, 1999-2011

African American age 20-24	7.10
Native American age 25-34	6.64
Native American age 35-44	5.91
African American age 25-34	5.58
Native American age 20-24	4.65
Average, all races, ages	1.18

Native Americans
are the most likely to be killed by law enforcement. With less than 1% of the population, Native Americans comprise nearly 2% of police killings

Source: Center for Juvenile and Criminal Justice

Figure 4.4 Police Shootings by Race.[35]

#BlackLivesMatter and #NativeLivesMatter have allied to address why these two groups are killed by police in disproportionately high numbers.

Conclusion: The Stakes of Difference

Western methods of ranking make inequity normal. They make difference negative rather than positive, constructing cultural others. Historically, they have exploited or oppressed cultural others. Without mass murder (genocide), nations could not conquer other nations; without resource extraction, unpaid labor (slavery), or poorly paid labor, they could not build empires. From the perspective of gender-balanced cultures, Western cultures use a terribly wrong schema—they organize and control the majority for the benefit of a few, at the ultimate expense of the Earth, affecting us all. Belief in the Great Chain of Being, which values white men above everything else in creation, cannot sustain equity; it cannot sustain life on Earth.

The stakes are high and the effects are enormous, so we need to learn to listen. Within Western culture, the only obvious choices are to perform within or against norms. We need schemas that don't divide us into valued norm/devalued other. These schemas already exist in Indigenous cultures. Societies organized around the value of difference shift as needed to benefit the whole. Difference places everyone within as a positive contributing member rather than an outsider. The only difference that would place you outside would be divergence from the Original Instructions. A key signal of that divergence is greed.

Why then do most Western feminists barely glance toward Indigenous cultures for clues on different ways of structuring societies? Most don't look seriously at Africans and Native Americans for advancements, since deeply ingrained cultural schemas (like Manifest Destiny) still consider them primitive. Westerners have an uphill battle against millennia of patriarchy. They or we have to dig deep into pre-history to unearth a layer of cultural history that it is truly egalitarian. On the other hand, gender-balance is still practiced or was in effect until relatively recently and is still remembered in many Indigenous cultures, who can turn to cultural practices, bodies of work like *Ifa*, and oral histories to restore equity.

Why should we consider this? Why can it succeed? It can succeed because gender oppression isn't natural; quite the reverse, it's a thin skin on the body of human history.

Before we turn to women-led movements in Part Three, let's dismantle certain assumptions that originally shaped much of Western feminist thought, action, and the academic field of WGSS itself (what Sellers referred to as "mainstream feminism"). Although we've definitely seen growth beyond these assumptions, they're worth consideration since they're still embedded in the title of the field.

Western, white, or mainstream feminisms have historically assumed that:

- Women have been universally oppressed by men throughout time and across places.
- US and European feminism initiated in the 19th century is central to women's rights.
- WGSS are primarily relevant to women and the differently gendered.

Let's take a logical, step-by-step look at the stakes of these assumptions.

- If we believe men have universally oppressed women, we must believe this is human nature.
- If we believe it is human nature, we must believe that working for gender equity is a battle against nature.
- We may therefore believe we need to evolve (a natural science concept) or invent alternative societies (a social science concept) to fundamentally alter (human) nature.
- Belief that evolution = improvement reinforces a core value of patriarchy (the Great Chain of Being).
- Belief that Westerners need to invent alternative societies erases the matriarchal and gender-balanced societies that patriarchy has tried to destroy.

Fortunately, none of these assumptions are true:

- There have always been and still are matriarchal and gender-balanced cultures, including in the US.
- There have been and are women-led movements around the world arising for different reasons depending on time, location, and culture.
- These movements tend to take into account conditions for all humans and the way humans and the natural world intertwine.

Western feminist assumptions keep us trapped in a battle against what we erroneously believe to be human nature, in ignorance of historical realities. This restricts possibilities for new learning and diverse alliances. It can cause us to expend considerable time and energy re-inventing wheels that have already been rolling for eons.

Removing these assumptions reveals that resistance to all forms of inequity, not just male oppression, has a better claim on universality. This aligns with contemporary scientific theories that humanity's deepest ancestral wiring is for compassion and cooperation. If we choose to believe and value this, we may ask: How did we humans relate all those millennia before the patriarchal problem arose? Where and how is that mode of relating remembered today? How have non-patriarchal cultures adapted and survived through millennia, leaving hints that drive scientific exploration about equity?

Feminisms have always changed and grown, and we are suggesting ways that can continue. Mid-20th-century liberal feminists like Betty Friedan offered astounding insights from within the master's house that gave middle-class, stay-at-home moms a view beyond his windows. However, she only addressed the man/woman schema, leaving it to Black, Latina, and Native feminists of the same period to offer an inclusive analysis of all the tools that maintain the master's house. The master's tools are clearly and consciously deployed in education, media, and politics to construct levels in the house, an upstairs/downstairs. By respecting differences and valuing what different feminisms offer, each of us can clearly and consciously choose methods that construct our shared lives differently. All we need to do to start is ask questions.

Now that we have new tools, we can explore how thinking has translated into action, looking at groups who challenged assumptions in various times and places. What are the stakes that concern you? What battles do you face?

Notes

1 Despite the ban being overturned, women have continued to be arrested for driving as late as May 18, 2018. See Kim Ghattas. "Saudia Arabia's Dark Nationalism." *The Atlantic.* June 2, 2018, https://www.theatlantic.com/international/archive/2018/06/saudi-arabia-nationalism-driving-ban-salman/561845/.

2 Kristine Beckerle et al. "Boxed In: Women and Saudia Arabia's Male Guardianship System." *Human Rights Watch.* July 16, 2016, https://www.hrw.org/report/2016/07/16/boxed/women-and-saudi-arabias-male-guardianship-system.

3 Jane Wells. "Who Owns Seeds? Monsanto Says Not You." *CNBC.* Feb. 15, 2013, https://www.cnbc.com/id/100464458. See also *Bowman vs. Monsanto,* Supreme Court. Oct. 2012, https://www.supremecourt.gov/opinions/12pdf/11-796_c07d.pdf.

4 Food and Agriculture Organization of the United Nations. Last updated 2019, http://www.fao.org/indigenous-peoples/en/.

5 Kirchberg V. Feenstra. 450 U.S. 455 (1981), https://supreme.justia.com/cases/federal/us/450/455/case.html.

6 Transcript of Dawes Act (1887). US National Archives & Records Administration. Last updated Mar. 14, 2019. http://www.ourdocuments.gov/doc.php?doc=50&page=transcript.

7 "What We Do." *Landesa Rural Development Institute.* 2019, https://www.landesa.org/what-we-do/womens-land-rights/.

8 Patricia Allen and Carolyn Sachs. "Women and Food Chains: The Gendered Politics of Food." *International Journal of Sociology of Food and Agriculture.* Vol. 15, No. 1, Apr. 2007, p. 1.

9 "The Cost of the Gender Gap in Agricultural Productivity in Malawi, Tanzania, and Uganda." *UN Women, UNDP, UNEP, and the World Bank Group.* Oct. 2015, http://www2.unwomen.org/~/media/headquarters/attachments/sections/library/publications/2015/costing%20gender%20gap_launch.pdf?v=1&d=20151015T142608.

10 Ibid., p. 7.

11 See "The Role of Women in Agriculture" (2011). Prepared by the SOFA Team and Cheryl Doss on behalf of the Food and Agriculture Organization of the United Nations. http://www.fao.org/docrep/013/am307e/am307e00.pdf.

12 "Women in Agriculture: Closing the Gender Gap for Development." The State of Food and Agriculture: 2010–2011. *Food and Agriculture Organization of the United Nations.* Rome. 2011.

13 Tonderayi Mukeredzi. "How Women Farmers Are Battling Climate Change in Zimbabwe." *Integrated Regional Information Networks.* Mar. 8, 2017, https://www.irinnews.org/feature/2017/03/08/how-women-farmers-are-battling-climate-change-zimbabwe.

14 "Breaking the Glass Ceiling: Empowering Women Farmers." *The World Bank.* Mar. 6, 2018, http://www.worldbank.org/en/news/feature/2018/03/06/breaking-the-grass-ceiling-empowering-women-farmers.

15 Belinda Goldsmith. "Female Farmers Gaining Ground in Rural India." *LiveMint.* Feb. 13, 2017, https://www.livemint.com/Politics/1iUQ4HpE8OvTdUfQ2HZQCJ/Female-farmers-gaining-ground-in-rural-India.html.

16 Indigenous Studies can include peoples who have maintained early traditional roots native to any continent. In this essay, Dr. Sellers focuses on the Americas.

17 "Machismo." *Merriam Webster Dictionary.* Last updated Feb. 18, 2019, https://www.merriam-webster.com/dictionary/machismo.

18 Nicholas Pineiro and Karanja Keita Carroll. "The Impact of Patriarchy on Latin American and Caribbean Cultures." May 18, 2012, http://www.academia.edu/6713964/The_Impact_of_Patriarchy_on_Latin_American_and_Caribbean_Cultures.

19 "Women Presidents of Latin America." *BBC News.* Oct. 31, 2010, http://www.bbc.com/news/world-latin-america-11447598.

20 Rosina Wiltshire. "Women in Political Office; LA and the Caribbean." Organization of American States. Last updated 2019, https://www.oas.org/es/sap/deco/jornada_5/present/RosinaWiltshire_e.pdf.

21 Nikhil Kumar. "The Machismo Paradox: Latin America's Struggles with Feminism and Patriarchy." *Brown Political Review.* Mar. 30, 2014, http://www.brownpoliticalreview.org/2014/04/the-machismo-paradox-latin-americas-struggles-with-feminism-and-patriarchy/.

22 "What Gender Inequality Looks Like in Latin America." *HuffPost.* Jan. 23, 2014, https://www.huffingtonpost.com/2014/01/23/gender-inequality-latin-america_n_4653710.html.

23 "The ILO in Latin America and the Caribbean." *International Labor Office.* 2014, http://www.ilo.org/wcmsp5/groups/public/---americas/---ro-lima/documents/publication/wcms_243878.pdf.

24 "Violence Against Women in Latin American and the Caribbean." *Hemisphere.* Vol. 22, No. 1, Article 1. 2013, 20, 2013, http://digitalcommons.fiu.edu/cgi/viewcontent.cgi?article=1007&context=lacc_hemisphere.

25 Catherine Lefevre. "Indigenous Feminism within Latin America." *Global Policy Watch.* Jan. 20, 2014, https://globalpublicpolicywatch.org/2014/01/20/indigenous-feminism-within-latin-america/; Ellen-Rose Kambel. "A Guide to Indigenous Women's Rights under the International Convention on the Elimination of All Forms of Discrimination Against Women." *Forest Peoples Programme.* 2004, p. 3, http://www.forestpeoples.org/sites/fpp/files/publication/2010/10/cedawguidejan04eng.pdf.

26 Menoukha Robin Case. "Last Report on the Miracles at Aazhoomog, Lake Lena." *All About Mentoring.* Vol. 50, 2017, pp. 20–24, https://www.esc.edu/

media/ocgr/publications-presentations/all-about-mentoring/AAM-50-Spring-2017.pdf.

27 Permission granted by authors, who now own all rights to the book.

28 Paula Gunn Allen. "History Is A Weapon." *The Sacred Hoop: Recovering the Feminine in American Indian Traditions.* 1986, http://www.historyisaweapon.com/defcon1/allenredrootsofwhitefeminism.html.

29 Roberto Borrero. "Mr. Roberto Borrero—International Treaty Council speaks at UN." *UN NGLS. YouTube.* Feb. 1, 2016, https://www.youtube.com/watch?v=8TH0FGD1rto.

30 Quinn Dombrowski, 2013, Creative Commons, https://commons.wikimedia.org/wiki/File:Idle_no_more_(9179654965).jpg.

31 Renee Elizabeth Mzinegiizhigo-kwe Bedard, "Keepers of the Water." *Lighting the Eighth Fire.* Ed. Leanne Simpson. Arbeiter Ring Publishing. 2008, pp. 89–106.

32 Ayse Gursoz. "Meet Josephine Mandamin (Anishinaabekwe), the 'Water Walker.'" *Indigenous Rising.* Sept. 25, 2014, http://indigenousrising.org/josephine-mandamin/.

33 Kady O'Malley. "Full Text of Declaration That Will End Attawapiskate Chief's Six-Week Protest." *Inside Politics.* Jan. 23, 2015, http://www.cbc.ca/newsblogs/politics/inside-politics-blog/2013/01/full-text-of-declaration-that-will-end-attawapiskat-chiefs-six-week-protest.html.

34 We're still working on permissions for these and had requested help from Routledge via Erik. We have permission from Ms Goodrich who is pictured, but not from the photographer.

35 Data is from Center on Juvenile and Criminal Justice. http://www.cjcj.org/news/8113 Approved: Renee Menart renee@cjcj.org
    However the table of the data was prepared by Aljazeera. Maybe need to make a new rendition of this but it is extremely basic, so it wouldn't really change.

Part Three

Times and Places

Introduction: Challenging Authority

Because cultures have distinct ways of thinking in different times and places, women's experiences of patriarchy differ widely. Indigenous and Western women, rich and poor women, old and young women, brown and white women, heterosexual and lesbian women, able-bodied and disabled women have different experiences, and so on. We saw that things that are positive in one culture may be negative in another (wealth: glory or greed); binaries that are evaluative in one place (gender) may be neutral in another place or not exist in another time (race). Here, we'll look at how women's movements have responded to these variations, shaping distinct feminisms around the world.

Humans are mobile and social. As we travel, cultures blend and clash and ways of thinking continually change. Yet, whatever the place and whenever the time, core biology remains the same. We are always in the midst of unfolding history, sparking movements to shift inequities and transform the world.

Part Three provides tools to identify how authority is maintained and examples of how people resist it. The previous case study examined corn's global impact on gender inequity; our next case study examines how the beauty industry effects women's experiences of patriarchy across the globe.

5 Power and Authority

How We See the World

Maps shape how we think of the world. If asked to picture the world, what would you see? Now, ask yourself why that's the image of the world you have. How might a map of the world have looked hundreds of years ago, before the advent of satellite imagery in 1959? One of the earliest world maps was designed in the 2nd century by Ptolemy. It looks pretty strange to us now. People in the 21st century are more likely to identify with a view of the Earth from space, like NASA's "Blue Marble" photograph, which was first taken in 1972.

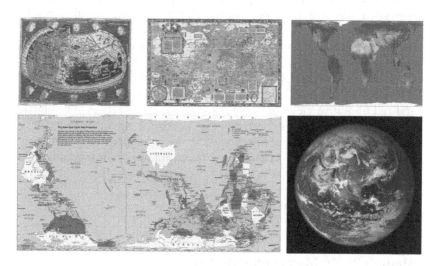

Figure 5.1 Map Projections.[2]
Top left to bottom right: Ptolemy (150); Mercatur (1569); Peters (1974); Hobo-Dyer (2002). Courtesy Richard Smith, TranspacificProject.com; "Blue Marble" (2002), NASA Goddard Space Flight Center Image by Reto Stöckli.

One of the best-known maps was created in 1569 by Gerardus Mercatur. This is what most people think of when asked to picture a world map. But what if they knew the Mercatur, like all maps, is a projection and isn't accurate? In fact, it doesn't claim to be. A projection is something geographers use to map three-dimensional objects onto a flat, two-dimensional plane. You can't make a spherical object flat without distorting it. That's why a flat map of a spherical surface is called a projection.

Map projections differ based on their aims. Mercatur's map was designed for nautical purposes. Because of the ocean's great expanse, ships needed to follow the most direct route from one point on the globe to another, and Mercatur's map provided clear latitude and longitude lines to do so. If the goal is to safely sail from one continent to another, the size of the continents themselves is less important.

Continent size in the Mercatur projection isn't just a little off, it's a lot off. Africa, for example, is far larger than Mercatur shows it. It's "bigger than China, India, the contiguous U.S. and most of Europe—combined!"[1] 1970s geographers showed that map projections don't just distort topography but also people's opinions: our idea of a continent's size shapes our attitudes toward its inhabitants. This is where other projections come in. The 1974 Peters projection is an "area accurate" map that attempts to show continents' relative size. Africa is clearly the largest of the seven continents. The 2002 Hobo-Dyer projection map goes further. Hobo-Dyer is two-sided, one with the Northern hemisphere up, making Africa central, and the other with the Southern hemisphere up, making Australia central.[3] You can research what the other differences are, and as you do, think about the ways your perceptions of the world might shift. The goal of Peters and Hobo-Dyer projections is to challenge popular perceptions of how we see the world. Keep this in mind as we explore how people's literal and figurative views of world shape beliefs and practices. The practice of projecting one culture's viewpoint on another is a master's tool that has been used to justify acts of domination. How is it supported by Mercatur? How is it challenged by Hobo-Dyer? In the masters' ranking, how much does size count?

Feminist Toolbox: Analyzing Systems of Authority

Master's Tools: Maintaining Authority

Hierarchy, a ranking system exemplified by The Great Chain of Being, is the foundation of Western culture. It enforces systems of supremacy or, as John Trudell describes it, systems of authority. It celebrates wealth rather than sharing and operates via exploitation rather than mutual thriving. It leads to beliefs like Manifest Destiny that valorize conquest. Conquerors may exploit a defeated nation's resources and labor in a variety of ways. **Imperialism** is the practice of extending a country's dominance beyond its traditional borders, usually beginning with military force and later employing economics and culture as weapons. **Colonialism** occurs when members of a dominant country establish settlements—farms, towns, cities, governmental, judicial, and military structures—on the subject country's land, displacing their traditional homesteads, earning activities, and governance organizations. Settling permanently in a foreign land is called **settler colonialism**.

Types of conquest are not always separate, nor are they locked to time and place. For example, conquest extended across time when children forcibly taken from their parents and raised as servants in military-style US and Canadian Indian Boarding Schools transmitted this trauma to future generations. This is known as intergenerational or historical trauma. Slavery, with its practices of rape and tearing apart families, also generated historical trauma. Capturing and enslaving people from one invaded country (an African nation) and exporting them to a settlement (colonial America) mixed imperialism with colonialism in distant places. Canada, with its continued ties to the British crown, mixes settler colonialism and imperialism. Colonists' primary focus is land ownership, while imperialism focuses on extracting resources, human and otherwise. The two go hand in hand because if you own the land, you can alter it or extract from it at will. Settler governments altered tribal governance, and cities, dams, and mines destroyed traditional ecosystems.

Because settlers are patriarchal and most Indigenous groups are egalitarian, the effect on Indigenous American women has been especially horrific; rape and domestic violence were unusual and harshly condemned in traditional societies, but sex-trafficking and even murder have become an all too common way for settlers to treat Indigenous women, even to this day. Similarly, Africans from matriarchal and gender-balanced cultures saw their women reduced to chattel and raped to produce more slaves in the US and Central and South America, and some of the attitudes about Black women that slaveholders used to rationalize this violence are still with us today.

Not everyone believed that non-European (non-white) people were not human. Some French supported Haitian independence, some Americans were abolitionists, and some whites respected Native Americans. But they were the minority, and the actions that resulted in the world we know today were based on the assumptions of white superiority and that imperial invasions and colonial settlements were the will of God. Europeans considered it their Manifest Destiny to conquer and rule not only the Americas but also other continents, such as Africa, and other nations, such as India, ignoring the already richly complex civilizations there. The extent to which beliefs can obscure our vision is remarkable. It is why, even though 15th-century Africa boasted cities with more sophisticated technology and governance than late medieval European cities, the tales "discoverers" brought back to Europe only described naked people in jungle huts. Even in today's media, the West largely shows negative images of Africa.[4] Rationalizing exploitation requires an us/them mentality, with us being the norm and them being the other.

Imperialism and colonialism work hand in hand, leaving almost no corner of the world untouched. All contemporary cultures are affected by Western cultures to some degree.

Hegemony refers to one group (and its beliefs) dominating another or beliefs within a group dominating its members. Yes, a culture can dominate itself. The field of Cultural Studies examines how institutions (schools, media, religion, laws, etc.) promote or enforce hegemonic belief systems. Perhaps the central beliefs most Westerners hold are (1) dominance is inevitable, and (2) ranking is valuable. These beliefs direct many political, monetary, and ecological decisions.

When cultural others challenge hegemonic beliefs, they're met with the master's tools. For example, African or Native religions are thought of as superstition. Beliefs about the cultural other are carried in stereotypes.

Stereotype is a tool for maintaining authority. When a culture defines a group as other, they go beyond differences in expression, such as cuisine or clothing, and imagine them as a different type of being. Stereotypes give positive or negative weight to cultural schemas, and because we are all raised with them, they are deeply connected with our emotions and affect how we understand each other.

Let's look at the dynamics of one stereotype. It began with Plato's schema, civilian/barbarian. Barbarian originally had nothing to do with race and just meant anyone not Greek. Here's how Europeans applied it to Indigenous people, one evaluative binary after another.

1 Because Western culture was hierarchical, they believed domination was superior to cooperation (domination-strong/cooperation-weak), and because violence is necessary to dominate, they believed it's basic to human nature.

2 "Natural" human violence is considered civilized when in the service of a monarch or nation (civilized-good/barbarian-bad).

3 When Europeans inserted race in the Great Chain of Being, barbarian was translated as "savage" and associated with the brown skin of Indigenous people. Brown skin had not previously been an issue and the hierarchical North African Moors were respected in 16th-century Europe, but Indigenous Americans were assigned a lower position on the Chain partly because they were egalitarian rather than monarchical.

Because of this, Europeans believed their violence was "uncivilized" (civilized-good/savage-bad).

4   This rationalized pro-active attacks against Natives to prevent their "untamed" violence. Attacks were considered defense even when Natives were welcoming and generous (well, yes, they also attacked because they wanted Native land or resources). This circles back to domination-strong/cooperation-weak.

Europeans distorted reality and created a feedback loop to project their own violence and map a stereotype onto Indians. This stereotype rationalized the many barbaric acts entailed in conquest as "civilizing force." Such force by their group was acceptable, yet when Natives defended themselves with the same force, settlers believed it proved their savagery. In this dynamic, if a group is cooperative, they must be "civilized," and if they are resistant, they must be conquered. There's no space for negotiation.

Stereotypes that project an ideal are also dangerous. The stereotype of the "noble savage" in a "pristine wilderness" arose from the second wave of east coast settlements. Stereotypes also control members of a group by promoting unrealistic ideals. For example, a life-sized Barbie is a physical impossibility.

Another stereotype holds that gay men are not masculine. But sexuality (hetero/non-heterosexual) isn't linked to gender (masculine/feminine) any more than gender is linked to anatomy. A woman may be as competitive as a man, and a gay man may be as masculine as a heterosexual man. We'll discuss how this mess of norms was untangled by feminist theorists in Part Four. What we want to point out now is that stereotypes are deeply woven through our ways of thinking.

Thinking about systems of power or, as John Trudell corrects us, systems of authority, and the practices and strategies that maintain or shift authority, helps reveal how that weaving takes place. Conquest emphasizes the physical. In order to force Indigenous children into Indian Boarding Schools,[5] settlers had to conquer their parents first. As Jacqui Alexander put it, the West did not attain global dominance because it's inherently superior, but because "they [beat] out [the] others" with their fists.[6] But it's important to understand how they maintained authority after conquest with effects that linger even after formerly conquered groups achieve independence.

Authority maintenance after conquest is as achieved through **structural oppression**. Structural oppression affects decisions from how we sit in a classroom to how we sit on park benches.[7] Ways to enforce authority include physical (walls, prisons, armed guards, gated communities), cultural (books, media, schools, exams), and spiritual (churches may promote beliefs such as the superiority of men). Aspects of each are directed at our emotional being, which, arguably, ties all the rest together and makes it stick. Hierarchical systems have characteristic modes of pressuring us to follow social norms. For example, we're required to look forward as we sit side by side in classrooms, churches, or watching media. The teacher at head of class and the preacher at pulpit see all of us, while we only see her or him. Similarly, while our gazes are fixed on media images instead of each other, ratings and data mining record our responses. Meanwhile, we may internalize and try to measure up to the "perfect selves" depicted in media images.

These modes of persuasion or control involve hierarchical authority. Whoever is in authority has the first and last word. In contrast, in the traditional Indigenous circle, everyone can see each other, and everyone is expected to listen more than they speak. Depending on the issue to be discussed, the person who makes the opening or closing remarks may vary. While egalitarian cultures connect individuals as equals and motivate them to develop and contribute their unique perspectives, hierarchy separates people and motivates them to conform to a social ideal or norm, often unattainable or stereotypical.

Feminists don't take the status-quo for granted. Tools for dismantling the master's house name common things in new ways. We keep a sharp eye on how beliefs, values, norms, stereotypes, and structural systems like hierarchy shape society and individual lives. We use vocabulary and methods of analysis that help us understand lines of authority. For example, in common use, norm means ordinary, average, or usual, but here, it means what's socially valued, while the opposite is devalued. That's why those who differ from norms are stereotyped. But, and this is important, norms are *not fixed*. They're the cultural tape on pause, marking reference points in historical processes. Examining American imperialism as a historical process reveals a Western stereotype of masculine norms:

> Power in America has always been about aggressiveness, what you can take and what you can control; . . . that's American manhood, Manifest Destiny, . . . we define manhood in America as dominating, as being in control, as having power, as taking over.[8]

Norms can manifest as **phobias**. For example, heterosexuality is a valued norm in Western culture. Even as laws change, other forms of sexuality remain marginally acceptable or unacceptable to many people. Unless specified otherwise, couples are expected to be made up of man and woman. This is called heteronormativity. Heteronormativity can lead to homophobia. Although the word phobia refers to fear, it usually generates fight instead of flight. A man who violates masculine norms by seeming feminine may be physically or verbally assaulted, as may a woman who seems "manly." People who don't comply with gender norms are even murdered simply because of their difference from expectations.

The suffix **ism** indicates a theory or philosophy. Ism as a stand-alone word can refer to any type of theory. Femin**ism** is a philosophy that advocates equality. On the other hand, heteronormativity leads to heterose**xism**, which perpetuates inequality. Isms that perpetuate inequality arise when schemas like race, class, and gender become so hegemonic that they shape not only beliefs, but also our social structures, resulting in racism, classism, and sexism (more on these and other isms in Chapter 8). This means that a belief (with its associated norms and stereotypes) reached a critical mass at some point in history and is now embedded in our social systems. When this happens, it's called an **institutional or systemic ism**. Institutional means it's embedded in laws, schools, places of worship, and other shared public venues. Systemic refers to how these institutions are interconnected even though they appear to work independently.

It's important to distinguish between **bias** (or prejudice) and ism. Bias is an individual feeling for or against something, generally based on stereotypes and misinformation. Anyone can be biased, but an ism requires the authority of belonging to a dominant group. Suppose a disabled individual is unable to enter a library because there's no ramp. S/he may express resentment at the privilege of the able-bodied who breeze in without a thought and even develop a feeling of bias toward them, believing they are all heartless and disrespectful. But bias doesn't reverse the situation. Reversal would be making the building inaccessible to the able-bodied. On the other hand, if able-bodied people failed to advocate for access, they have passively participated in institutionalized ableism, regardless of whether or not they feel any personal bias against disabled people. That's why reverse racism is a misnomer. It's a matter of institutional authority.

Isms affect us all regardless of our individual beliefs or biases, and they persist even though all people may not feel or act biased all the time. They shape inequities such as pay rates, incarceration rates, educational opportunities, and the questions raised in scientific studies.

Stereotypes are always linked to isms—they reproduce and reinforce each other. Even a stereotype that masquerades as positive, such as ideal images of women, conveys sexism.

For an ism to remain institutionalized, it must be reinforced by cultural texts that portray a group stereotypically. **Cultural texts** is another example of special use of a word in academia. It refers to how we organize information according to cultural schemas. Texts can include "objects, actions, and behaviors,"[9] and examples range from maps to movies and governmental studies to social policy.

For example, the cultural text called supplemental nutrition assistance program (SNAP) is associated with the stereotype that recipients are "lazy Blacks" or "welfare queens" who fraudulently trade in benefits for cash. Some politicians assert they are gobbling up your tax dollars. First, SNAP fraud is extremely low, and it's not predictable by race. Second, SNAP hardly gobbles up our tax dollars: the program's 2016 cost was 2% of the national budget, and it costs the average American tax payer $196 per year to assure that everyone gets nutrition, a basic need for life itself.[10]

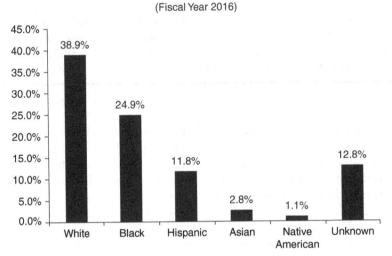

Food-Stamp Rolls by Race

(Fiscal Year 2016)

Figure 5.2 Race and SNAP (Food Stamps).[11] Copyright © Matt Trivisonno.

Poverty statistics are another example of a cultural text shaped by stereotypes. Poverty is almost always presented as a percent *of* a race. We can easily find figures on what percent of Blacks, Latinx, and whites are poor, but looking at poverty for all Americans paints a different picture. We had to do extensive research and calculations to reveal that the majority of poor people are white. In 2016, 76.9% of Americans identified as "just white," and their poverty rate was 8.8%. This means that 6.8% of Americans are poor whites. Latinx are 17.6% of the US population and their poverty rate is 19%. This means that 3.3% of Americans are poor Latinx. Blacks are 13.3% of the population and their poverty rate is 22%. This means that 2.9% of Americans are poor Blacks. Clearly, there are more poor whites than all poor people of color combined,[12] yet Black and brown faces are the public face of poverty pictured in information about social services, such as the Children's Health Insurance Program (CHIP) and SNAP.

What's at stake by promoting such groundless stereotypes? It comes down to another specialized word set: issues and interests. You're already familiar with special uses for words; that's why you don't put on a pair of Doc Martens and kick your computer to "boot up." **Interest** refers to investment in a belief and value system. You act according to your beliefs because you expect a return on your actions. It yields benefits for you, so it's a vested interest. The benefits can be monetary or psychological; for example, you can have a vested interest in feeling your group is superior to others. These are polarized examples, but even within homogenous groups there can be differing interests.

When interests clash, they create an issue. The Cultural Studies use of the word is not synonymous with problem (I have an issue) or disagreement (I take issue). **Issues** can be analyzed according to the beliefs and values that drive conflicting vested interests. Sometimes, issues get so heated that analysis and facts fall to the wayside. If your self-worth relies on the belief that you're better than Blacks, and you justify this with the "lazy Black" stereotype, you may vote for someone who vows to end SNAP benefits, even though your vote will affect white people (possibly including your family). The stereotype diminishes compassion, and candidates get the votes of those who believe in it. Such a vote will hurt many more whites than Blacks, most of them elderly and children. The heated debate around this issue can cause you to vote against your own interests because stereotypes, phobias, and isms divide and conquer.

Indigenous Tools for Power Sharing

Indigenous neutral binaries lead to carefully structured methods of where everyone has a role. They may include spokespersons for plants, animals, and even weather phenomena. At an Anishinaabe council, a person responsible for ensuring the well-being of beavers may speak. This person would know whether the beavers are thriving or challenged and how many can safely be harvested without compromising their community. Rivers, trees, and thunder may also choose to speak through a human representative. Larry Matrious, mentioned earlier, was named Nagan Wewidang, which he translated as First Thunder to Speak. This kind of inclusive structure can be found in many Indigenous cultures. The Western word for it is heterarchy.

Heterarchy is "a governance system composed of collective actors at multiple levels with overlapping authority, linked together through various kinds of networks."[13] "Collective actors" means there may be councils of men, women, and children, and of artists, fishers, and farmers. "Multiple levels" doesn't mean higher and more authoritative versus lower and less authoritative. It means there are councils for different-sized groupings, such as extended family, village, tribe, and associations of tribes. "Linked networks" means stakeholders for each group arrive at agreements that are conveyed to the next size level. Each group sends a delegate to share their decisions at a larger council, where conclusions that affect the entire community are made together.

The matriarchal Haudenosaunee believe that women can best select spokespersons who will consider the well-being of the whole family. Therefore, their Council of Elder Women traditionally appointed the men who filled responsible positions such as diplomats. These women step back and trust decisions to the appointees. They keep watch for consideration of the whole and leave details to other councils.

The Ojibwe are gender-balanced and believe that leadership is best conducted by someone with skill in the required task:

> In the past when we needed a warrior we made a warrior our leader. But when the war was over and we needed a healer to lead us, [s/]he became our leader. Or maybe we needed a great speaker or a deep thinker. The warrior knew his time had passed and he didn't pretend to be our leader beyond the time he was needed. He was proud to serve his people and he knew when it was time to step aside. . . . A leader is a leader as long as . . . [s/]he is the best person to lead us.[14]

Most importantly, leadership isn't authority:

> You can only lead as long as people will follow . . . leaders never ordered people to do anything because they strictly adhered to the principle that people have a right to self-determination . . . leadership was neither coercive nor hierarchical.[15]

It makes sense that the person best at an activity helps direct that activity and should step back when it's time for another activity, at which time the person best at that steps forward. Authority is horizontal, always changing, and democratic. Individual and community have a reciprocal relationship: you must develop your unique nature to fulfill your role in a heterarchical society. Heterarchy closes an inclusive loop: because respect for uniqueness is a fundamental principle, difference is valued, and valuing different natures, talents, and concerns is best expressed when heterarchy is the organizing structure.

Systemic Conflicts

What kinds of issues arise when heterarchical and hierarchal cultures meet? As indicated by the term "Native Americans," the continent and surrounding islands were fully populated long before Columbus and Ponce de Leon (in the East) and Balboa and Cortez (in the West) found their way to what Natives call Turtle Island. Long before the US was even a concept, clashes, diseases, and other radical changes had occurred that affected both Europeans and Natives. When cultures clash, either one model takes over the other or the two models bend and blend. The US was conceived and influenced by both Indigenous and settler cultures, and much has been written about the impact of the Haudenosaunee Constitution on the US Constitution. Upon formation of this nation, the British settlers had been exposed to two modes of governance: their own and the First Americans'. Their home country was patriarchal, monarchical, and feudal. Except for an occasional Queen of England, women's decisions, along with group decisions, were made almost exclusively by men, and children belonged to their fathers. Only men could own land, and only landowners could exert authority. Despite the English Magna Carta, in the feudal system, the monarch ruled. Monarchs might listen to advice brought to the royal council (later parliament), but they were not beholden to do so. Although nobles, clergy, and knights gained more say in governance as parliament developed, the king retained absolute rights such as collecting feudal taxes. Petitions submitted to the king's ministers were often ignored and the king had the final say on all issues. The success of parliament rose and fell according to the strength and character of the monarch. Even to this day, only the monarch can summon and dissolve British Parliament.

So, when the British settlers came to Jamestown in the 17th century, they were walking away from several centuries of power struggles between monarchy and wealthy nobles. Although many migrated later, the founding fathers of the 18th century were men like John Adams, whose father had migrated from Britain in 1638, and Benjamin Franklin, whose father had migrated from Britain in 1682. Washington's grandfather arrived here in 1657, and Washington himself was only the third generation of his family born on Turtle Island. They all had roots in the period when the stranglehold of the monarchy was finally loosened. Their home government had moved from zero representation (absolute monarchical rights) to partial and carefully hedged representation, reliant on money for a voice, and a new method of legislation somewhat affected by elite voters.

The US Constitution is a hybrid between hierarchy and heterarchy, but the blend was not easy or comfortable:

> The 1789 US Constitution arose from a long process of intercultural exchange marked by tenets that were at odds from the outset. American exposure to Indigenous peoples began through quests for wealth, power, and cultural expansionism. The Indigenous peoples' impressively egalitarian lifestyle captured European imagination and initiated thirst for broader powers than monarchy, feudalism, and even parliamentary government permitted. Still, . . . true egalitarianism . . . would have required them to forego the patriarchy and racialism that allowed them to accumulate the very wealth for which they had ventured forth. As the founding fathers . . . mused over how to gain power without giving

it away to everyone . . . they adapted a Haudenosaunee/Iroquois governmental structure that was originally designed for inclusiveness. Drafting and re-drafting . . . to accommodate vested interests culminated in a paradoxical document that, on the one hand, limited privilege to select groups, and, on the other hand, carried egalitarian sensibilities that would lay the groundwork for [future] US Constitution[al amendments].[16]

Systemic conflict can lead to radical misunderstandings. After conferring with the Council of Elder Women who conveyed the decisions of all the people, Haudenosaunee men were sent forth to meet European settlers like Ben Franklin. Since Europeans refused to listen to women, other tribes likewise sent men to discuss their collective decisions with newcomers even if their spokespersons had previously been women. Because Western organizations are hierarchical and patriarchal, settlers believed each tribe had a sole male leader. They therefore mistook Indigenous diplomats for rulers in the Western model, called them "chiefs," and expected them to make binding agreements without further consultation with the people. Such agreements typically involved land ownership, but in Indigenous cultures, no one could own the land in the European sense.

These are just a few of the many misunderstandings that led to conflict and resistance in early American history. Meanwhile, on the Pacific, the clash between Spanish and Aztec traditions led to armed resistance followed by cultural resistance.

Feminism, Patriarchy, and the Aztec Empire: Conquest and Resilience by Rhianna Rogers[17]

After they lost control of the marketplace, Aztec women fought for their traditional lifestyles. "They tucked up their skirts and dressed in the regalia of war"[18] and "command[ed] . . . their own men."[19] But the Spanish had horses and guns. The Aztecs were forced to reorganize their Indigenous gender customs and expected to internalize Spanish ideologies. According to 16th-century Spanish Christian roles, women were to be virgins until marriage, respect their husband and obey his commands, and be subordinate to men.[20] They were forced to succumb to patriarchal subjugation, especially in major population areas. Rural settlements had less Spanish presence. Non-royal women were non-entities in Spanish culture, and Aztec women used this loophole to retain reciprocity. Believing the balance between men and women was essential to a well-balanced society, local Aztec communities provided women opportunities to make significant contributions. Another factor affecting women's power was the depopulation of Aztec males due to war and disease. By outnumbering Aztec men, women gained authority within kin groups, political offices, and at home, which initially enabled them to excel in activities the Spanish ascribed to males.[21]

Unfortunately, this was short-lived. The Spanish deemed strong females sinful and forcefully implemented Christian ideals. "They depicted native women as promiscuous which made them . . . [rapeable] within . . . prevailing code, thus extending . . . conquest to . . . the realm of sex."[22] This distressed gender parallelism, destroyed the strength of balance, and allowed the Spanish to dominate Aztec women socially, economically, politically, and sexually, while weapons and diseases allowed them to dominate militarily.

Missionaries taught Christianity in terms already familiar to the Aztecs, encouraging correlations between native deities, symbols, in order to more effectively convert them, and the Aztecs found covert ways to maintain gender reciprocity and cosmic dualism. They prayed to Christian female saints and the Virgin Mary to maintain the significant female worship required for gender balance. They appeared Christian in public but maintained traditional beliefs at home, worshipping pre-Columbian gods such as Huitzilopochtli and Coatlicue.

On the one hand, the prominent roles Aztec women once held were no longer socially acceptable. Conquest transferred them to the lowest position in the social pyramid. On the other hand, Aztec women adapted to their difficult circumstances and resisted gender marginalization through accommodation of their traditions. In spite of the enormous odds against them, they found ways to combat the oppressive nature of patriarchal rule and reinstated cosmic dualism and gender parallelism.

In this globalized age in which women fight to retain access to land, property, and wealth, it is important to analyze the ways in which they historically fought racial and gendered stereotyping to create space for themselves in society. Aztec women continue to combat gender oppressions in Mexico today. In the modern era, they use *Chicanismo* to mobilize against Latin American patriarchy, continuing Aztec women's colonial defiance of Spanish gender subjugation.

Issues don't always spark movements, but movements are always based on issues. Movements can respond to tensions within a culture (#MeToo responds to patriarchy) or between cultures (#WaterIsLife responds to US corporations invading sovereign Native nations). The stakes, methods, and agenda of each are shaped by a mix of internal and external tensions. Now that we have an overview of the complicated forces of conquest and maintaining authority, we can focus on tensions in the 19th and early 20th centuries, when some of the best-known movements took place. During this period, in the US and around the world, women often initiated change on behalf of themselves and their entire societies.

Internal Tensions

A primary tension within patriarchal cultures is unequal rights between males and females. Mainstream feminism, therefore, traditionally focused on gender issues. Depending on time and place, the gap between men's and women's rights has been absolute or relative. Women settlers in the US had no vote and could not own property, and their wages went to their father, brother, or husband. Today, we can vote and own property, but we still get paid less than a man for doing the same job.

Men are also negatively affected by patriarchy. Conforming to masculine norms to stay at the top of a hierarchy comes at a price as men are discouraged from expressing feelings or vulnerability. They must control themselves because patriarchy depends on men controlling women's unpaid labor in the home and low-paid labor in the workplace. Because control relies on distinct gender roles, non-heterosexuals and those who don't comply with gender norms violate the patriarchal pact and suffer accordingly. Homophobia may be directed at gay men for failing to dominate a woman and at lesbian women for not supporting a man. Changing sides or refusing to take a side is a threat to a system that depends on ranking.

Internal clashes don't end there because cultures that rank gender generally rank in other ways, too. Patriarchal cultures have always elevated the rights of the wealthy over the poor, and the primary task of the non-wealthy is producing more wealth for the wealthy. In the patriarchal schema about class (rich/poor), wealthier people have a dominant voice and hand in making the rules and norms for the rest of us, while the testimonies of those with less money often go unheard. Since the 15th century, Western cultures have also elevated one race over another. Schemas like class and race are part of a grid of cultural intelligibility that clarifies our different experiences within patriarchy. Pointing at the way race, gender, and class are linked, bell hooks calls our socialist economic system white-supremacist-capitalist-patriarchy. Efforts to resolve internal tensions need to address these kinds of links.

External Tensions

External clashes are even more complex because different beliefs and values lead to different systems for organizing and governing. Generally, societies following the Great Chain of Being organize by vertical ranking, and those in accord with The Circle of Life organize with horizontal connections. Patriarchy is vertical because it places men above women. Matriarchal and gender-balanced societies are horizontal because they are egalitarian.

There were tensions between some Indigenous nations, often because circumstances forced them to share space. Shared space can arise through migration and intermarriage with minimal conflict. If groups have enough similar values, tensions may be resolved over one or two generations. We saw in Part Two that Ojibwe and Dakota, who had clashed over territory, adopted each other as family when the US government intervened. But, if a group is subjected to an outside group with different values through invasion and conquest, tensions can persist for centuries. Tensions between European settlers and natives of the Americas are ongoing today. In a radio interview, Nish Nung Matrious, a Mille Lacs Ojibwe elder, describes "how we live today" as a difficult navigation of racism and violated treaties.[23] He makes it clear that treaties are not lost in mists of the past. Similar to the way Americans continue to respect the Constitution, treaties signed between European and Indigenous ancestors are as vital today as when they were written. Yet Indigenous sovereign nations today still struggle with the US and Canada when their treaty-protected rights are dishonored. Native diplomats like Roberto Borrero bring these concerns to the UN.

Case Study: Beauty and Authority

Some conflicts lead to war and some persist in times of peace. Conflicts over the meaning of beauty persist at all times; ideas of beauty, like gender, changes according to time, place, and culture. Beauty becomes an issue through internal tensions (authoritative pressure about how to look within a given society), external tensions (clashing beauty standards between societies with unequal authority), or both. In Korea, there is a tradition called *hwarang*, roughly translated as Flower Warriors. They were elite royal guards who mastered martial, visual, and literary arts and were renowned for their beauty. When they put their lives on the line, they wore elaborate makeup and jewelry. Flower Warriors were instrumental in conquering, or "unifying," as they called it, multiple tribes that extended Korean rule into parts of China, connecting ideas of beauty to imperialism; at the same time, this unification enabled Korea to resist Chinese and Japanese imperialism. When we think "soldier," we don't think "pretty." But beauty norms are not always gendered, and a male warrior can have what we think of as a feminine appearance.

Many white feminists have written about beauty pageants such as Miss USA and Miss Universe. Objections voiced by Robin Morgan in 1968 are still discussed today. Taté Walker, in an article on Native American women and feminism, describes how Miss Indian World contests require participants to showcase "talents ranging from tribal language mastery to nation-specific know-how in clothing, ritual practices, storytelling history, and more."[24] In the Miss Navajo contest, women must show their skill in sheep butchering, something much of the US would not consider a feminine virtue.[25] Norms of how a woman should look, what she should know, and how she should behave vary from culture to culture.

There are different ideas of beauty (masculine, feminine, neither/nor) and different ideas of who should pursue beauty (men, women, either/or), but we can all agree that beauty has become an industry. So, what do feminists think about the beauty industry? Depending upon the person's location, life conditions, and way of thinking, different interests and issues are at stake. Mainstream feminists address a wide range of topics (from anorexia to xenophobia, from makeup to the Islamic hijab) that may be understood differently around the world. But we all have a shared feminist stake in how beauty standards affect us. Let's dismantle beauty norms (attractive/different looking) that drive the $326 billion global beauty industry.[26] The US, which is 4.4% of the world population, accounts for $50 billion or 15.3% of that industry, reflecting an enormous vested interest.

We've seen how corn assured some Indigenous women economic status. In contrast, women in contemporary Western cultures earn markedly less than men. We have to wonder where women's value lies. According to media, it's largely based on her attractiveness to men, as if she were a product for them to consume. But attraction is not universal; it's affected by beauty norms. Since media has spread Western beauty norms far and wide, that's a good place to begin. Ideal body images that originally varied according to culture have become largely white (straight hair, light skin, angular features).

In many countries, there's tension between traditional and European standards. The Yoruba saying *iwa l'ewa* (character is beauty) is representative of many African traditions, but European standards contribute to skin lightening, hair straightening, and weight loss industries in Africa.[27]

The tradition of *hwarang* is echoed today in popular Korean "flower boys." These media stars often have flowing hair, immaculate skin and features, and wear pastel colors and ruffles. At the same time, plastic surgery to make East Asian faces more Western has sky-rocketed. Another break in tradition is that today, if men must be beautiful, women must be more so.

Beauty, like any norm, entails a hidden evaluator, a desired norm, and a devalued other: for someone to be considered beautiful, someone else must be thought of as plain or even ugly. Images of how you should want to look are at the heart of advertisements for products that will supposedly get you there. Advertisements gender (women should be feminine) and racialize (women should look white). But there are a few more steps that have to be in place before norms generate the profits necessary to industry.

- Profits are maximized by mass production. Until small Black companies began to take up market share, big companies catered to the lighter skin tones that they advertise as beautiful. To this day, no major cosmetic company matches every single color.
- Wage stratification also maximizes profits. While CEOs may be well paid (the L'Oreal CEO is paid $2, 323,000 per year plus stock shares),[28] laborers on production lines are poorly paid (about $20,000 per year),[29] sending economic ripples throughout communities.

- Profits also require mass consumption. In order to sell products and services, people need to want to meet a beauty norm, and they need to believe a product will help them get there. So, we come full circle back to advertisements and media representations.

We're encouraged to internalize dominant beliefs about beauty through cultural texts like films, TV, news, and advertisements. But no matter how much you buy, you may never meet the beauty norms proposed in advertisements. So, despite billions of advertising dollars promoting feminine norms, some women just don't buy it—or not all of it all the time, anyway. Some (like the Navajo) assert their own traditional standards, while others create their own industries, such as makeup brands that match a range of darker skin tones. We could make a pretty complicated grid of the beauty industry. The morning mirror is a good place to discover the effects of norms and stereotypes. How do beauty norms affect you?

It takes community, vigilant awareness, and continued engagement to overcome stereotypical norms and any other form of domination.[30] We can work together to dismantle the master's house in many ways. As we move to women's movements, keep in mind that though you may not be the face of a movement, your own face is important in daily life.

Notes

1 Mark Fischetti. "Africa Is Way Bigger Than You Think." *Scientific American*. Jun. 16, 2015, https://blogs.scientificamerican.com/observations/africa-is-way-bigger-than-you-think/.

2 Hobo-Dyer Equal Area Projection Map. TranspacificProject.com. Last updated 2019, http://www.transpacificproject.com/wpcontent/uploads/2011/06/ SouthUpMapr.jpg.

3 Ekra Miezan. "Media Images of Africa and African Americans' Attitudes toward Africa." *Doctoral Dissertations Available from Proquest.* 2000, https://scholar works.umass.edu/dissertations/AAI9960774.

4 Children were taken from their parents and raised in military-style work camps. Due to this, they never learned how to function as a family member. The trauma affected following generations. See "Impact of Historical Trauma," The National Native American Boarding School Healing Coalition, https://boardingschoolhealing.org/education/impact-of-historical-trauma/.

5 Jacqui Alexander. *Pedagogies of Crossing: Meditations on Feminism, Sexual Politics, Memory, and the Sacred.* Duke U. Press. 2006, p. 327.

6 Ruha Benjamin. "From Park Bench to Lab Bench—What Kind of Future Are We Designing?" *TEDxBaltimore.* Feb. 2015, https://www.youtube.com/watch?v=_8RrX4hjCr0.

7 Byron Hurt. *Barack & Curtis: Manhood, Power, & Respect.* 2008, http://www.bhurt.com/films/view/barack_and_curtis.

8 Suzanne Blum and Ames Hawkins. "3a—Examining Culture as Text." *Engaging Communities.* http://www.engagingcommunities.org/proposing-the-ethnographic-research-project/3a-examining-culture-as-text/.

9 Scott Greenberg. "Summary of the Latest Income Tax Data." *Tax Foundation.* Feb. 1, 2017. https://taxfoundation.org/summary-latest-federal-income-tax-data-2016-update/.

10 "Percent of Population in 2016 by Race." US Census, https://www.census. gov/quickfacts/fact/table/US/PST045216; "Percent in Poverty by Race in 2016." US Census. http://federalsafetynet.com/us-poverty-statistics.html.

11 Matt Trivisonno. Chart compiled from data in "Characteristics of Supplemental Nutrition Assistance Program Households: Fiscal Year 2016." Report No. SNAP-17-CHAR. USDA. Nov. 2017, https://fns-prod.azureedge.net/sites/ default/files/ops/Characteristics2016. pdf. Copyright © Matt Trivisonno.

12 Ronnie D. Lipschutz and Judith Mayer. *Global Civil Society and Global Environmental Governance: The Politics of Nature from Place to Planet.* SUNY Press. 1996, p. 113.

13 Tracy Becker. "Traditional American Indian Leadership." *American Indian Research and Policy Institute.* 1997, pp. 3–4, http://www.navajocourts.org/Har monization/Traditional%20American%20Indian%20Leadership.pdf.

14 Ibid.

15 Menoukha Robin Case and Rhianna Rogers. "Iroquois Influence on the US Constitution, 1789." *50 Events that Shaped American Indian History: An Encyclopedia of the American Mosaic.* Ed. Donna Martinez and Jennifer Williams Bordeaux. ABC-Clio. 2016.

16 Rhianna Rogers, excerpt adapted with permission by Menoukha Robin Case, "The Spider Woman Rules No More? The Transformation and Resilience of Aztec Female Roles" MA Thesis. Rhianna Rogers MA Thesis Florida Atlantic University. 2004.

17 Miguel León-Portilla, ed. *The Broken Spears: The Aztec Account of the Conquest of Mexico.* Expanded and Updated Edition. Beacon. 2006, p. 137.

18 Gonzalo Fernández de Oviedo. *Natural History of the West Indies.* Trans. and ed. Sterling Stoudemire. U of North Carolina Press, 1959, pp. 44–45.

19 Robert M. Carmack, Janine Gasco, and Gary H. Gossen. *The Legacy of Mesoamerica: History and Culture of a Native American Civilization.* Prentice Hall, 1996, p. 327.

20 Louise M. Burkhart, *The Slippery Earth: Nahua-Christian Moral Dialogue in Sixteenth-Century Mexico.* U of Arizona Press, 1989, p. 52–54.

21 Brenda M. Romero. "The Indita Genre of New Mexico." *Chicana Traditions: Continuity and Change.* Eds. Norma E. Cantú and Olga Nájera-Ramirez. U of Illinois Press. 2002, p. 76.

22 Deb Regers, Brian Matrious, and Jim Beard. "Noodin and Nish Nung on Moccasin Tracks," Mar. 28, 2018, https://www.podomatic.com/podcasts/ radiowithdeb2/episodes/2018-03-28T14_19_29-07_00. This show has one error: Noodin says Indians gave up the right to hunt off their reservations. While some did, many did not. The Anishinaabe Ojibwe retained usufructuary rights—the right to hunt and fish on ceded territory. In effect, they said, you can live here and play at selling the land among yourselves, but we retain the right to derive our livelihood as we always have in these woods, meadows, streams, and rivers. Therefore, an activity like mining, which pollutes the water where wild rice grows and fish thrive, is a treaty violation.

23 Taté Walker. "These 4 Phenomenal Native Women Will Totally Make You Re-examine Your Relationship to Feminism." *Everyday Feminism.* May 16, 2015, http://everydayfeminism.com/2015/05/native-women-feminism/.

24 Billy Luther. *Miss Navajo, The Film.* PBS. 2007, http://www.pbs.org/inde pendentlens/missnavajo/film.html.

25 "Market Size of the Beauty Industry Worldwide: 2005–2015." *Statistica: The Statistics Portal,* https://www.statista.com/statistics/667909/global-market-value-of-the-beauty-industry/.

26 Akinyi Ochieng. "Challenging Beauty Standards: Ng'endo Mukii's Yellow Fever." *Ayiba.* 2015, http://ayibamagazine.com/challenging-beauty-standards-ngendo-mukiis-yellow-fever/.

27 L'Oréal Financial Statement 2016. L'Oréal. Last updated Apr. 19, 2018, https://www.loreal-finance.com/_docs/remuneration-mandataires-sociaux/News_Release_2018_04_19_EN.pdf.

28 "L'Oréal Salaries in USA." *Neuvoo*. 2019, https://neuvoo.com/salary/?job=L+Oreal.

29 bell hooks. *Teaching Community: A Pedagogy of Hope*. Routledge. 2003.

30 Ptolemy Map 15th Century. Wikimedia Commons. https://commons.wiki media.org/wiki/File:Ptolemy_map_15th_century.jpg.

Gerardus Mercatur. Mercatur 1569. Wikimedia Commons. https://commons. wikimedia.org/wiki/File:Mercator_1569.png.

Gall-Peters Projection SW. Wikimedia Commons. https://commons. wikimedia.org/wiki/File:Gall%E2%80%93Peters_projection_SW.jpg.

Hobo-Dyer Projection: South-up, Pacific-centered, Equal-area Map. Courtesy of Richard Smith, TranspacificProject.com. The Decolonial Atlas. https://decolonialatlas.wordpress.com/2014/11/04/hobo-dyer-equal-area-projection-map/.

"The Blue Marble." Visible Earth NASA.gov. https://visibleearth.nasa. gov/view.php?id=57723.

6 Justice Movements

#WTF: What's That Feminism?

The Americas

The Americas are home to many feminisms such as white, Black, Native, and Latinx. Any examination of women's participation in US movements includes the issue of slavery and treaties between the young American nation and the much older sovereign Native nations. Likewise, it includes women's roles in abolition movements and, later, in civil rights movements.

Latin America and the Caribbean

"Latin America" refers to areas of the continent and surrounding islands invaded by the Spanish as well as Brazil, invaded by the Portuguese. The Caribbean includes islands invaded by France (Haiti), England (Jamaica), Holland (Aruba), and Denmark (Virgin Islands). Since invaders brought enslaved Africans and, as in the US, raped both African and Native women, some of the peoples of Latin America are called mestizo or mixed. In Mexico, they are referred to as Chicano. Another term we hear today is Afro-Latino. Native, African, and mixed resistance took place wherever Europeans dominated. Women were deeply involved in these movements.

The United States

One of the first US feminist movements concerned women's right to vote. To understand issues preceding our time, let's look at pre-suffrage beliefs.

Start with the belief that Eve cost Adam the Garden of Eden, even though he too bit that apple. A higher value is placed on the original male than on his rib, the subsequent female. Because of this, a good 19th-century woman believed in male superiority and valued her father's and husband's opinion above her own. The word "good" is an evaluative binary, a cultural schema that threads society with the weight of moral judgment. If you believe in men's superiority, then you must believe women's opinions carry little value. Opinions of little value were not welcome in the political realm; therefore, women could not vote.

But the Indigenous egalitarian sensibility that influenced the US Constitution, along with Africans' goal of equality, continued to drive a series of suffrage changes:

- 1776: white male landowners can vote
- 1856: all white men can vote
- 1868: African American men can legally vote, but state and local laws prevent many from doing so
- 1920: White women can vote, but state and local laws prevent African American women from voting
- 1947: Native Americans can vote, but state and local laws prevent many from doing so
- 1965: The Voting Rights Act overrides state and local prohibitions
- Early 21st century: New state and local laws and locations of voting centers prevent many people of color from voting

Movements arose because the Constitution proposed in contradictory norms. It became evident that "mankind" excluded women and that we needed to consider race as well as gender. Although separations aren't hard and fast, we can distinguish between interests and issues important to white and women of color's feminisms. Nineteenth-century white Suffragettes and Progressives aimed to change gender laws and practices. Women of color focused on issues of freedom, such as abolition and Indigenous sovereignty. Since white feminism is better known, we'll begin by reviewing what people already know about US women's movements.

The Suffrage Movement grew from internal gender clashes. It consisted of long, sometimes violent battles fought largely by educated white women from prosperous families. Some suffragettes allied with those working to abolish slavery, but too many held racial biases. Elizabeth Cady Stanton said, "What will we and our daughters suffer if these degraded black men are allowed to have the rights that would make them even worse than our Saxon fathers?" Anna Howard Shaw complained, "You have put the ballot in the hands of your black men, thus making them political superiors of white women. Never before in the history of the world have men made former slaves the political masters of their former mistresses!"

They were concerned with dismantling what Barbara Welter (1966) called the "Cult of True Womanhood," the belief that a "true" woman's sole responsibilities were to home and family, under her husband's "guidance." The Suffragettes' main agenda was to achieve the same legal rights as their well-to-do white fathers, brothers, and husbands: to work in a profession of their choice, own property, and have a say in politics. The vote would give them a public voice and political power. After they had power, they could address what was to them the secondary issue of Africans. Therefore, their main emphasis was sexism. Their main accomplishments were the 17th and 19th amendments to the Constitution, which gave women the right to vote.

The Progressive Movement responded to internal class clashes. Its activists, who never had the luxury of being "true women," already worked outside their homes to support themselves and their families. They also advocated for abolition, unlike the Suffragettes. Nineteenth-century Progressives focused on the concerns of impoverished factory workers who didn't own property. They wanted to end governmental and industrial corruption and gain rights for themselves as well as their children, fathers, brothers, and husbands. They fought for social services, child labor laws, and other labor reform legislation. Therefore, their main emphasis was classism. Some successes include the Interstate Commerce Act (1887) and the Sherman Antitrust Act (1890).

Each group had its own agenda crafted from a collection of issues that changed as historical forces unfolded.

Waves—The changing agendas of US feminism are often described as "waves." The first wave is associated with the mid-19th century to 1920, when women won the right to vote; the second with the mid-to-late 20th century; and the third with the late 20th into the 21st century. Some call the second decade of the 21st century the beginning of a fourth wave. Here are a few key accomplishments:

Table 6.1 Western (Mostly White) US Waves, with Alice Lai

Wave	Agenda	Public Sphere Accomplishments
First	Suffragettes and Progressives worked on ending legal inequities, promoting legislation, gaining political power, and improving social welfare through labor rights.	Women acquired voting rights, right to own property and execute a will, and union-supported rights at work.
Second	The Women's Liberation movement critiqued history, laws, and popular cultural representations of gender roles. They worked on ending cultural inequities in order to gain equal educational, professional, and personal opportunities. "The Personal is Political" promoted wider choices and equity in power relations in daily life: reproductive rights, sexual freedom, and marriage equality.	Laws and court decisions supporting rights, such as equal pay (Equal Pay Act), employment (Civil Rights Act), educational equity, equal credit opportunity, equal admission to military academies, reproductive rights (*Roe v. Wade*), Violence Against Women Act, and media such as *Ms.* Magazine.

(Continued)

Wave	Agenda	Public Sphere Accomplishments
Third	Term coined by Rebecca Walker. Less about organizations and more about personal narrative, action over theory, multiple versions of feminism, multivocality, contradictions, grrrl power, and new cultural images of women.	Gender fluidity and equity, such as trans rights and same-sex marriage, were championed during this wave and were successfully legislated at the start of the fourth wave. Addressed ongoing problems through anything from a Flash Mob to a Disney Princess video to Punk Rock and Zines.
Fourth	Grrrl Power continues and morphs (be yourself). Social media diminish virtual gaps between different communities, while real gaps remain.	Same-sex marriage supported by SCOTUS, women permitted in military combat, and extended Violence Against Women Act gives new rights to Native Americans, lesbians, and immigrants.

Criticism of Waves—While the wave concept is useful for listing accomplishments, it can be misread as if there were distinct stops and starts. But quests for equality preceded the waves and agenda items such as voting rights remain issues today. Also, each period built on previous waves. For example, the Stonewall riots began the public fight for LGBTQ+ rights in 1969 (first wave), the first legal challenge to same-sex marriage took place in 1971 (second wave), and in 2015 the Supreme Court of the US finally upheld its legality (fourth wave). Women like Eleanor Roosevelt bridged waves—she didn't stop or change her goals as so-called waves rolled. Roosevelt was involved in the Women's Trade Union League to abolish child labor and institute a 48-hour work week in the early 20th century and later participated in Kennedy's Presidential Commission on the Status of Women. Changes to de jure (legally accepted) and de facto (illegal but common) realities are uneven. Today, you can meet people who represent the core missions of any of the four waves. The beliefs and values that drive movements exceed suggested dates.

Another criticism of the wave framework is that it centralizes mainstream feminism and prioritizes the patriarchal problem. If there's any way that feminism, a counter-hegemonic concept, could be turned to the use of hegemony, mainstream feminism is it because addressing only one aspect of hegemony leaves the system intact. For example, when suffragettes addressed sexism, they left racism and classism intact, so only white wealthy women were aided. Though some women like Sojourner Truth bridged the color-gap, for the most part, the wave frame tends to ignore movements by women of color—Blacks, Latinx, Asians, and Native Americans—with different agendas and timelines from the mainstream. Not only did each group understand gender differently, they also experienced different kinds of problems. Given how people tend to be most aware of their own vested interests, it isn't surprising that feminist descendants of colonists didn't consider the devastating effects colonialism had on Indigenous and Black women. After all, many of them had gained their status from precisely that devastation— they were living on Indian land and benefiting from their husbands' wealth which, directly or indirectly, drew from slavery and imperialism.

Roots of Black Feminism—There is continuity in Black feminisms from Harriet Tubman to Sojourner Truth to today's Black Lives Matter. Kimberly Foster, founder and editor of the digital community "For Harriet," explains that "Black women in the United States have been organizing around progressive gender politics for 200 years. Each generation picks up where the last left off."[1]

Black women were feminists before the word was invented. One of the earliest autobiographies addressing women's rights was by Jarena Lee, born 1793. The African Methodist Episcopal Church thought only men should preach. She responded, "If the man may preach, because the Saviour died for him, why not the woman? Seeing he died for her also. Is he not a whole Saviour, instead of a half one?"[2]

Women like Ida B. Wells helped found the National Association for the Advancement of Colored People (NAACP) in 1909 in response to lynching. In 1917, they held a Silent Protest Parade in New York City. Women were out in force. Other photos show an equally large cadre of girls also in white dresses.

The International Council of Women of the Darker Races was founded in 1920. They studied women's concerns in Haiti, Liberia, and Sierra Leone, eventually extending to China, Japan, and India. Small but effective, this group "organized for mutual international cooperation . . . among women

Children in the "Silent Protest" Parade, New York City   *Underwood & Underwood*

Figure 6.1 1917 NYC Silent Protest.[3]

and children of the darker races of the world."[4] Like Progressives, they worked on behalf of entire communities, including fathers, brothers, sons, and husbands, but focused primarily on women of color. They included some wealthy members, and their main mode of activism was education. They were one of the earliest groups to describe how sexism, classism, and racism work together. By including international affairs, they also addressed colonialism.

In 1974, Black, Latinx, and Indigenous women created the Combahee River Collective. Their 1977 statement argued that "If Black women were free, it would mean that everyone else would have to be free since our freedom would necessitate the destruction of all the systems of oppression."[5] In 1982, members Gloria Hull, Patricia Bell Scott, and Barbara Smith edited a collection of essays, memoirs, and poems called *All the Women Are White, All the Blacks Are Men, But Some of Us Are Brave* that foregrounds the value of testimony and articulates current feminist theory.

The 20th century continued to see a rise in African-based approaches to intersecting issues, and Afrocentricity became an academic term in the 1980s and 1990s. Since white feminism didn't include Black women's experiences, Alice Walker, a novelist, poet, novelist, and activist, coined the term Womanism, re-defining feminism with her sense of Black women's concerns.[6] Unlike Black Feminism, it doesn't have to be preceded by the word Black because it refers exclusively to Black women in relationship to Black men and children. A womanist loves other Black women and celebrates their creativity and power. Walker's poetic definition concludes, "Womanist is to feminist as purple is to lavender" (1983).[7] Womanism has become a rich and complex theory further developed by women such as Chikwenye Okonjo Ogunyemi and Clenora Hudson-Weems.

Women of color feminism can be envisioned as a continual river rather than waves, so the following is a timeline. It highlights a few key accomplishments.

Resistance movements like suffrage arise when people are dissatisfied with their position in a grid of cultural intelligibility. They resist the beliefs and values that shape the way society sees them, and they resist the way it "keeps them in their place." "Their place" changes according to time and location.

Table 6.2 US Women of Color Timeline

Period	Agenda	Public Sphere Accomplishments
15th–17th c.	Women in Native tribes such as the Haudenosaunee Clan Mothers in the east and the Pueblo Clan Mothers in the west were instrumental in retaining sovereign rights.	Over 500 hundred treaties were signed. Some have fueled movements, from the Walleye Wars (the right to continue to hunt, gather, and fish on ceded lands) to Standing Rock (the right to protect water, sacred sites, and graves).

(Continued)

Table 6.2 (Continued)

Period	Agenda	Public Sphere Accomplishments
18th c.	Pre-Civil War activism	Harriet Tubman and Aliquippa (Seneca) are examples of women who actively protected their people.
19th c.	Post-Civil War Activism. NAACP agenda was implementation of the 13th (end slavery), 14th (equal protection under the law), and 15th (adult male suffrage) amendments; International Council of Women of the Darker Races was concerned with global conditions for women of color and their families.	While some proposed legislation failed (Dyer Anti-Lynching Bill), NAACP was and remains an effective educator and organizer. Their work led to Brown versus Board of Education and the school integration. The ICWDR aided groups outside the US and pressured school superintendents within the US to order books about Africans in diaspora.
Early 20th c.	Women's strong participation in Civil Rights organizations helped pass bills and make changes, but they began to protest sexism in the movement. In 1977, the Combahee River Collective advocated liberation for all.	In 1964, 24th amendment (abolished poll tax); Civil Rights Act of 1964 and 1968; Voting Rights Act of 1965; Combahee was highly successful in their goal of educating through Kitchen Table Women of Color Press
Late 20th c.	Two sites among many: academia and media. Some hip-hop musicians and artists echo earlier academic work such as Lorde's "Uses of the Erotic: The Erotic as Power" (1978); academics strengthened presence and publications.	Higher visibility of Black women academics; emergence of Latina, Afro-Latina, and Native leaders such as Gloria LaRiva, Zenaida Mendez, and Winona LaDuke.
21st c.	Black Lives Matter; continued arts and media education. The 2018 midterm elections.	#BlackLivesMatter and #NativeLivesMatter bring attention to police killings; artists like Beyoncé proclaim themselves feminists; educators like Franchesca Ramsey (MTV) and Kimberly Foster (blog) bring digital education to the public. Black Twitter becomes a prime political site. An unprecedented number of women of color are elected in 2018.

Global Women's Movements

Global women's movements are often offered as proof of universal oppression of women. But as with Indigenous women in the US, racism, classism, and sexism were introduced to many cultures by colonialism or imperialism. If we don't study global movements alongside Western movements, mainstream assumptions can distort the gender schemas of other cultures, unwittingly erasing their issues. To avoid that pitfall, let's look at historical processes that combine internal and external tensions.

China

Chinese women's stance against foot-binding was sparked by internal clashes. Despite exceptional women warriors, scholars, and politicians, patriarchy was endemic in most of China. It was more absolute among the elite than peasants, roles often determined by ethnicity. Peasant women performed strenuous physical labor. Their feet could not be bound because with bound feet, it's hard to walk, let alone work. Elite Chinese women with class and ethnic privilege had to fight for something peasant women already had—the freedom to walk on natural, fully grown feet. One lesson from China is that male privilege versus female oppression isn't always the cornerstone of a culture, and hegemonic assumptions about class don't always apply across cultures. The ways norms intersect—who is privileged, who oppressed, and how—can be complicated and surprising.

Chinese Feminism by I I "Kathy" Chou

I see feminism in China as a confluence of two bodies of water—the seawater of the west and the freshwater from the rivers within. The star-crossed cultural phenomenon in the late 19th to early 20th centuries created an estuary, and it was a wholly organic process—predisposed conditioning, geographic position, a little bit of luck, and chance encounter—to be infected by it. The idea that women can have independent lives and work as well as men started with Qiu Jin. She was born into a southern Fujian family of scholars in 1875 and went to Beijing all the way in the north in 1903 where she encountered the raging radical nationalism in the capital. She sold her dowry and went to Japan the following year, further immersed herself in the revolutionary community for two years, and finally joined Sun Yat-sen's Revolutionary Alliance, becoming one of the first female members of an organization that built the foundation for new China.[8] Without the ability to travel, Qiu Jin would have remained domesticated in the traditional women's role, and her coming of new age pattern can be seen in all the women pioneers of that time. She did a whole bunch of gender bending things—cross-dressing as a man, writing feminist novellas, and even experimenting with bomb making and army building. In her essays, which were written like speeches, she passionately defended women's right to fight in battles, claiming there is nothing a man can do that woman can't and that gender equality is only achievable when women pick up weapons and fight alongside men. But Qiu Jin's outrageous feminist conduct was little known in the Chinese population. She was immortalized as a martyr for the republic, many stories were written and films were made about her heroic actions, but other than a few feminist scholars in the west, no one knew about her feminist core.

Feminism in China is also a who comes first question. Was it the proliferation of women's schools that sprang up in urban centers throughout China in the early 1900s that opened women's mind to bigger things? Was it the male reformists—many taught in women's schools—who used women's issues in the reform discourse that revolutionized the country's thinking? Was it the importation of ideas and theories from the west? And conflictingly, was it the lack of colonialism on Chinese soil that allowed the seeds to grow into something local? If we look through that foggy window of feminism in the third world (back then, China was the third world), similar patterns can be seen in the Arab world, in the Southeast continent, but feminism in China evolved on a different trajectory and across the strait that separates China and Taiwan.

Two decades after Qiu Jin's birth, a second wave (some would claim this is the first wave) was born, and for the first time in Chinese history, women traveled mostly alone to the nearest city to attend women's schools. There were two major centers for women's schools—Beijing and Shanghai—that attracted women from the nearby provinces. Women from progressive households (mostly in the south) were already forward thinking and eager to take their place on the new stage, but women from traditional households (mostly in the north) that still practiced foot-binding, had to climb a higher wall. Physically, these women had to go through the painful process of unbinding their feet in order to go to school, and emotionally, living among strangers was as unthinkable as nine suns in the sky. They helped each other to acclimate in the new world order, sisterhood formed spontaneously and unquestioningly, and once they finished school, most of them would be summoned home to fulfill pre-arranged marriage agreements. The May 4 movement (1919) saw women students marching on the street for the first time. Thus began the phase of women's mobilizations and publications that lasted in Beijing until the 1927 crackdown against women activists, when the center of gravity moved to Shanghai, where the progressive climate and economic growth allowed a brief renaissance of women's writings (both translated texts from the West and homegrown "subjective writing" by local writers) to flourish until the mid-1930s. The New Women of the May 4 era re-invented their appearance—bobbed haircuts and loosely fitted Cheongsam dresses—and revolutionized women's gender identity using the power of writing. Traditionally, Chinese women have always been active privately in cultivating literary skills: in elite families, women formed poetry circles, mastered calligraphy and ink painting;

rural women used various crafts and storytelling to pass on their female knowledge; there is even a women-only-can-read writing system—Nu Shu—that existed in the Hunan countryside with the sole purpose of sharing isolated experiences with other women. The New Women writers took this tradition onto the public stage by fervently publishing personal journals, letters, and fictions that centered around women's realities in newspaper columns, popular and literary magazines, and periodicals. For a short time, between 1933 and 1936, a woman's bookstore found lifeblood in Shanghai through the donated time and money from a community of women writers.[9] Their collective effort told stories from women's perspective and tackled issues of free love and marriage, poverty, and anxieties that many young women faced when they rebelled against the norm. It was like an enormous Conscious Raising Awareness campaign. The ensuing civil wars in China silenced and shamed women writers as self-serving, lacking political awareness of the time, and the few remaining women writers found refuge in two political camps, the Communist Party of China (CPC), leader of the People's Republic of China, and the Kuomintang (KMT), coleader of the Republic of China, Taiwan. With women's voices silenced, China's feminist movement seemed to have vanished under the banner of nationalism, but little attention was paid to a small group of 80 female KMT members, who presided over the drafting of the new constitution in 1946 and fought for and succeeded in guaranteed seats for future female politicians, albeit their dream was realized only decades later in another landscape.

The fruits of the effort of the early Chinese feminists can be seen abundantly in recent women's advancement in Taiwan, including the public election of the first female president, Tsai Ing-Wen. From 1970s onward, a handful of feminists began to till the ground for change. Among them was Annette Lu (Hsiu-lien), who published a series of feminist essays that was collected in the first Taiwanese feminism book, *New Feminism* (*Xin Nüxing Zhuyi* [1973]). She founded Frontier Publishing, organized women's study workshops, mobilized women students, and established the first helpline for needy women.[10] Lu was one of the eight dissident leaders in The Kaohsiung Incident who rallied and criticized the KTM government openly, and she was imprisoned for 5 1/2 years for the 20-minute speech she gave. This experience cemented her position and influence in the Democratic Progressive Party (DPP) which is now the co-ruling party of Taiwan, and as DPP gained power, Lu was elected vice president from 2000 to 2008, serving alongside the first DDP president Chen Shui-bian. Because DPP needed to grow and expand rapidly, just like the Reform movement did back in 1919, women were given free rein to be radical, and many entered politics through Legislature Yuan, the guaranteed path that was paved by the 80 KTM female members.

Outside the government, an educator named Li Yuan-chen began a grassroots movement that eventually transformed the Formosa landscape. Li founded *Awakening* magazine that became the launch pad for legal reforms aimed at gender and sexual equality for women. Li was very pragmatic in her tactics, and between 1987 and 2009, her advocacy achieved a number of important laws that changed women's lives for good: legalized abortion, criminalized rape, incest, human trafficking, and sexual harassment, equal wage and employment opportunities, paid maternity leave for both sexes, and women's right for child custody, marital properties, alimony, and child support.

For matriarchies and gender-balanced societies, male privilege was an alien practice. If a society was also heterarchical, class stratification may have been minor or nonexistent. We'll find movements were often driven by newly disempowered women resisting the culture of invaders in order to restore social balance. They were, at heart, anti-colonial movements, initiated by clashes between imperial and Indigenous values. Such is the case with many African nations.

African Nations

In *African Women's Movements: Changing Political Landscapes*, Aili Mari Tripp and Isabel Casimiro explain that women's movements today draw on "indigenous women's strategies that were part of African societies before colonization."[11] Although traditions vary between 3,000 ethnic groups and 54 nations, most African cultures include powerful roles for women. To consider this in a culturally specific way, we offer the example of Nigeria, a multi-ethnic, multi-religious state with all the internal tensions that implies. We'll start with Yoruba society: the ethnic group already introduced is traditionally gender-balanced. Oyeronke Oyewumi, a Yoruba feminist scholar, argued that the idea of the Yoruba "woman" is a European invention.[12] Gender neutrality begins in childhood, as both girls and boys are called *omo* (child), not son or daughter. In order to specify the sex of the child, one must say *omo ti a bi li obinrin* (child who is female) and have a reason to do so. Motherhood is privileged differently than in the West. Rather than referring to the nuclear family, Yoruba speaks of *omoya*, children of one mother, which includes children of the mother's siblings. Words like *onile* (owner of the home) refer to Mother Earth as well as a society of elders represented by twin male and female figures.

Titi Ufomata says that "in Africa the idea of a full-time housewife is alien."[13] Olajubu adds that "it is difficult to find areas of social life from which either men or women were completely barred in the Yoruba society."[14] Like the Aztecs, Yoruba women ran the markets. Margaret Drewal adds,

Women are economically independent of their husbands and have the opportunity and potential to acquire great wealth. It is possible . . . for a woman to be wealthier than her husband, and he may be a nonentity in the town. [. . .] [A] woman's status derives largely from her reputation in trading, her craftsmanship, and her wealth, rather than from her husband's importance.[15]

Candace Johnson-Phipps concludes that in Africa,

> Historically, women were included in all aspects of decision making . . . through colonialism and its enforcement of the patriarchal society . . . women began to lose their prominent places. Men were given more power and women were put in positions where they were expected to have to look to their men for guidance and become . . . subordinate[16]

Although ethnic groups vary, many have similar principles. A famous example of trans-ethnic Nigerian women's resistance occurred in 1929. Thousands of women from six ethnic groups traveled to urban centers in a tightly organized "Women's War" that covered about 6,000 square miles and lasted a year. They protested colonial restrictions that revoked their traditional social, political, and economic rights, especially their right to govern. They employed a strategy called "sitting on a man," traditionally enacted when a man mistreated his wife or violated market regulations. They mobbed the men who had imposed restrictions, singing derisively as they danced around them, following them everywhere, eventually forcing some to resign their posts and pressuring the colonial governor to incorporate their recommendations into new policy. Women chiefs were appointed and they also re-gained seats in the courts. This success was followed by three decades of protests that ultimately contributed to independence. But British colonizers did not give up their patriarchal beliefs:

> The British [had] outlawed *Iyaami* [mothers' society] because the women of *Iyaami* have the power to remove a Yoruba king from office. Because the British wanted puppet kings to rule they made *Iyaami* illegal and systematically destroyed many of their shrines throughout Nigeria. In the fifties . . . just before the British left Nigeria, they sponsored a Christian crusade . . . [to burn] down *iroko* trees based on the belief that speaking with your ancestors is the work of the devil. . . . The *iroko* tree is . . . the meeting place for *Iyaami* . . . in Ode Remo . . . a Christian church was built on the sacred site. . . . When the church was completed the women of *Iyaami* burned it to the ground and continue to use the site for the rituals.[17]

Many African nations have worked hard to reinstate women's status. In fact, Rwanda tops the world in female governmental representation, and 48% of African countries exceed the US which is tied for 78th place. Until the 2018 midterms, even Saudi Arabia, famous for its patriarchy, had a higher percentage of female representation than the US.[18]

Arab Countries

In *Opening the Gates: A Century of Arab Feminist Writing*, Margot Badran collected Arab women's responses to colonialism. Arab feminists thrived in the late 19th century, and essays and fiction from the Arabic Women's Press detailed their beliefs and activities. They described how women who had previously "participated with the men in work and wars" were now confined by patriarchy. They theorized that Arab men accepted Western patriarchal norms because they had lost their own status. Through patriarchy, they retained some internal control and privilege (over women), although they had lost their external power as heads of areas or states.

As early as the 19th century, Arab feminists strove to restore their rights by calling on Islam. Zainab Fawwaz, from Lebanon, wrote in 1891:

> We have not seen any[thing] . . . among the corpus of religious law (in Islam), ruling that woman is to be prohibited from involvement in the occupations of men. Nature has nothing to do with this: I do not think that if this were to happen the sun would change its path . . . woman is a human being as man is . . . with equivalent [capacities].[19]

Huda Shaarawi presented the opening speech at a Pan-Arab Feminist Conference held in Cairo, Egypt, in 1944, asserting,

> The advanced nations, after careful examination into the matter, have come to believe in the equality of the sexes in all rights even though their religious and secular laws have not reached the level Islam has reached in terms of justice towards the woman. Islam has given her the right to vote for the ruler and has allowed her to give opinions on questions of jurisprudence and religion.[20]

Some highly respected Muslim men agreed. In a 1952 essay, Duriya Shafiq quoted His Eminence Shaikh Alam Nassar, Mufti of Egypt: "Islam looks at the woman as it looks at the man with respect to humanity, rights, and personality. . . . Woman and man in the judgment of Islam are equal."[21] As in every religion, these feminists say, there are fundamentalists who espouse patriarchy, but it isn't intrinsic to Islam.

To this day, Islamic women in the US say the same thing. One source of misunderstanding about women's power in Arab countries comes from Western assumptions that the hijab, or head-covering, is a sign of oppression. Dalia Mogahed clarified this issue for Trevor Noah. She said:

> When we talk about oppression . . . that concept's really important and interesting because oppression means the taking away of someone's power. What hijab does is it basically privatizes women's

sexuality . . . so what are we saying when we say that by taking away or privatizing a woman's sexuality, we're oppressing her. What is that saying about the source of a woman's power?

Noah answered, "We're saying that woman is only strong if she's sexy in public?"[22] Bingo.

Transnational Feminism

Thanks to global interactions, we have a rich growth of feminisms today. Global connections allow us to learn from multiple generations, multiple voices, and multiple cultures. Transnational feminism is associated with scholars and activists like Chandra Mohanty, Jacqui Alexander, Inderpal Grewal, and Caren Kaplan. They build bridges between cultures and nations that have undergone similar experiences. Rather than using terms like international that emphasizes nation states (many of which have had borders drawn by imperialists) or global (sometimes associated with white second wave feminist ideas of universal women's experiences), they choose the term transnational. Their main point is that even though different cultures have divergent gender norms, global capitalism, a modern form of economic imperialism, affects all non-white cultures in specific ways. This feminism has a strong presence in academia and is active in public organizations and non-governmental organizations (NGOs), such as Association for Women's Rights in Development (AWID), which addresses "gender equality, sustainable development, and women's human rights."[23]

#WTF: Who's That Feminist?

Elizabeth Wiltse

I Am Happy to Say I've Found My Voice Again

> I do not wish them [women] to have power over men, but over themselves.
> Mary Wollstonecraft, *A Vindication of the Rights of Woman, 1792*

My interest in a feminist perspective of history began during my junior year of study at SUNY Empire State College. Many of the history classes that I completed early on focused on broadly constructed survey courses of time periods or geographic regions, such as Western Civilization and Early American History. One of the themes that became apparent to me during this time was that all of the histories focused predominantly—almost exclusively—on the history of men, written by men. What happened to all the women in history? And more importantly, why were they left out?

Seeking to answer these questions became the driving force behind my later studies and why I chose to seek out the female voice and to consider the implications of studying history from a feminist perspective. While there are many different lenses through which historians might examine history, such as social, cultural, or political, I was drawn in particular to the feminist lens.

My interest in a feminist approach to history developed somewhat unintentionally and in many ways was influenced in a large part by my own history. My grade school education during the 1970s and 1980s was rather typical in many ways. My hometown of Allegany, nestled among the foothills of Western New York, could have been any small town in America. I was a straight A student, played soccer, was in the band, planned to attend college, get a job, buy a house, raise a family, to live the quintessential American dream. However, the actualization of this vision for my life would not be so easy.

I did go to college for a short time, but I dropped out after a year and a half. My high school boyfriend (and later first husband) and I struggled on our own from the outset. I was 17 when I left home. Wholly unprepared for the challenges that I would face, my idealistic visions of adulthood quickly vanished. Those early years found us moving across the country and back again in the search for something better. I had my son at the age of 21, my oldest daughter three years later. My relationship with my ex-husband suffered terribly from the financial strain of relocating and job changes. I struggled to find my place and was excruciatingly lonely and unhappy. We did eventually buy a house. I got a job. We raised a family. Twenty years came and went but at some point, along the way, I had lost myself and my voice.

After 20 years of marriage, I made a bold decision: I left. I rented an apartment for the first time on my own at the age of 42 and enrolled at SUNY Empire State College. My first class was English Literature, and I stumbled upon Mary Wollstonecraft's *A Vindication of the Rights of Woman* in a hefty English anthology. Two things struck me in that initial reading: first, the date of the piece, 1792, and second, the word *vindication*. There are several meanings of the word *vindicate* but one in particular stood out to me at that time: "to claim for oneself or another." In other words, the title of Wollstonecraft's piece could be understood as "to claim for oneself or another the rights of woman." This definition implies ownership of a thing, in this case women's rights, and I felt passionately that I needed to claim for myself my own rights as a woman.

I became fascinated in the history and scholarship surrounding Wollstonecraft. I was struck by the amount of time that had passed, 200+ years, and the relevance of the issues that Wollstonecraft had written about to modern feminist discourse. I drew many parallels between Wollstonecraft's turbulent and often contradictory personal life and writing, and my own life and views. She was a flawed and fragile woman at times, just like I was, but yet she persisted in her dedication to the rights of women and speaking up when it was "not a woman's place." Her story inspired me to rethink the beliefs that I had formed about women's lives historically and to seek out women's voices in history.

I am happy to say I've found my voice again. I continue to grow and learn and experience everything I can. I continually seek out those stories that I have not discovered yet but that are intrinsically valuable, feminist or otherwise. The ongoing discourse on women's rights in modern society will continue to develop and I am grateful to be able to participate in the conversation, just like Wollstonecraft did in 1792.

MaryNell Morgan

My Feminist Consciousness Was Expanded

I will focus on a point when my feminist consciousness was expanded because that is more memorable than my entry point. My interest in feminism was broadened by reading "The Damnation of Women," Chapter 7 in *Darkwater: Voices From Within the Veil*, William Edward Burghardt Du Bois's first book-length autobiography. In that chapter, published in 1920, he champions women's rights in the areas of education, work, political rights, family roles, and reproductive freedom. From there, I explored his writings about women's issues in *The Crisis Magazine*, the organ of the NAACP that he founded and edited for the first 25 years of its publication (in 2018, it is still published by the NAACP).

Through my exploration, I found that Dr. Du Bois had devoted three special issues of *The Crisis Magazine* to advocating for the passage of the Nineteenth Amendment to the Constitution of the USA. The first suffrage issue was published in September 1912. It featured contributions from four suffragettes, two Colored—Mary Church Terrell and Adella Hunt Logan—and two White—Fannie Garrison Villard and Martha Gruening. The second suffrage issue came in August 1915. It was a symposium of leading thinkers of Colored America. A total of 26 contributors were featured, 11 men and 15 women. The contributions of three White suffragettes were presented in the third suffrage issue in November 1917. Dr. Anna Howard Shaw, Carrie Chapman Catt, and Mary Garret Hay focused on the parallels between the Women's Rights Movement and the Civil Rights Movement.

By pairing the voices of Colored women with those of Colored men as well as with the voices of White women, Dr. Du Bois highlights the dual suppression of Colored women because of racism and sexism. This dual suppression carries forward the two-ness or double consciousness theme that is featured in his most popular book, *The Souls of Black Folk*, first published in 1903. And for me, it demonstrated that W.E.B. Du Bois was a pioneer in the struggle for social, political, and economic justice for women.

Finding Yourself in the Feminist Landscape

Feminist stories help identify the goals of specific feminisms. MaryNell Morgan recalls "when my feminist consciousness was expanded because that is more memorable than my entry point." She has described how she became aware of race from an early age and how awareness of one oppression facilitated critical thinking about other forms of oppression. Her "expansion" story speaks to the goal of men and women of color progressing together.

Scholars within every feminism have done remarkable work researching women and movements that would otherwise have been lost to history. Because there've been so many feminists since the term was coined, we'll highlight a few who demonstrate key positions. However, they're the foam on the tidal roar of an enormous swell of women. They can help you locate yourself in the feminist landscape.

The Americas

Famous stories of how women resisted or negotiated invasion include La Malinche, an enslaved Aztec girl who grew up to act as a buffer between the invaders and her people.

La Malinche: Statesperson or Traitor?
by Rhianna Rogers[24]

Almost immediately upon contact with the Aztecs in 1519, the Spanish began reconfiguring traditional Aztec social and religious norms. By subjugating, evangelizing, and converting the Aztec peoples, conquistador Fernando Cortés drastically changed women's ability to impact and function in colonial Mexico. Using Indian translators to establish trust with New World inhabitants as well as promote alliances with various native groups, Cortés intentionally used natives to dominate Mexico. One such translator and later mistress of Cortés was La Malinche or Malintzín Tenepal.[25] An inhabitant of the Vera Cruz region and a native speaker of Nahuatl, the language of the Aztecs, Malinche accompanied Cortés on his trip to Tenochtitlan, the Aztec capital.[26] The first documented case of a woman to excel in post-contact Mexico, Malinche's experience foreshadowed the path followed by women attempting to maintain their societal status (or survive) among the conquerors.

In the account by Bernal Díaz del Castillo, *Historia verdadera de la conquista de la Nueva España*, Malinche was secretly sold by her mother and stepfather to the people of Xicalanco as a way to provide more inheritance for her younger brother.[27] Once in Xicalanco, Malinche was again sold to inhabitants of the Chontal Maya area near the base of the Yucatan peninsula. Offered as a gift along with 20 other women, Malinche was then given to Cortés by the Mayans in order to appease relations with the Spanish. On the one hand, some state that as a slave Malinche had few choices. They speculate that she was aware of the superior military strength of the Spanish and used her linguistic and diplomatic skills to broker agreements that saved lives.[28] Others state that, given away by her family and sold by her own people, Malinche was more than willing to help Cortés in order to escape the shackles of slavery. In either case, unlike other native women who were mistreated by the Spaniards, Malinche improved her social status.

"Doña Marina's [Malinche's] invaluable multilingualism distinguished her from the other women who fell in the hands of Cortés and his men. She was not branded on the forehead, gambled for, fought over. She survived to be made the legitimate and dowried wife of a conqueror . . . [she] is a gifted woman in impossible circumstances carving out survival one day at a time."[29]

In fact, many historians and Mexicans today portray Malinche as a traitor, even coining the term *malinchismo* for those who dishonor the Mexican nation.[30] As feminist scholar Adelaida R. Del Castillo states, Malinche's negative portrayal in history can directly be attributed to "an unconscious, if not intentional, misogynistic attitude towards women in general, especially towards self-assertive women, on the part of western society as a whole."[31] It is uncertain if Malinche would have taken part in the conquest of Mexico had she known what would happen to her people, but it is clear that her relations with Cortés and ability to interpret multiple languages made her an influential participant in the early days of the post-contact Aztec world.

Feminists Influential in the US

Mary Wollstonecraft (1759–1797)
by Elizabeth Wiltse[32]

Eighteenth-century British author Mary Wollstonecraft is well recognized as an early champion of women's rights, publishing her second political treatise, *A Vindication of the Rights of Woman*, in 1792. Outspoken and controversial, Wollstonecraft advocated for equality of the sexes, demanding equal access to education for girls, stressing the importance of financial independence for women, and encouraging relationships between men and women built on mutual respect and moral values. She also publicly supported Enlightenment ideologies, which were at the heart of the revolutionary movements in France and the American colonies. Initially, her political writing was accepted positively, but that reception quickly changed following the violence of the French Revolution. Soon, her political works caused critics to label her as a "hyena in petticoats" and an "unsexed female," and the *Anti-Jacobin Review* (1798) to label her under "P" for *Prostitute*.[33] Modern readers might find it difficult to relate to the level of animosity that her calls for female equality fomented in her time. While women's suffrage and the subsequent feminist movement have guaranteed many of the social and political rights that Wollstonecraft advocated for, Wollstonecraft has earned a permanent place in our collective memory because she so passionately fought for the rights of women through the use of her pen.

The political and social ideologies as presented in her writing include discourse on men's and women's rights, education, class, marriage, and childrearing, which later inspired controversy and labeled her as a radical in her time.[34] Wollstonecraft's personal life, as detailed by her husband William Godwin after her death, quickly became a source of debate and controversy, especially her liberal views on marriage.

Modern scholarship includes discussion of Wollstonecraft's influence as a political reformer, her role as a proto-feminist to later feminist movements, her importance as an author during the Romantic period, and biographies framed around her personal and political life. Wollstonecraft's written works span a relatively short period of time beginning in 1773 and ending in 1797. They include personal letters, political tracts, educational and moral instruction, literary reviews and translations, travel literature, and fictional novels.

Titles by Wollstonecraft include *Thoughts on the Education of Daughters; Mary, A Fiction; A Vindication of the Rights of Men; A Vindication of the Rights of Woman; An Historical and Moral View of the French Revolution; Letters Written During a Short Residence in Sweden, Norway and Denmark*; and *Wrongs of Woman, or Maria*. The personal letters of Wollstonecraft can be found in *The Collected Letters of Mary Wollstonecraft*, edited by Janet Todd (2003). These varied written sources have provided scholars with a rich background of primary sources in which to study the life and philosophy of Wollstonecraft.

Wollstonecraft died in 1797 of complications resulting from the birth of her second daughter, Mary Wollstonecraft Shelley, the author of *Frankenstein*; a tragic ending to a life which continues to intrigue and inspire scholars and students today. Modern feminists might argue that the goals and ideals that Wollstonecraft had presented and debated with the men and women of her time have come to fruition. Certainly, she would be pleased with the many political, social, and economic rights and privileges that modern women enjoy today. But history is not static and certainly the history of significant figures such as Wollstonecraft undergoes changes over time. Wollstonecraft's legacy continues to have significance and influence modern feminist thought and movements. This is what makes the feminist history and legacy of Mary Wollstonecraft so meaningful—that we can understand her place at once among the British radicals and Enlightenment *philosophes* of her time and yet outside of them, "the first of a new genus" as Wollstonecraft herself said.[35]

Emma Goldman (1869–1940)

J. Edgar Hoover, director of the FBI from 1924 to 1972, named Emma Goldman "One of the most dangerous people in America." She was such a powerful speaker that she was called "sledgehammer" and "Little Joan of Arc." She saw herself differently, saying she was fighting for "everyone's right to beautiful radiant things." Goldman, an anarchist, rejected all forms of institutional repression, and her fight for labor rights and women's rights ended with her in prison several times. She was at odds with suffragettes because she believed the vote was part of a system that should be dismantled. She advocated women's free rule over their own bodies, birth control, and the right to love as one pleases and was one of the earliest advocates for gay rights. Equally important to Goldman were labor rights. Her citizenship was revoked and she was deported to Russia. Never an adherent to political systems, she spoke out against Hitler's extreme right and Stalin's extreme left.[36]

Claudia Jones, née Claudia Vera Cumberbatch (1915–1964)

Cumberbatch was born in Trinidad, moved to the US as a child, and grew up to become an activist, Black nationalist, and member of the Communist party. She fought for job training, equal pay, and childcare programs to equalize opportunities for women. She took the name Jones because the Communist Control Act of 1954 made party membership illegal. However, even some Communists considered her too radical because she didn't believe economics was the only cause of racism and sexism. Her best-known writing, "An End to the Neglect of the Problems of the Negro Woman!"[37] appeared in 1949. Her theory of "triple oppression" was a major:

> contribution to feminist thought . . . she formulated . . . a universal emancipatory politics that would free . . . all humans. . . . She [argued] that true freedom lay in the demolition of class, race, and gender oppression. What better way to do that than to focus on the emancipation of the group that suffered from all three . . . by freeing black women, you would free *all* women, and by struggling to free the most downtrodden, *all* would be freed. Jones's theory of socialist feminism was a universal idea for global emancipation.[38]

Jones was arrested in 1948, convicted of "Un-American activities," and deported in 1955. Trinidad rejected her, but Britain accepted her on humanitarian grounds because she had suffered severe illness in prison. She founded Britain's first Black newspaper, *The West Indian Gazette*. Her activism in Britain was central to the 1950–1960s British Civil Rights movement, and the newspaper addressed a wide range of issues, from women's rights to West Indian rights to the release of Nelson Mandela. She also continued to write for *Freedomways*, a journal founded by a group that included WEB DuBois. She founded what later became the Notting Hill Carnival. It's not enough to criticize problems; we need to celebrate solutions. Her slogan for the carnival, "A people's art is the genesis of their freedom," was no doubt inspirational to Lorraine Hansberry, a young writer for *Freedomways*.

Lorraine Hansberry (1930–1965)

Hansberry was born to an upper middle-class Black family. She recalled

> early "memories of fighting white supremacy in America" in a "hellishly hostile" white Chicago neighborhood that include . . . [her] mother patrolling the house all night with a loaded German luger while her father "fought the respectable part of the battle in the Washington court." Teachings on colonialism by her well-known Africanist uncle engendered global understanding of this local struggle. She worked to impart this understanding in the face of entrenched contemporaneous norms of racism, sexism, classism, and homophobia.[39]

Hansberry was the first Black woman playwright to author a Broadway play. She was also the first African American and the youngest playwright to receive the New York Critic Circle Award for Best American Play. Her best-known work, *A Raisin in the Sun*, premiered in 1959. "It was the McCarthy era: Communists, Blacks, and gays were jailed as equally un-American." Hansberry, a gay Black Communist woman, was radically "un-American." The period espoused a fantastical "heterosexist upper middle-classism,"[40] and *Raisin* demonstrates the relationships between white and Black, rich and poor, men and women, old and young, and American and African characters. A later play, *Les Blancs*, explores this in international context.

Hansberry was active in labor rights, civil rights, and gay rights, as evidenced by publications in journals such as *Freedom, Freedomways*, and *The Ladder*, and organizations such as the Labor Youth League, Young Progressives of America, and The Daughters of Bilitis.[41] Her early 1950s journalism addressed imperialism (African liberation movements in Kenya, Ghana, Egypt), sexism (women's rights), the combination of racism and classism (conditions in Harlem Public Schools), stereotypes ("Representation of Negroes in Same Old Roles)," and invasive government surveillance—she herself was in FBI files. She raised money to buy a station wagon for the voter registration drive happening in the South. This was the car that was burned when Goodman, Chaney, and Schwerner were murdered.

Part of her genius was the ability to instigate "imaginative acts in which whites see themselves as Blacks see them."[42] Michael Anderson explains how "you had white audiences applauding the Younger family moving into a white neighborhood who would have been appalled had a Black family moved in next to them."[43]

National Organization for Women Founders

Pauli Murray (1910–1985), Betty Friedan (1921–2006), Muriel Fox (1928–), Shirley Chisholm (1924–2005)

The National Organization for Women (NOW), founded in 1966, initiated the legal activism of the 20th century. It was originally composed of seven task forces—Equal Opportunity of Employment; Legal and Political Rights; Education; Women in Poverty; The Family; Image of Women; and Women and Religion—and by 1967 had proposed a "Bill of Rights for Women." Some of the legal victories are listed in Table 6.1. Muriel Fox notes they were inspired by the Civil Rights movement—Betty Freidan had called for "an NAACP for women"—and she credits over 300 men and women as founders. The organization quickly took on a hierarchal structure since its main goal was to change laws.[44] A Google search for founders reflects this hierarchy, and the four names are imprinted in American memory; the NOW site itself refers to 49 founders.[45] It could be interesting to research unmentioned founders. NOW continues to be active, with a political action committee (PAC) that supports women and women-friendly candidates.

Lawyer Pauli Murray has been called "the most important legal scholar you've likely never heard of." Along with women's rights, Murray was active in civil rights, arguing that "separate but equal" was discriminatory. She coined the term "Jane Crow" and, in her essay "Jane Crow and the Law," argued that the Equal Protection Clause should be applied to sex as it was to race, thus crafting the legal foundation for addressing multiple issues. Ruth Bader Ginsburg credits Murray with inspiring her approach to sex discrimination. Murray was also an advocate of class equity and a gender non-conformist.[46]

The iconic writer Betty Friedan's 1963 book, *The Feminine Mystique*, spurred mid-20th-century feminism. She challenged the heritage of the Cult of True Womanhood, calling the discontent of stay-at-home housewives "the problem with no name." Her analysis mainly applied to middle-class white women since poor women already worked outside the home as they always had.[47] Betty in the TV series *Mad Men* personifies this discontent and this era.

Muriel Fox helped Friedan draft the Statement of Purpose. She wanted to "make history" with her skills as a wordsmith, was involved in public relations, and did much to further Affirmative Action and Equal

Employment Opportunity. There is an award in her name, the "Foxy," for Communication Leadership Towards a Just Society. She currently serves as chair of Veteran Feminists of America.

Shirley Chisholm, a congresswoman for seven terms, was the first African American woman elected to this office. She also pre-dated Barack Obama as the first African American to run for president in a major party and Hillary Clinton as the first woman to run for president. Her book, *Unbought and Unbossed*, was the basis of a film by the same title made in 2004.[48]

International Feminists

China: Lu Yün Zhang (1892 or 1893–1974) by I I "Kathy" Chou

Lu Yün Zhang was my grandmother. During the time I knew her, she was paralyzed from the waist down and blind, but she was still in command of our household and held the seat of legislator for the Republic of China, Taiwan, until her death. Lu's feet were bound in childhood, but she was one of the lucky ones who broke away from that traditional bondage and entered a woman's school in Beijing at the age of 19. She was one of the women students who marched in protest against the Treaty of Versailles in 1919 and studied new Chinese Literature under the iconic reformist writer and thinker Lu Xun. In the photos I found buried in her "Daughter's Trunk" made of Camphor wood, the young Lu always wore a bob-cut hairstyle and, Chiongsam dress under a long coat, and stood with her head held high among important-looking men. She had a keen interest in promoting women's education, worked as principal for a number of schools, and held the position as the first female Inspectorate of Education, though the wars in China pulled her into the Nationalist movement, where she worked underground and traveled extensively as the party's trusted liaison on women's mobilization. She was a single mother of two children, a loyal Nationalist, and one of the 80 against 1,700 female KMT members who fiercely defended and insisted on guaranteed seats for women in the new government. Her famous last words on the issue were plain and logical: "How can you expect women to follow a constitution that doesn't have fair representation of the female population?"

Africa: Waangari Matthei (1940–2011)

Wangari Maathei was the first East African woman to earn a PhD (1971) and the winner of many awards, including the 2004 Nobel Peace Prize. In her books, she describes her life-long campaign for "Africa, Women, and the Environment"[49] that culminated in the Green Belt Movement.

She was department chair and associate professor at the University of Nairobi, where she campaigned for equal benefits for women employees. She was highly active in many organizations, including the Kenya Red Cross, the Kenya Association of University Women, the National Council of Women of Kenya, and the Environmental Liaison Centre. Her work in these organizations led her to focus on effects of and remedies for environmental degradation. She founded Envirocare Ltd., a group that worked with local communities to plant trees. This responded to women's reports that "their streams were drying up, their food supply was less secure, and they had to walk further and further to get firewood for fuel and fencing."[50] Saplings from local forests were planted to honor local elders and women were encouraged to plant nurseries. Seed money from the UN Voluntary Fund for Women allowed her to offer a stipend when trees from local nurseries were transplanted throughout the country. Trees not only provide habitat for traditional communal agriculture and animals as well as cooking fuel, they also prevent the spread of deserts, reduce floods, conserve watersheds through shade, and filter ground water.

This was the start of the Pan-African Green Belt movement. The results were so beneficial that representatives from numerous African countries studied with Dr. Maathai so they could set up Green Belts in their countries. But at home in Kenya, she faced challenges. The government tried to privatize some of the areas she had reforested, leading to international protests. The government ended up banning the privatization of public land. This was the first of many battles, which included Maathai running for and winning a seat in parliament. Ultimately, the Green Belt Movement planted 51 million much-needed trees in Kenya and millions more in Uganda, Malawi, Tanzania, Zimbabwe, and Ethiopia.

Egypt: Nawal el Saadawi (1931–)

Nawal el Saadawi is an Egyptian writer, activist, physician and psychiatrist. She wrote several dozen books, some translated to English and other languages, positioning her as one of the contemporary Arab world's feminist spokespersons. She fled Egypt to the US for a time due to threats from Islamic fundamentalists, but returned to Egypt and resumed her activism.

Saadawi began her career as a medical doctor. She attributed the women's suffering she saw to a combination of patriarchal and imperialist oppression. She worked to better women's conditions when serving as Egypt's Minister of Health. As a writer, most of her work addressed women in Islam. She was particularly concerned with the harm of circumcision (both male and female) and the benefits of education. She was also concerned with poverty and women's work, having raised her eight siblings from the age of 25.

In *Woman at Point Zero* (1973), a psychiatrist interviews a poor Egyptian girl, Firdaus (Paradise), who suffers the worst of patriarchy, from childhood sexual abuse to prostitution. The novel depicts how Firdaus's critique of patriarchy, Islam, and businessmen culminates in mental and spiritual freedom. Feeling liberated, she kills a man who tries to harm her and ends up in prison. In 1981, Saadawi herself was imprisoned for being critical of the Anwar Sadat regime. While incarcerated, she used toilet paper and eyebrow pencil to write *Memoirs in a Woman's Prison*.

Saadawi continues to speak out. In 2010, she was involved in Arab Spring events that ousted President Hosni Mubarak. In a 2014 interview, she said, "the root of the oppression of women lies in the global post-modern capitalist system, which is supported by religious fundamental-ism,"[51] echoing Firdaus's analysis in *Woman at Point Zero*.

Conclusion: Movements Spark Theories

Women's experiences in different times and places led to the creation of varying movements. Both grassroots and academics have theorized the causes of these movements. Theories—how each works, how they relate to each other, and what you can do with them—is the topic of Part Four.

Notes

1 Kimberly Foster, "Thank a Black Feminist." For Harriet. *YouTube*. Jan. 17, 2017, https://www.youtube.com/watch?v=fdjpY9gm_GA.

2 Anita Little. "How Many of these Early Black Feminists Do You Know?" *Ms.* Feb. 19, 2014. http://msmagazine.com/blog/2014/02/19/how-many-of-these-early-black-feminists-do-you-know/.

3 Silent Parade, Underwood & Underwood, 7/28/1917, Creative Commons, https://commons.wikimedia.org/wiki/File:1917_Silent_Parade,_first_blood.jpg

4 Sharon Harley and Rosalyn Terborg-Penn. *The Afro-American Woman: Struggles and Images*. Black Classic Press. 1997, p. 104.

5 Combahee River Collective Statement. April 1977, https://combaheeriver-collective.weebly.com/the-combahee-river-collective-statement.html.

6 Alice Walker. *In Search of Our Mothers' Garden: Womanist Prose*. Harcourt Brace. 1983.

7 "Why Black Feminism?" *In Search of Our Mothers' Garden: Womanist Prose*. Harcourt Brace. 1983, https://beyondthemoment.org/wp-content/uploads/2017/03/Why-Black-Feminism2.pdf.

8 More about Qiu Jin's life and read novella experts from "Stones of the Jingwei Bird" in Amy D. Dooling and Kristina Torgeson, *Writing Women in Modern China*. Columbia U Press. 1998.

9 Ibid.

10 The first English language book about the Women's Movement in modern Taiwan: Doris T. Chang, *Women's Movements in Twentieth-Century Taiwan*. U of Illinois Press. 2009.

11 Aili Mari Tripp, Isabel Casimiro, Joy Kwesiga, and Alice Mungwa. *African Women's Movements: Changing Political Landscapes*. Cambridge U Press. 2008, p. 25.

12 Oyeronke Oyewumi. *The Invention of Women: Making an African Sense of Western Gender Discourses*. U. Minnesota, 1997.

13 Candace Johnson-Phipps. "Review of Nigerian Videos: Born Again and Submission." *Ijele: Art Ejournal of the African World*. Africa Resource Center. Issue 5, 2002, p. 6.

14 Oyeronke Olajubu. *Women in the Yoruba Religious Sphere.* State U. of New York Press. 2003.

15 Henry John Drewal and Margaret Thompson Drewal. *Gelede: Art and Female Power Among the Yoruba.* Indiana U. Press. 1990. p. 182.

16 Candace Johnson-Phipps. p. 6.

17 Falo'okun Fatunmbi. Personal Conversations with Menoukha R. Case. 2008.

18 "Women in National Parliaments." *Inter-Parliamentary Union.* June 1, 2018, http://archive.ipu.org/wmn-e/classif.htm.

19 Margot Badran. *Feminists, Islam, and Nation: Gender and the Making of Modern Egypt.* Princeton U. 1996, p. 15.

20 Margot Badran and Miriam Cooke. *Opening the Gates: A Century of Arab Feminist Writing.* Indiana U. 1990, p. 338.

21 Ibid., p. 355.

22 Dalia Mogahed on "The Daily Show." *Comedy Central.* Jan. 8, 2016, https://www.youtube.com/watch?v=nYzkHVu6Gwc.

23 Association for Women's Rights in Development. *AWID.org.* 2019, https://www.awid.org/.

24 Excerpt adapted with permission by Menoukha Case from "The Spider Woman Rules No More? The Transformation and Resilience of Aztec Female Roles." Rhianna Rogers MA Thesis. Florida Atlantic University. 2004.

25 Adelaidia R. Del Castillo, "Malintzín Tenepal: A Preliminary Look into a New Perspective." *Chicana Feminist Thought: The Basic Historical Understandings.* Ed. Alma M García. Routledge. 1997, p. 122.

26 Frances Karttunen. "Rethinking Malinche." *Indian Women of Early Mexico.* Eds. Susan Schroeder, Stephanie Wood, and Robert Haskett. U of Oklahoma Press, 1997. p. 302.

27 Ibid., p. 299.

28 Jacqueline Gerson. "Malinchismo: Betraying One's Own." *The Cultural Complex: Contemporary Jungian Perspectives on Psyche and Society.* Eds. Thomas Singer and Samuel L. Kimbles. Routledge. 2004.

29 Ibid., p. 312.

30 John Greenway. "Introduction." *Fernando Cortes: His Five Letters of Relation to the Emperor Charles V.* Trans. and ed. Francis Augustus MacNutt. Rio Grande Press. 1977, p. 21.

31 Del Castillo. p. 126.

32 Author note: "While MW greatly influenced women's suffragists, she cannot be considered a US feminist in a geographic sense. I consider her as transnational, as her Vindication was available in the US very early on." Elizabeth Wiltse.

33 Claudia L. Johnson, ed. *The Cambridge Companion to Mary Wollstonecraft: Cambridge Companions to Literature.* Cambridge U Press. 2002, pp. 1–2

34 Ibid., pp. 1–6.

35 Ibid., p. 31.

36 Anita Sarkeesian. "The Revolutionary Life of Emma Goldman." *Feminist Frequency.* Sept. 12, 2016, https://feministfrequency.com/video/the-revolutionary-life-of-emma-goldman/.

37 Beverly Guy-Sheftall. *Words of Fire: An Anthology of African-American Feminist Thought.* The New Press. 1995.

38 Denise Lynn. "Claudia Jones' Feminist Vision of Emancipation." *African American Intellectual History Society.* Sept. 8, 2016, https://www.aaihs.org/claudia-jones-feminist-vision-of-emancipation/.

39 Menoukha Robin Case. "Lorraine Hansberry: Writing Between Rocks and Hard Places." *Black Writers and the Left.* Ed. Kristin Moriah. Cambridge Scholars Publishing. 2013, p. 135.

40 Ibid.

41 "Lorraine Hansberry: Sighted Eyes/Feeling Heart." *PBS*. Jan. 19, 2018, http://www.pbs.org/wnet/americanmasters/lorraine-hansberry-sighted-eyesfeeling-heart-film/9846/.

42 Case. "Lorraine Hansberry: Writing Between Rocks and Hard Places." p. 145.

43 Tracy Heather Strain. "Lorraine Hansberry: Sighted Eyes/Feeling Heart." *PBS*. Jan. 19, 2018, http://www.pbs.org/wnet/americanmasters/lorraine-hansberry-sighted-eyesfeeling-heart-film/9846/.

44 Muriel Fox. Makers. *Verizon Media*. 2019, https://www.makers.com/muriel-fox.

45 "Honoring Our Founders." *NOW*. 2019, https://now.org/about/history/honoring-our-founders-pioneers/.

46 Brittney Cooper. "Black, Queer, Feminist, Erased from History." *Salon*. Feb. 18, 2015, https://www.salon.com/2015/02/18/black_queer_feminist_erased_from_history_meet_the_most_important_legal_scholar_youve_likely_never_heard_of/.

47 Debra Michals, ed. "Betty Friedan." *National Women's History Museum*. 2017, https://www.womenshistory.org/education-resources/biographies/betty-friedan.

48 "Remembering Shirley Chisholm." Interview with Shola Lynch and Barbara Ransby. *NPR*. Jan. 26, 2010, https://www.npr.org/templates/story/story.php?storyId=122984022.

49 Wangari Maathai. *The Canopy of Hope: My Life Campaigning for Africa, Women, and the Environment*, Lantern Books. 2002.

50 The Green Belt Movement. 2019, http://www.greenbeltmovement.org/.

51 Arian Fariborz. "They Don't Want Any Really Courageous People." Interview with Nawa El Saadawi. Ed. Aingeal Flanagan. Trans. Jennifer Taylor. *Qantara.de*. July 5, 2014, https://en.qantara.de/content/interview-with-nawal-el-saadawi-they-dont-want-any-really-courageous-people.

Part Four

Theory Today

Introduction: What Is Theory?

Why do feminists make theories, and how do we use them? Many people think of theory as something overly intellectual, something that you think about but don't do anything with. But the purpose of theory is quite the opposite. Theory is defined as "a system of ideas intended to explain something," "a set of principles on which the practice of an activity is based," and "an idea used to account for a situation or justify a course of action."[1] How we think about the world determines how we act in it, and theory is basically a formalized way of thinking about our actions. Theory influences our everyday lives, whether or not we are conscious of it. Being aware of how we think and learning different ways to think allows for better thinking and empowers us to take actions are aligned with our goals.

You know a lot more theory than you probably realize, whether or not you know what those theories are called. Some of the theories you already know come from science class: Einstein's theory of relativity, which the discipline of physics revolves around; plate tectonics, the theory about how Earth's surface moves that allows scientists to predict earthquakes; and, of course, the big bang theory, which theorizes how the Earth itself came to be. In Parts Two and Three of this book we proposed cultural theories about the nature of meaning and social theories about the ways societies can be structured.

Cultural and social theories follow much the same method as scientific ones. They start with careful observation of phenomena, usually a question or problem in need of explanation. They generate a hypothesis, which means an idea of what's happening and why. And then, they test the hypothesis. This test is an educated guess about what will happen. And although testing needs to confirm that the hypothesis makes sense, it also seeks to finds where things *don't* make sense. When does it make sense, and when doesn't it? Will it happen in the way we think it will, for the reasons we think it will, in different circumstances? A theory is the name given to a sufficiently tested hypothesis.

Not only do cultural and social theories have the same purposes as scientific ones—to solve problems—they face some of the same challenges.

The challenge of space travel would have been a lot easier if simple math were all that was needed to get to the moon and back. If you know about the book or film *Hidden Figures*, you know Black women were the "human computers" responsible for crunching those numbers, but because of their race, their accomplishments were long ignored. Katherine Johnson, who was awarded the Presidential Medal of Freedom in 2015 by President Barack Obama, was particularly important in the process, computing the launch window and double-checking the reentry trajectory of John Glenn's Friendship 7 capsule, the US' first crewed suborbital flight.[2] The math involved for human spaceflight goes far beyond simple addition because so many factors are involved. In addition to addition (pun intended), you need algebra, geometry, orbital mechanics, and astrophysics, and a whole host of theoretical, applied, and computational mathematics. Cultural studies and social sciences aren't divided into the same types of branches as math, but similar to advanced math, it takes advanced ideas to solve complicated problems. As we move into theory, don't get daunted if the language describing some ideas seems advanced. It will become clear step-by-step. We're doing introductory work, not rocket science!

Those dedicated to studying feminist issues formalize their ideas in order to test them and arrive at the wisest possible solutions to their questions. They share knowledge with others who can further refine the ideas and/ or build on them as time goes by. Scholarly wisdom can be passed down orally, visually, through the arts, or as writing. The kinds of theories that feminist scholars develop attempt to explain why people and societies behave as they do so as to remedy inequities. They may ask: How do words carry meaning and shape societies? What are the demographics of violence against women? Why is the gap between rich and poor higher now than it was 50 years ago? Why are some societies based on ranking while others are more egalitarian? The benefit of theory is that those who ask complex questions are constantly in conversation with each other, and the theories they develop come from years of inquiry and collaboration. Part of the purpose of sharing theory is that we don't have to all do the same experiments ourselves to arrive at productive solutions. Our thoughts and actions benefit from wisdom passed on.

Feminist actions can be personal (choosing to boycott a certain company, choosing to dress a certain way) or collective (Women's March on Washington). A series of collective actions can become a movement. There are many different kinds of justice movements, women's movements, and feminisms. Some respond to inequities within a culture, and some arise when one culture strives to dominate, alter, and exploit another. People in justice movements talk, write, and make art to organize the meaning of their experiences and seek paths of change and solutions. This talking, writing, and art explain connections between multiple injustices, suggest principles for achieving change, and justify proposals for changes. For example, we presented data organized to reveal pay inequities and proposed the principle of equal pay for equal work. When this proposal was originally made, it justified and resulted in the Equal Pay Act of 1963 which addressed pay discrepancies between men and women. As feminists addressed related inequities, data was sought to also address pay discrepancies according to ethnicity. This demonstrates that theory is an ongoing conversation during which participants may both stick to and stretch their ways of thinking. Different ways of thinking clash and blend, are exchanged and change, and change us. When we organize and explain the concerns of feminist movements, we're making feminist theory. The results make their way into college textbooks that discuss feminist thought and action.

7   Feminist Theories

Feminist Theories: Tools and Methods

There's a saying: "if all you have is a hammer, everything looks like a nail."
It doesn't work to swing a hammer at everything that needs changing; you
want the most effective tool for each job. Similarly, it's important to know
exactly what each theory in the wide range of feminist thought is designed
to accomplish. Theories can be tools for dismantling and changing a singular part of the whole, theories can combine several tools to broaden our
perspective, and theories can generate methods for using multiple tools
together for maximum effectiveness. Each kind of theory has value. So,
instead of ranking them, we are going to group them according to function, considering stand-alone theories as tools and combined theories as
methods.

Theoretical tools reveal the workings of a specific concern. To address
gender inequities, feminist thinkers crafted a tool to differentiate between
anatomical sex, behavior and characteristics, and social identity. This theory, called the social construction of gender, arose within Western thinking because men in Western cultures have treated women unfairly for at
least 6,000 years, long before race became a question. Western societies
had and still have laws that enforce men's political power and practices
such as unequal pay that maintain men's economic power. Because there
are vested interests at stake, inequities extend beyond male/female and
limit opportunities for all those who don't fit gender norms (male = masculine = man/female = feminine = woman). For example, in the fashion
industry, thin and white has been the dominant feminine beauty norm
for about 50 years. Model and body activist Ashley Graham broadened
opportunities for women by working hard to make the industry accept
her curvy figure ("Plus size? More like my size!"[3]). As we saw in our
case study on the beauty industry, even when Western norms affect non-
Western areas, cultures can retain their own values. Therefore, theory
about the social construction of gender can be adapted to reveal how beliefs vary according to culture, time, and place.

Clearly, this effective tool that reveals the workings of gender is important: It helps feminist activists change conditions that lock anatomy to

social expectations and rights, and we'll look at it more deeply. Still, gender alone doesn't account for all women's experiences of injustice. We'll also look at theories about race, class, sexuality, disability, and other aspects of identity listed in Table 3.1. Each is a crucial tool for understanding injustices and inequities.

Theoretical *methods* go beyond tools for defining a problem (sexism, racism) or analyzing the workings of that problem (words, schemas). To make theory into method, we need to think about why we need each tool and how they can best work together to dismantle the entirety in which we live and breathe, what Audre Lorde called "the master's house." Methods instruct us when to pick up a hammer and when to put it down and pick up a saw. We'll introduce feminist identity theory and discuss how identity politics empower us to understand multiple issues. We'll discuss intersectionality, which is the primary feminist method for effectively using multiple tools. In this way, we can avoid pitting different problems against each other and form mutually supportive alliances.

You yourself can refine theory. You can apply, combine, and add premises of your own to make new tools, theories, and methods that address your experiences and understanding. You can help shape the blueprint for dismantling the master's house.

Before going into specific theories, we'll start with two tools that apply to them all. **Privilege and oppression** describe conditions in society where some have more rights, material wealth, safety, acceptance, and status than others simply because they do or don't fit particular norms. On one hand, if a society values difference, it creates norms such as we saw in the Indigenous Table 3.2—generosity and equity are valued; wealth is considered greed—that lead to less privilege *and* less oppression. On the other hand, if a society measures difference as better/worse, discrepancies between the privileged and oppressed increase. Norms measuring better/worse lead to hierarchy, and since almost none of us fits each and every norm, each of us may be limited or attacked according to our position in that hierarchy.

If a society believes that hierarchy is natural, then it believes privilege is natural, deserved, or earned. In the US today, some people believe the wealthy are inherently superior to others. Although some of us think differently, as a society we've accepted this belief, which has led to "eight men owning the same wealth as half the world"[4] and "the top 1 percent of households own[ing] more wealth than the bottom 90 percent combined."[5]

Members of privileged groups are more or less invested in a belief and value system that supports their privilege. We say "more or less" because from time to time someone's natural empathy awakens. A person can feel beyond personal interests or expand her/his sense of the personal to realize we're all connected. If you believe anyone's suffering affects everyone in some way, it's wise to consider the well-being of the whole. For people

include in discussion.

with such beliefs, the drawback that privilege is always based on someone's oppression becomes clear. They can move beyond fearful or aggressive defense of their positions and instead be motivated by compassion, sharing, reciprocity, and "giving back," all parts of our natural biological wiring. They can then invoke fight/flight appropriately and only as needed.

For most, simply disproving a belief or asking that people adjust a value is rarely effective, because privileged members of inequitable systems benefits from their privilege. Generally speaking, they protect these benefits for two reasons. The more obvious is that adjusting privilege and oppression means someone must give up something they believe they're entitled to even though they gained it at someone else's expense. For example, corporations could pay more taxes so that all children can eat, but the benefit of a rising generation of healthy children isn't part of their profitability calculations. If corporations don't pay, ordinary citizens could pay $196 per year in taxes to support SNAP to assure children don't go hungry, but some believe poor families "deserve" poverty. The less obvious reason is that those who have more than they can use are often driven by fear (fight/flight/freeze) of losing their status in the hierarchy. Whether or not this fear is driven by our deeper wiring for empathy is debatable, but, if you're a billionaire who still feels the need to accumulate more wealth, then any change to the system that privileges you can feel like a threat. To the privileged, a move toward equity can feel like oppression.

The good news is, because belief in the value of a norm is cultural, not natural, we can change it. The bad news is that unless we change how it works in the system is more difficult.

Language is therefore another important feminist tool. Words, the basic building blocks of thought, shape not only what we know but how we know. You might be wondering if words really make that big a difference. You've probably heard someone defend something they've said as "just a figure of speech" or with "I [or they] didn't really mean it." Language is sometimes dismissed because measuring its impact isn't easy or straightforward. But words are never just words. We give them meaning that drive values, and those meanings can change and evolve over time and location. If two people are using the same word, but with a slightly different definition, they may have trouble understanding each other. They may disagree and not even know why!

Sometimes, it's true that the impact of words is minimal. A single incident of someone saying something offensive or derogatory isn't the same as a pattern of behavior. But when the full force of authority is used, how one speaks and what one is allowed to speak can become what Gloria Anzaldúa called "linguistic terrorism." In "How to Tame a Wild Tongue," about growing up in the US speaking Chicano Spanish, Anzaldúa writes, "If you really want to hurt me, talk badly about my language . . . I am my language."[6] Prohibition against speaking one's native tongue has long been used as a tool of domination. Erasure of a language removes ways to think about many important things. For Native American children in boarding schools, this sometimes included the sense of relatedness to each other and the natural world. Loss of a language can eradicate important ecological knowledge as well as ideas such as diverse understandings of gender.

Words are used in many ways: there is the common use and misuse of everyday language, and there are technical definitions appropriate to a field of study. Different levels of meaning can get complex when academics define words to express theoretical ideas. Therefore, contrary to popular opinion, a dictionary cannot offer the "correct" definition for a word. Dictionaries record and store the shifting meanings of words, so they're a good place to study how language changes according to time and place. This is why you'll often find multiple definitions of a single word.

Here's an example. If you look up the word "racism" in the online Merriam-Webster dictionary, you'll find three entries. The first is "belief that race is the primary determinant of human traits and capacities and that racial differences produce an inherent superiority of a particular race." The words "race" and "determinant" are hyperlinked and have multiple definitions of their own. The second definition has two parts: (a) "a doctrine or political program based on the assumption of racism and designed to execute its principles," and (b) "a political or social system founded on racism." The third definition is racial prejudice or discrimination, with the word "prejudice" hyperlinked to its own multipart definition.[7]

You might notice that all three of these definitions rely heavily on individual beliefs. The third especially does something most social scientists, and most feminist scholars, in particular, are careful *not* to do, which is equate the social system of racism with individual racial prejudice or bias. But "isms" that perpetuate inequality are systems of oppression, and racism is a system of oppression based on race. In *"Why Are All the Black Kids Sitting Together in the Cafeteria?" and Other Conversations About Race*, Beverly Daniel Tatum defines racism and discusses why individual racial prejudice is only part of it. She draws on David Wellman's definition of racism, "a system of advantage based on race," explaining that "prejudice doesn't offer a sufficient explanation for the persistence of racism."[8]

This doesn't diminish the significance of racial prejudice but rather clarifies that, on its own, it's an incomplete explanation. Racial prejudice maintains structures, policies, and cultural messages that make up a racist system, but what we call overt racism—the acts or statements individual people make based on prejudice—are only part of that system. Tatum compares the system with a moving walkway in an airport. There are three ways to engage: actively racist, passively racist, and actively antiracist.[9] Someone walking faster than the walkway in the direction it's already going is actively racist. Someone walking faster than and against the direction of the walkway is actively antiracist. Regardless of whether or not they intend to support the system or are even aware of it, most people do exactly what it's designed for: they stand still and let the walkway carry them along. This is the passively racist category. Passively racist people might not agree with racial prejudice and may believe themselves to be unbiased but nevertheless allow the system to roll on as is. They might mistakenly believe their approach is neutral or even beneficial ("I don't see race"). Racism doesn't persist because an overwhelming number of actively racist white people believe they're superior to people of color, but because so many people fail to recognize that the system functions on more than their personal beliefs. It may not be perpetuated by their actions, but by their lack of action. Think back to the barriers to entry a person in a wheelchair faces getting into a non-accessible building. You or I may not have planned to cause this problem, but by failing to advocate for a ramp we allowed it to happen. The systemic components of isms are easy to overlook when we're taught to believe that people must have made bad choices and are personally responsible for their misfortunes. But the person in the wheelchair did not choose to omit a ramp from the building design.

You might be left wondering why the definition of racism in a regular dictionary is incomplete. Why isn't the "right" definition there? Does this mean dictionaries are suspect? It's complicated, or at least it's complicated if we think words are just words. But even Merriam-Webster knows language isn't neutral. If you scroll down the racism page, you'll see "The History and Dictionary Definition of Racism." They discuss how the presence of racism predates the term itself and how the role of dictionaries is not to fully explain terms but to record how people use them. They write that a "lexicographer"—someone who makes dictionaries—explain[s] how words are (or have been) actually used, not how some may feel that they should be used, and they say nothing about the intrinsic nature of the thing named by a word, much less the significance it may have for individuals.[10] Words are not simply empty containers that carry fixed meanings. The struggle over the meaning of a word often reflects how controversial an idea is. Struggles reflect stakes, what the outcome of believing in one thing or another will be. For racism, the stakes are extremely high, which makes the definition an intense site of struggle.

Because words are living and changeable, it's important to recognize how dictionaries may inadvertently foster discrimination and systemic injustice. Words shape how we think, and yet we're often unconscious of how they affect us on a daily basis. The words we use fit into an entire network of beliefs and values (beliefs, you'll remember, are the stories we tell ourselves that shape our worldview, and values are the thoughts and behaviors we think are right or wrong). The more conscious we become of how our thoughts are shaped, the more able we are to choose actions consistent with our beliefs.

The dictionary and the popular use of a word cannot always convey its full meaning, but that's not the end of the problem: there is also popular misuse. Sometimes, misuse arises over time for reasons that have become hidden, and sometimes, it's an intentional expression of prejudice. Earlier, we noted how some refer to feminism as the F-word. Some people are so threatened by the idea of feminism they don't even want to mention its name. But how can a single word cause so much fear? Because words are always connected to beliefs and values, what we feel about a word is less about its meaning and more about associations with it—this is why feelings are a good place to start reflexivity. A man who recoils from being handed a tampon isn't actually afraid of sterile cotton, for instance, but of a variety of associations he's internalized about menstruation. Fear of feminism taps into various anxieties. For some men it might be about losing control and power over their environment. For some women, it might be not knowing what social role to play other than the one they know best. The fear brought about by associations, however, is just one indicator of a larger issue: privilege and oppression. Those at the top of a hierarchy along with those who believe they could or should be high in a hierarchy are often most opposed to changing that hierarchy.

When we use the term oppression, we aren't using the everyday definition. Commonly, people use it to refer to individuals, meaning one person making another person suffer through an abuse of authority. But when feminists talk about oppression, we mean **social oppression**, "a concept that describes a relationship between groups or categories of people in which a dominant group benefits from the systematic abuse, exploitation, and injustice directed toward a subordinate group."[11] In social oppression, a group or category of people is privileged above all others and receives benefits other groups don't, usually at the expense of and to the detriment of those groups. In her famous essay, "White Privilege: Unpacking the Invisible Knapsack," Peggy McIntosh lists 47 privileges white people are given, often without noticing them, from "I do not have to educate my children to be aware of systemic racism for their own daily physical protection" to "If I have low credibility as a leader I can be sure that my race is not the problem" to "I can choose blemish cover or bandages in 'flesh' color and have them more or less match my skin."[12] A "flesh"-colored bandage is an example of privilege and oppression maintained through words. It seems minor, but in fact, it functions as a weapon. Someone with darker skin has to devote time and energy to think past this idea that her or his flesh isn't, in fact, normal human flesh.

So, when someone speaks or writes, how do you know what they're saying? Are they following popular usage? Are they following a discipline-based usage? Or are they intentionally misusing a word to undermine its cultural power? And what kind of damage can a word actually do? A key way to examine which way language is being used is to pay attention to contradictions. **A contradiction** is present when a word or phrase is used to indicate the opposite of what it usually means, and with the F-word we see a definite contradiction. Those who use it believe feminists are extremists who want to replace the patriarchy with matriarchy. But matriarchies are not hierarchies with women on top; they're egalitarian. The F-word twists feminism into its opposite, so that rather than exposing and eradicating injustice, feminism itself is said to be unjust. Start paying attention when you notice this kind of reversal, whether it's in person, on social media, or elsewhere. It's a window into how words, beliefs, and values lead to action. The more vehemently people deride feminism, the more likely they are to act in ways that keep traditional power structures intact.

You've read how many of our contributors overcame this derision and embraced the term feminist. The act of claiming makes feminism more than a word: it becomes a value-generating action. Habitual actions—like cleaning your home—make a practice. The aim of regular cleaning is to maintain a healthy, functional environment, and the aim of feminist practice is to remedy systems of inequity. Some situations require a deep remedy, much as elements of a house sometimes needs to be taken apart for renovation or repair. Dismantling a system, whether an actual house or the metaphorical master's house, requires structural knowledge. We need to carefully analyze how the house was built before we dismantle or remodel. Theory provides an X-ray/blueprint that lets you see past paint and wallpaper to reveal the structure of the master's house. It organizes feminist thought and informs feminist action.

Theoretical Tools

These foundational tools, privilege, oppression, and language are used in all feminist theories. Now, let's look at gender, sexuality, class, race, and disability theories. Because WGSS is interdisciplinary, they draw from the sciences and the humanities.

Advocating for equality between men and women was the original basis of academic feminism, so it makes sense that gender and sexuality theories occupy a central place in feminist theory. We've used the term gender throughout this book in ways that reflect **feminist gender theory**, which takes as a starting point the idea that sex and gender cannot be thought of interchangeably.

In the 1970s, theorists like Simone de Beauvoir, Kate Millett, and Gayle Rubin were among the first feminists to suggest that sex doesn't equal gender. Female and male are sex. Masculine and feminine are gender. Woman and man are gendered social identities. They demonstrated that someone who's anatomically female doesn't automatically act feminine but that femininity, the idea of being a woman, is behavior a female person is taught. Similarly, males don't behave in "manly" ways because of their DNA but are taught how to be men. Feminist gender theories, therefore, state that the connections between sex and gender are more cultural than biological. There may be social expectations for males to act in masculine ways and for females to act in feminine ways—the acting part is called gender expression—but whereas sex is coded in our genes, gender is a social spectrum that varies across cultures. Ask yourself what gets labeled masculine or feminine and why? The next time you're in a clothing or toy store, look at the way items are gendered. Why aren't men supposed to wear dresses or cropped jeans? Why are women's shirts so short and frilly? Why are boys allowed to play with GI Joe but not Barbie? Why is one called an "action figure" while the other is a "doll"? How are these distinctions made? Who makes them? The way poles of each binary in the gender grid are valued and devalued is part of this labeling (Figure 3.6). Think also about how gender expression could or couldn't be accounted for in cultures that use non-gendered languages. Decoupling gender from sex was a crucial starting point for feminist gender and sexuality theories.

We can say with some certainty that sex is usually determined genetically through DNA, while gender is taught, but there's still a lot to learn about the entire range from sex to gender to sexuality. First, let's look at what we do know. Biologically, sex in humans is usually determined by chromosomes, which isn't the case for all animals nor even all mammals. We know these sex-specific codes as XX for female and XY for male. It might surprise you to know that the Y chromosome and its significance in determining sex was discovered by an American woman, Nettie Stevens, in 1905. The credit for the discovery was, however, given to Edmund Wilson, the head of the biology department where she studied. Stevens's work led her to believe that chromosomes function in pairs and that the sex-specific Y chromosome she discovered was paired with the sex-specific X found some 15 years earlier by Hermann Henking. Her work greatly influenced Thomas Morgan, who went on to win the Nobel Prize for his work on chromosomes and sex determination.

Despite agreement that sex is coded in our DNA, it's not always completely straightforward. Anatomy can have a range of expressions that may or may not match chromosomes. There are also other chromosomal combinations referred to as intersex. So-called "sex hormones," estrogen and testosterone, can also be present in ratios that differ from what anatomy or chromosomes would usually indicate. A famous example is the South African Olympic sprinter, Caster Semenya, an anatomical female with high levels of testosterone. The stakes of gender—that someone must comply with expectations for a man or woman—are so high that the Olympic authorities demand blood tests of athletes like Semenya and can even prohibit them from competing. An April 2018 international ruling (which only applies to Semenya's events) now demands that athletes take drugs to align their hormones with the norms. Semenya has appealed the ruling.

To make matters even more interesting, some non-mammalian animals don't have chromosomal sex markers. Some fish, birds, and amphibians can change back and forth between sexes during their lifespan, including reproductive organs. Because scientists want to understand the implications of human sex-changes, they've successfully experimented with changing mice's sex through altering how chromosomes function. What we know about the human genome is still relatively new, so we still have much to learn about biology's relationship to sex and much more to learn about the relationship between sex, gender, and reproductive sexuality.

Sexuality isn't just for reproduction, though, but includes a complicated range of attractions, pleasures, and identities that are beyond the scope of science. Feminist gender theories start with the idea that sexuality isn't biologically linked to sex, or gender for that matter. French feminist Simone de Beauvoir's *The Second Sex* (1949) described the many ways women in patriarchy are subordinate to the male sex. Her work on gender, specifically how one isn't born a woman but made one, laid the groundwork for other important contributions to theories on feminist sexuality.

Similar to the ways gender is explored as a spectrum, **feminist sexuality theories** explore a wide range of sexual expressions and activities. They include Kate Millett's 1969 *Sexual Politics*, Toril Moi's 1986 *Sexual/Textual Politics*, and Judith Butler's 1990 *Gender Trouble*. This ushered in what became popularly known in feminist criticism as the "sex wars." Concerned about the major causes and contributing factors to violence against women, feminist scholars debated the pros and cons of sexuality, pornography, and sex work.

Work in this area spurred the Rape Crisis Movement, including Susan Brownmiller's groundbreaking claim that rape was not a crime of sexual passion but an assertion of power and an essential element of patriarchal domination of women. This movement attempted to redress high-stakes life and death problems. For example, women are often discouraged from reporting being raped or sexually assaulted by laws that required witness corroboration and proof of physical resistance to one's attackers.

Since the rape crisis of the 1970s, reported incidents of rape in the US have declined significantly, down 85% by some estimates.[13] As we found in regard to poverty, it's important to analyze what statistics actually measure. Reports and rapes are two different things. Rape and sexual assault are still an enormous problem, as evidenced by the statistic that "[e]very 98 seconds an American is sexually assaulted."[14] Below are some of the most recent US statistics gathered from the Rape, Abuse, and Incest National Network (RAINN):

Table 7.1 Rape and Sexual Assault

Ages 12–34 are the highest risk years for rape and sexual assault.
One out of every six American women has been the victim of an attempted or completed rape.
One out of every ten rape victims is male.
Eighty-two percent of all juvenile victims are female. Ninety percent of adult rape victims are female.
Women aged 18–24, who are college students, are three times more likely than women in general to experience sexual violence. Females of the same age who are not enrolled in college are four times more likely.
Twenty-one percent of TGQN (transgender, genderqueer, nonconforming) college students have been sexually assaulted compared to 18% of non-TGQN females and 4% of non-TGQN males.

Abuse rates in the US are not consistent across all groups of women. Poverty plays a key role, as "[t]he prevalence of sexual assault increases dramatically as annual household income decreases."[15] According to current research, "[t]he poorest Americans are 12 times as likely to be sexually assaulted as the wealthiest."[16] Kathryn Casteel of the Pennsylvania Coalition Against Rape explains that "Abusers are more likely to target victims who are less likely to report their abuse . . . [that] low-income women (or men) have fewer resources . . . puts them more at risk to experience both repeat-offenses and unpunished perpetrators."[17] Abusers typically isolate victims and create financial dependency; you may even rely on your abuser just to eat every day. Leaving the situation may be difficult or impossible without resources to relocate, which is why feminists created domestic violence shelters.

Racial disparities play another key role. Although "80% of rapes are reported by white women, women of color are more likely to be assaulted than white women."[18] The following statistics on prevalence rates for rape, broken down by race and ethnicity in the US, is compiled by EndCampusRape.org. These and other statistics can be found on their webpage.

Table 7.2 Rape by Ethnicity

Asian/Pacific Islander: 6.8%
Hispanic/Latina: 11.9%
White: 17.7%
Black: 18.8%
American Indian/Alaska Native: 34.1%
Mixed Race: 24.4%

Note that "American Indians are twice as likely to experience rape/sexual assault compared to all other races."[19] More troubling, although overwhelmingly rape and sexual assault are committed by someone the victim knows, this isn't the case for Indigenous women: "41% of sexual assaults against American Indians are committed by a stranger; 34% by an acquaintance; and 25% by an intimate or family member."[20] Because Natives are a small percent of the population, most of these strangers and acquaintances, as well some intimates, are white men. Until 2013, reservations were known as a "free zone" where white men could literally get away with murdering Indian women. If a man attacked a woman on her own reservation, the tribe had no authority to prosecute him. The crime was in the jurisdiction of the FBI, who didn't consider such cases a priority.

Sovereignty over what happens on one's land and what happens to one's body is a high-stakes issue. Rape swells to epic proportions wherever national sovereignty battles are ongoing. Both US Natives and the Democratic Republic of the Congo (DRC) reflect how rape is deployed as a weapon in battles over land. During the height of the DRC conflict in 2011, it was reported that "48 women [were] raped every hour," leading it to be called the "rape capitol of the world"[21] by the UN. Dismantling the acceptability of rape, especially during wartime, will take a lot of doing. Making it harder is the horrific idea that such acts are justified by way of race, nationality, and ethnicity.[22] But there is hope. The Violence Against Women Act as amended in 2013 gives tribes more authority in crimes committed by whites against Native women on reservations. And in 2016, Congolese Vice President Jean-Pierre Bemba was tried by the International Criminal Court. Although his conviction was overturned for other reasons, it was the first time ever that rape was officially recognized as a war crime.[23] Feminist sexuality theories contributed to this recognition and continue to address both national and individual sovereignty.

Additional sexuality issues addressed by scholars include Hortense Spillers's assertion that racial prejudice alienates black women from their own bodies, thus denying them a claim to their own sexuality.[24] Gayle Rubin wrote about the ways sex was legislated through moral codes like the 1873 Comstock anti-obscenity act, sodomy laws, and civil codes enforced out of homosexual panic. Rubin argued that because "[t]he realm of sexuality has its own internal politics, inequities, and modes of oppression . . . sex is always political."[25] What was radical may become normal and mundane, only to be challenged again in another time or place.

Defining Sexualities

Let's switch gears and look at how sexuality terms have changed over time. If you look up the word sexuality in the dictionary, you might feel as though you're being led down a rabbit hole of meanings, especially when you find yourself redirected to terms like sexual identity, sexual orientation, and sexual attraction. The origin and development of key terms might surprise. "Sexuality" was coined in 1797, "homosexual" in 1891, and "heterosexual" in 1892. Table 7.3 shows a brief list of terms from the Oxford English Dictionary (OED), along with definitions from the dates they are first known to appear in written English.

Table 7.3 Sexuality Terms

Lesbian (1732)—a woman sexually attracted to other women; derived from the 1550 term meaning inhabitant of the island of Lesbos
Asexual (1862)—someone not sexually attracted to other people
Homosexual (1891)—someone sexually attracted to the same sex
Heterosexual (1892)—someone sexually attracted to the opposite sex
Bisexual (1907)—someone sexually attracted to males and females
Intersex (1916)—someone with a combination of male and female biology or anatomy
Pansexual (1977)—someone for whom sex or gender isn't a defining factor in sexual attraction
Gay (1922)—a man sexually attracted to other men

Etymology is the study of how words originate and how their meanings change through history. Because meaning is social—people decide what things mean—language is always changing. Sometimes, the changes are minor, but sometimes they can be quite substantial. For instance, most people know that gay once meant happy before it became synonymous with homosexual, but did you know it also once

Figure 7.1 Nepal Pride Parade.[26]

meant a man who frequented prostitutes and, at other times, the art of poetry? Etymology raises useful questions about how and why a word's meaning changes over time. The following timeline is a snapshot of entries for the word "gay" from the OED which is known for its etymological references.

Table 7.4 Changing Meaning of "Gay"

(1225) Bright or lively looking, especially in color; brilliant, showy.
(1325) Noble; beautiful; excellent, fine.
(1387) Finely or showily dressed.
(1400) Of persons, their attributes, actions, and so on: lighthearted, carefree; manifesting, characterized by, or disposed to joy and mirth; exuberantly cheerful, merry; sportive.
(1405) Wanton, lewd, lascivious.
(1590) Of a horse: lively, prancing.
(1597) Originally of persons and later also more widely: dedicated to social pleasures; dissolute, promiscuous; frivolous, hedonistic. Also (especially in "to go gay"): uninhibited; wild, crazy; flamboyant.
(1693) The gay science: the art of poetry; (also in extended use) poetical or literary criticism.
(1703) With implied sense of depreciation: offhand, airy.
(1795) Frequently *euphem.* Especially of a woman: living by prostitution. Of a place: serving as a brothel.
(1842) (With) gay abandon: (in) a carefree or expansive manner; (with) lack of consideration for the consequences of an action.
(1922) Originally US slang. (a) Of a person: homosexual; (b) (of a place, milieu, way of life, etc.) of or relating to homosexuals.

What do you notice about how the meaning of the word gay changed over time? What questions could such an etymological timeline raise about how people understand and apply the word today? What other words could you look up that might raise similar questions?

Because beliefs and values about gender vary from culture to culture, and many cultures around the world refer to gender minimally or differently than the West, words like "gay" may be inaccurate beyond Western cultures. Some cultures assign gender roles within a family regardless of sex in order to balance activities. If a family has no sons, a daughter may be taught by an uncle or father to take on traditionally male activities so that the family has all it needs met.

Many cultures also have more than two gender identities, and sometimes this is associated with sexuality. In Mojave culture, there are traditional man's and woman's social roles, but they're not assigned by anatomy. *Alyha* refers to a male who chooses to live as a woman and *hwame* refers to a female who chooses to live as a man. A *hwame* may marry a female and an *alhya* may marry a male. While some might think of this as same-sex marriages, the Mojave don't, because roles follow character rather than anatomy. A *hwame* is a social man, so his marriage to a woman is unremarkable.

In *Diné* (known as Navajo), children born with ambiguous genitals or who demonstrate multiple gender traits are called *nádleehi*. Those with anatomical difference are sometimes called "real" and those who later identify differently from their anatomy may be called "pretend," but "the distinction was not necessarily important—both 'real' and 'pretend' *nádleehi* were . . . accorded respect."[27] The way *nádleehi* is expressed varies from group to group. From a Western perspective, *nádleehi* may seem to dress as a woman when doing woman's work and as a man when doing man's work, but all these categories are Western. From a *Diné* perspective, *nádleehi* demonstrates the equal value of both genders (Figure 7.2).

We can also turn to the ancient Asian Indian tradition of *hijra*, today a community of about two million people whose heritage has been "enshrined in Indian literary epics" since as early as 400 BCE. *Hijras* are anatomical males who choose to become women. This transition can range from dressing as female to undergoing surgery. Today,

Figure 7.2 Hijra Protest.[28]

hormones may be added. While they were originally respected and appreciated, they encountered severe oppression as India suffered invasions from both the West and East, so *hijra* today are often "runaways or evicted by their families."[29] In April 2014, India's Supreme Court officially adopted the word transgender to recognize *hijras'* human rights. India wouldn't have had to add a new term if their culture had not been impacted by British conquest. Even though India achieved independence in 1947, the results of colonization continue to affect India much as they do the US.

In Western patriarchy, the dominant trend is to fit the man/woman binary. But many terms have been developed to show how binaries don't equate to bodies (male/female), gender expression (masculine/feminine), and social identities (man/woman). One such term is nonbinary, which challenges the idea of gender as a basis for identity.[30]

Western cultures are still in the early stages of understanding the wide spectrum of gender identities, especially in relation to sexuality, and gender terminology tends to be much newer than sexuality terminology. And yet they've probably been around longer than you think. Some words, like transsexual, date back to the beginning of the 20th century, while others only gained recognition by the general population in the last few years. As we saw with the word gay, the meanings of words that have been in the social lexicon have changed over time. For example, in 1907, the word transsexual was associated with living as a gender opposite one's anatomy; in the 1970s, transsexual was associated with sex confirmation surgery; and now, it refers to those whose biological sex and gender don't match, regardless of whether or not they have had or plan to have surgery.

Similarly, associations with the term queer have changed over time. It became a derogatory term, but now, at least within the LGBTQ+ community— LGBTQ+ stands for lesbian, gay, bisexual, transgender, and queer (or questioning), and the plus keeps it open-ended as definitions continue to change—it's a legitimately recognized sexual and/or gender identity. According to GLAAD (formerly the Gay & Lesbian Alliance Against Defamation) intern Cleo Anderson,

Figure 7.3 Trans Day of Visibility. Lexi Adsit, Mia "Tu Mutch" Satya, Shawn Demmons, and Nya. San Francisco 2016.[31]

"Queer is anything that exists outside of the dominant narrative [and] means that you're one of those letters (LGBT), but you could be all of those letters and not knowing is OK."[32] Those who recognized a need for broader gender and sexuality terminology outside the binary of "gay" or "straight"

Table 7.5 Gender Terms

Agender (1996)—someone who doesn't identify by a specific gender identity
Aporagender (2014)—someone who sees themselves as "separate from male, female, and anything in between (unlike Androgyne) while still having a very strong and specific gendered feeling"
Cisgender (1997)—someone whose personal identity and gender corresponds to his or her sex at birth
Gender-fluid (1987)—someone who doesn't identity with a single gender
Genderqueer (1995)—someone who doesn't identify with traditional gender distinctions, but identifies with neither, both, or a combination of male and female genders
Queer (1914)—once associated primarily with male homosexuals but now more associated with someone whose gender orientation is fluid
Transgender (1974)—a person whose sense of personal identity and gender doesn't correspond to that person's sex at birth or which doesn't otherwise conform to conventional notions of sex and gender
Transsexual (1907)—a person born with the physical characteristics of one sex but who identifies as belonging to the other sex; living or wishing to live as a member of the opposite sex

The *Oxford English Dictionary* dates the term queer to 1894 but notes its derogatory use lasted until a circa 1980s, when a more positive association came into being.

reclaimed the term queer from its derisive use, as popularized in the chant: "We're here, we're queer, get used to it!"

Table 7.5 lists some gender identity terms recorded in written English. You'll find many of these in the OED and can research how their meanings have changed with time. Some, like aporagender, haven't yet found their way into the OED, which is another lesson in how meanings are socially constructed. Who decides if a word goes in the dictionary? And by what criteria is such a decision made? Because social understanding of gender beyond the binary is still relatively new, terminology and meanings are in flux. If gender terms haven't made it to the dictionary, that makes them no less important.

For more gender and sexuality terms, check out GLAAD, GLSEN (Gay, Lesbian & Straight Education Network), and/or the Human Rights Campaign websites.

What is the relationship between a person's identity and the social construction of gender? This is where the nature/culture interaction becomes slippery. Gender is socially constructed—each culture has its own definition of male and female character and behavior (that's culture)—but people don't choose their personal qualities, their mix of "masculinity," "femininity," both, or neither—these are inborn (that's nature). What, then, are the stakes of gender and sexuality identity?

You may recall an earlier description of a traditional Indigenous culture where men generally hunted bigger game and women snared rabbits. Let's replace he and she, her and him, with xyna (xy chromosomes not applicable) to mimic gender-neutral language, and tell the story of a girl, born athletic, who loves deer hunting and freely shares her opinion:

Xyna was born lively, curious, and active. Like all children, xyna was encouraged to develop athletically. It was a matter of survival. As a teen, xyna preferred the peaceful solitude and long treks of deer hunting. As an adult, the nurturance xyna provided in winter was greatly admired and appreciated. Xyna's voice, like everyone's, was valued at the council fire. (Whether xyna was sexually attracted to men or women is a separate question altogether. The point is, xyna's identity was not called into question because xyna liked to hunt deer, and xyna never had to choose a gender or a pronoun.)

Now, let's say xyna is born in a patriarchal culture. Xyna—the inborn person—will be called she but considered masculine. She might be called a "tomboy," coached all her life to "tone it down," "act like a lady." Her parents may do this protectively: she must learn to suppress her nature to fit gender norms or risk cultural or physical attack. S/he may decide, "I was born in the wrong body"—from her culture's perspective, she was—and identify with a term such as agender, genderqueer, or transsexual.

Gender identity fits the definition of an issue because it's based on conflicting interests. The conflicts are multidirectional, not a simple either/or. In an article about gender pronouns, Ashleigh Shackelford explains why she uses the female pronoun, even though she identifies as nonbinary. Because she's a large Black girl, she doesn't fit the white, thin feminine ideal, so to peers in school, she was sexless. On the other hand, predatory older men subjected her to sexual harassment and assault. Despite her inner identity as nonbinary, she claims the female pronoun as an act of solidarity with all women who have been assaulted.[33]

Binaries are intrinsic to the English language, but reality cannot be reduced to opposite extremes, and this affects gender in specific ways. Living in a culture that begins every thought about a person with gender can cause personal turmoil for anyone who doesn't relate to binary poles. Even if we want to, almost nobody measures up to such extreme ideals. On a personal level, this turmoil can lead to depression or suicide, and on a social level, it generates issues such as what bathroom a transgender person should use. Tension between inner and outer sense of self leads 41% of transgender people to attempt suicide at least once in their lives compared to 5% of the general population.[34] Finding a term isn't a complete solution to these problems but can offer a sense of belonging to a group. Terms can also educate those in the norm.

As Shackelford noted, gender is never neutral in our culture. A white nonbinary person explains how she responded to norms:

My Gender Identity by Menoukha Robin Case

I tried to make it neutral. I mean, I was a skinny kid who was always mumbling to herself, "I'm not a boy but I'm not a girl but I'm not a boy but . . ." and as an adult "I'm not a man but I'm not a woman but I'm not a man but. . .." I began to identify as queer and made up the alternative pronoun xyna years before 2015 when the word nonbinary hit the dictionaries. I acted out the struggle in musical performances.

Figure 7.4 Menoukha Robin Case, *Cost of Living*, circa 1983.[35]

This image is part of a show where I started off wearing a blonde wig and feminine clothes over a Barbie/Marilyn Monroe-ish pink plastic body I had sculpted. I would do a striptease over several songs and eventually rip off the body itself (it had frontal velcro closures). I ended up looking like a boy with dregs of femininity (one stocking, a thong over my pants). It meant so much to me when I encountered actual non-gendered pronouns and learned that in gender-balanced cultures, a person's unique individuality supersedes anatomy. I imagined if I was raised like that, I wouldn't have had to say, "I'm not a . . . " because I would have been busy learning to express who I actually am as a human being. After I spent time as an adopted family member in an actual gender-balanced culture, I started to identify as a woman because in such cultures, a woman can be whatever the F she wants to be.

Queer Theory, a term coined by Teresa de Lauretis, challenges conventional ideas of gender and sexual identity that construct fixed grids, elevating norms and devaluing cultural others. But rather than just rearranging binary poles, queer theory inserts fluidity as a schema and value. This displaces normativity altogether, because the opposite of fluidity isn't normativity, it's fixity. Yes, norms can change, but fluidity is the mode of change, which makes this tool especially dynamic. What fluidity refers to is really no-norms. No-norms, unlike cultural others, have no containable identity, so they're not as automatically or easily devalued. Queer theory replaces cultural others with a spectrum of identities allowing infinite individual expressions, something that brilliantly resonates with the American value of individuality.

The idea of no-norms has applications beyond gender. It provides a tool for dismantling grids of intelligibility with far-reaching effects in Western culture. As discussed in "Case Study: Beauty and Authority," stable norms allow for mass production/mass consumption of products and services that can be advertised in predictable ways. Another binary, rich/poor (class), depends on wealth-building, which depends on profit, which relies on effective advertising of mass-produced items. By making target markets less predictable, queer theory potentially disrupts the smooth flow of money from individual consumers to corporate producers.

Feminist Class Theories, such as Marxist and materialist feminism, address economic conditions. People often think class is just a matter of how much money one makes, the difference between rich and poor, or one's place in society: working class, middle class, upper class. Class determinations are not straightforward and change over time. Although there's never been a definitive line designating wealth, social scientists do assess the amount of income adequate for survival. In 2017, someone in the US who made less than $12,060 in a year was considered to be living below this minimum level, the "poverty line." For a family of four, the amount was $24,600. How much money it takes to be considered rich, on the other hand, often depends on where you are on the financial spectrum. Making $50,000 a year would seem rich to someone in poverty, yet among people with a net worth of a million dollars, only a small percentage—28% to be exact—consider themselves rich.[36] Perhaps this reflects the drive for higher ranking.

Class can also differentiate between a caste system—whatever class you're born into is where you remain for your lifetime—and class mobility—the ability to change one's life conditions by moving from one class to another. The American Dream is built on the idea of improving one's class. The belief that even if you start out poor, you can end up rich, was made famous by Horatio Alger. His 19th-century stories about poor boys becoming financially successful through grit and hard work became popular precisely because they were so unlikely. President Herbert Hoover used the phrase "rugged individualism" to encourage the same concept. Leaving it up to the "rugged individual" takes the steam out of solidarity.

This idea of exceptional hope became a normative goal. And while it's not impossible to improve—or diminish—one's class conditions in the US, hard work isn't the most significant factor. In an episode of MTV's *Decoded*, "How Hollywood Misrepresents the Working Class," Gabe Gonzales discusses how television depicts class status. The key takeaway is how ideas about class are distorted and stereotyped: "[w]hen poverty or working-class lifestyles are shown exclusively as a personal failure, we start to imagine financial stability as only a reflection of your character" and not as a reflection of structural obstacles such as declining class mobility, wage stagnation, a globally competitive workforce, and skyrocketing college tuition.[37]

If you were raised in a neighborhood with poorly funded schools, you may not make it to college. The most accurate predictor of class mobility in the US is the zip code where you're born.[38] How and why your zip code affects your opportunities is part of what feminist economists study.

Feminist Economics by Katharine Ransom

Feminist Economics has become a mostly academic movement, but it originated during the second wave of feminism with writers, activists, and educators who realized there was not enough discussion about the economics of being a woman. Those in the field of Feminist Economics examine economic issues that mainstream economists do not address or cannot address accurately due to the methods that are used. Feminist Economists not only address women's reproductive rights, women and the environment, what it's like for women in the workplace, the well-being of children, how relationships affect career choices, and the options women have when they cannot find a job, they also show how traditional economic models and methods cannot provide an accurate view of women's lives because women's voices were not considered when these models and methods were created.

Some of the most notable scholars are Ester Boserup, Marianne Ferber, Marilyn Waring, Nancy Folbre, and Silvia Federici with Waring's 1988 book *If Women Counted* being called the founding document of the field. Feminist Economics has grown significantly over the past 20 years, with the creation of multiple organizations and a journal to promote the work of these scholars and activists. The *Feminist Economics* journal is the publication of the International Association for Feminist Economics (IAFFE). The journal was founded by Diana Strassman, Professor of Humanities at Rice University, and co-edited by Günseli Berik, Economics Professor at the University of Utah. The journal publishes articles and book reviews from many different fields and has a global audience. Some of the articles from the 2017 publications address sex work, violence against women, women and farming, women's behavior when looking for a job, and financing women's small businesses.

Feminist Economics also relates to Ecofeminism, which is the combination of feminism and sustainability. Ecofeminists believe that the male domination of nature and women has the same root cause and should be addressed together. Many Feminist Economists write about sustainable methods for economic growth and development that will protect the land, air, and water for future generations. Unlike traditional economists, Feminist Economists and Ecofeminists understand that there are limited resources on this planet and that economic growth cannot go on forever.

If class is relative, how do we make sense of it? It's true that the famed American middle class is more an idea than an actual category, but class isn't just a state of mind; it's an indicator of social status that includes income; access to resources; behaviors, including dress and appearance; and, perhaps most importantly, power or authority. Power in this case can be thought of as how much authority one has over our social and economic conditions. Because of the steadily increasing gap between

Figure 7.5 Working Class.[39]

rich and poor, wealth and authority seem to go hand in hand, but as John Trudell points out, access to power goes beyond social authority. Still, because we're in a hierarchical system, it can be hard to access that power while struggling to make ends meet. Class can be addressed through "unity" or "solidarity" among non-wealthy groups working together across differences in race, gender, and other factors.

Race is also crucial to feminist theories. While it's a global phenomenon, it's especially active in the US, the first nation on earth that originally enshrined whiteness in its constitution. Outside, the US racism is sometimes called colorism, and its history differs. Race and color account for much economic disparity. While colonists put internal pressure on imported and enslaved Africans, imperialists put external pressure on nations of color. Both types of pressure caused a wealth gap between whites and people of color.

The origins of the racial wealth gap in the US may seem obvious. Native American lands are the foundation of cities, farms, railroads, in fact any and every thing that has become America's wealth—somebody did the math in 2013 and arrived at a land value of $23 trillion. Africans were enslaved from 1619 to 1865, and their unpaid labor during those 246 years was a primary source of white wealth. Estimates based on financial documents in historical archives place the 1863 value of enslaved people and their labor at: "three times greater than . . . all capital, North and South combined, invested in manufacturing, almost three times the amount invested in railroads, . . . seven times the amount invested in banks . . . [and] seven times the total value of all currency in circulation in the country. . . ."[40] It's no wonder that the *Explained* episode, "The Racial Wealth Gap," begins with Confederate money featuring images of enslaved Blacks picking cotton. And while this took place in the South, the entire nation's economy was driven by slavery. For example, textile factories in the US North and Great Britain that wove and sewed cotton were also beneficiaries.

Explained also discusses how the causes of continuing issues are more complex and how "past injustices breed present suffering."[41] We know from Table 1.1 that wage gaps affect other races, but they define the racial wealth gap as the difference between median white and Black households. Measured by adding savings plus assets and subtracting debts, the gap of $153,400 in 2016 is still growing. How did this happen?

When slavery ended, much of the US was considered "unsettled" (although Natives still had homelands everywhere), so the solution was to deed each Black family up to 40 acres of tillable ground. After Lincoln was assassinated, Johnson reversed this order and they were evicted from these lands. To survive, they worked anywhere they could, as sharecroppers, miners, and other jobs where they had to meet quotas or become indebted. The books were set-up, so their debt continued to grow, effectively continuing slavery. Meanwhile, whites got to keep and invest wealth they had already gained from cotton growing, textile manufacturing, and cloth export, all reliant on slavery. Compound interest means that $100 of that money invested in 1863 is worth $3,584,970 in 2018.[43] So, even if we closed wage gaps, centuries of compounded wealth would leave the racial gap intact.

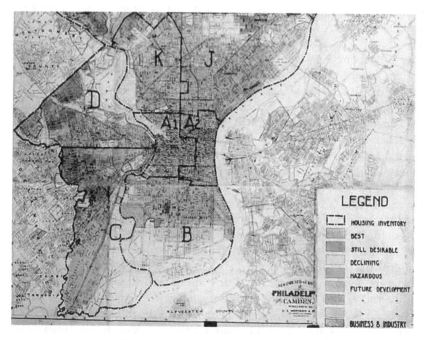

Figure 7.6 Redlining.[42]

Many whites who arrived in the US after slavery created wealth through land ownership—again, always at the expense and pauperization of Native Americans. Whites who lost property during the Depression (1929–1933) benefitted from a federal mortgage program. But Blacks were not only prevented from purchasing homes in white areas; they could not buy homes in Black neighborhoods either. The Federal Housing Association marked off Black neighborhoods in red to indicate areas where banks should not offer mortgages. This was called redlining. Preventing Blacks from buying homes put them way behind in wealth-building. Since a house purchased in the 1960s for $20,000 is worth more than half a million dollars today, and property accounts for two-thirds of white middle-class wealth, the racial wealth gap continued to grow because of this federal policy of segregation. Although redlining became illegal in 1968, it persisted through social and banking practices. To this day, where you live affects where you can work and where your children attend school. This affects the kinds of educational and extra-curricular activities that benefit future generations.

The global racial wealth gap arose from similar histories. If we look at Haiti, for example, we find that their poverty is rooted in debt dating from and compounded since the Haitian Revolution. France agreed to recognize their independence only if they paid the equivalent of the profit France had expected from slavery—they had to buy their own freedom. In all these cases, Blackness and whiteness are at issue, but racism also affects Latinx and Asian communities and nations, who also contributed to white wealth in the US through severely underpaid labor and continued housing discrimination. Many Latinx and Asian nations have had experiences similar to those in Haiti. And Indigenous peoples are at the bottom of the hierarchy in every nation.

Critical race theory was developed because of these kinds of problems, and **Feminist Critical Race Theory** (FCRT) was developed to address the gap between critical race theory and feminist gender theory. As Theodora Berry put it, FCRT "acknowledges, addresses, and accepts my Black experiences as different from those of my brothers (critical race theory) and my womanhood as different from those of my sisters (feminist theory)."[44] Discussions of racism have often marginalized women, and discussions of sexism have often marginalized women of color. FCRT makes women of color the center of discussion rather than a footnote in the margins. For example, it moved the discussion of Wages for Work from a limited focus on white women's 80 cents on a white man's dollar to include the lesser wages of women of non-white ethnicities.

Feminist Disability Studies challenge stereotypes about bodies and seek to remedy how we define ability and disability. Feminism and disability studies make a strong pairing, given how the female body and mind have often been seen as inferior to male. One of the foremost feminist disabilities theorists, Rosemarie Garland-Thomson, asks us to fundamentally "reimagine" the relationship between bodies and society. Another key purpose of disability studies is to draw awareness to the fact that all people are temporarily able-bodied. We may or may not lose functions through disease or accidents, but we all age. Even if we age in perfect health, there will be things we can no longer do. Another key purpose is to "question our assumptions that disability is a flaw, lack, or excess."[45] For too long, people with disabilities, such as the blind or deaf, were considered second-class citizens (remember the able-bodied person being unaware of the obstacles to a person in a wheelchair entering a building?).

A famous predecessor to feminist disability studies is American author Charlotte Perkins Gilman's *The Yellow Wallpaper*. This short story, published in 1892, described a woman going mad, ironically as a result of psychiatric treatment she underwent for what we now know as post-partem depression. The story became an iconic feminist text that led to important critiques of gender bias in medical treatment. Though the account is fictional, Gilman herself had been diagnosed with "hysteria" and prescribed the "rest cure" like her main character. The word "hysteria" comes from the Greek and literally means "wandering womb." Doctors of the time believed that the uterus detached and moved through the body, inflaming emotions and creating a "nervous condition." While it sounds ridiculous now, there are still traces of this belief. For example, women were not officially allowed to compete in the Olympic marathon until 1984, largely because (male) physicians thought the grueling physical activity would cause a woman's uterus to fall out of her body. The winner of that marathon, American Joan Benoit, continues to compete in the marathon today and she hasn't once lost her womb. Another lingering effect is that insurance companies in the US sought to classify pregnancy as a pre-existing condition, like cancer or asthma.

A hallmark moment for US disability activists came with the passage of the Americans with Disabilities Act (ADA) in 1990, "a civil rights law that prohibits discrimination against individuals with disabilities in all areas of public life, including jobs, schools, transportation, and all public and private places that are open to the general public."[46] The ADA defines disability as "a physical or mental impairment that substantially limits one or more major life activities, a record of such an impairment, or being regarded as having such an impairment."[47] In 2008, the ADA was amended because disability had been too narrowly defined and interpreted. According to Garland-Thomas, "[t]he disabled body is a body whose variations or transformations have rendered it out of sync with its environment, both the physical and the attitudinal environments."[48] Unfortunately, currently proposed legislation like the so-called ADA Education and Reform Act could make it harder for people to get the accommodations they need. Feminist disability studies is thus not only about the body, but also about identity and overall quality of life, which has led disability activists to the forefront of today's feminist movements.

Theoretical Methods

When people think of significant events in feminism, they often think of how suffrage movements led to women "getting the vote" in the UK and US. They might think of the phrase "the personal is the political," which emerged during mid-20th-century feminism to challenge the mistaken notion that women's "personal" (domestic) labor was inferior to men's "real world work." Making the personal political challenged gendered social norms and laid the groundwork for the iconic 1960s and 1970s images of hairy-legged hippies and bra-burning patriarchal protests made famous by some members of the National Organization for Women (NOW). But suffragists fought for white women's votes only, and staying home to do domestic labor is a luxury that only the well-to-do can afford. These are examples of how non-intersectional feminism prioritized gender and failed to take other factors into account. If we don't take them into account, significant feminist events look like a series of disconnected breakthroughs.

Intersectionality remedies this failure and offers us a way to ally and connect. Alliances are crucial because there's always work to do. Within a hierarchical system, who's on top may shift, but there is always inequity. If it's you today, it may be me tomorrow. Intersectional analysis equalizes voices that have been historically silenced. Listening to these voices can help us locate the power of our connections. If we ally to protect our rights, we can move together toward heterarchy's egalitarian cooperation. Alliances begin with recognition of different identities.

Identity Politics

Identity politics began with the Combahee River Collective, a group of Black lesbian feminists. They named their group as an homage to Harriet Tubman's Combahee River Raid. If you've ever seen Comedy Central's *Drunk History*, you might recognize the name of this Civil War-era event from the "Harriet Tubman: Superspy" episode, offering a humorous take on one of Tubman's many amazing accomplishments. The narrator explains that while they likely know Tubman helped free enslaved Blacks during the Civil War, they probably don't realize she was a Union spy or that the Combahee River Raid was "the first military operation that was executed and led by an American woman, and it was planned by a former slave, who could not read or write, who was only five feet tall, and who was Black."[49] It was hugely successful and led to additional raids by the North. The Boston *Commonwealth* newspaper described it in glowing terms in 1863:

> Colonel Montgomery and his gallant bank of 300 black soldiers under the guidance of a black woman, dashed into the enemy's country, struck a bold and effective blow, destroying millions of dollars worth of commissary stores, cotton and lordly dwellings, and striking terror into the heart of rebeldom, brought off nearly 800 slaves and thousands of dollars worth of property, without losing a man or receiving a scratch. It was a glorious consummation.[50]

Considering Tubman wasn't even named in *The Commonwealth* article or that many people today still don't realize the scope of her role in the Civil War, you can see why the name Combahee River Collective is a fitting tribute.

The Combahee River Collective Statement was published in 1977 and made the case for "focusing upon our own oppression [a]s embodied in the concept of identity politics." This came from the Collective's belief "that the most profound and potentially most radical politics come directly out of our own identity, as opposed to working to end somebody else's oppression."[51] Identity politics includes and builds on "the personal is the political" to examine how people's lived experiences are affected by their race, class, and gender. One of the hallmarks of identity politics is that personal experience and point of view are essential to developing political action. This is especially true for those in marginalized groups. For example, an identity politics approach to women's reproductive rights would be that women need to be included as decision makers, from laws and policies to medical practices. That may seem like such common sense that identity politics wouldn't be necessary, but the problem is that "common sense" assumes other people think just like we do and ignores the fact that experiences vary substantially.

Margaret Prescod, a speaker in a new documentary, explains the need for identity politics:

> I was teaching in CUNY . . . and there was a lot of organizing among the students of color and the faculty of color. . . against racism and access and that sort of thing. We were working with some of the welfare mothers who had gone into City University under a special program to help bring in poor and minority students, and there were various problems, including the fact that the women needed childcare. There wasn't any. We . . . got space in the Women's Center. Now that was frowned upon by the men . . . who . . . considered themselves . . . third-world revolutionaries and academic heavies. It's like, ". . . you're separating yourself from the black community by going into the women's Center." Because we know there are a . . . white women over there and a bunch of them are lesbians, right? And we were like, "So what? We don't care." There was that tension and we had to make that fight to say that yes, we are anti-racist and we are for women's rights. . . . I was part of the first congressionally-mandated US Conference on Women held in Houston in 1977. Women of color got together and ran a slate. We felt that the concerns of mothers on welfare, of poverty, of the forced sterilization of women of color wasn't really getting a look in. I got to the floor to raise a resolution opposing the forced sterilization of black, Native American, and Puerto Rican women and my mic was shut off. We were told not

to raise these issues because if we did, it would jeopardize choice, which we all supported . . . [but] we were saying, "No, you can't do that on our backs." Women are going into hospital, they come out and they're sterilized. How the hell are we supposed to keep our mouth shut about that?[52]

This example also shows people too often don't recognize that their privileges come at the expense of others.

Intersectionality

We now turn to intersectional analysis, a method that draws from multiple theories and provides a way for them to work together as an interconnected system. If we're aware of our interrelatedness, we understand that anyone being devalued is a concern for us all.

As we saw in Part Three, women of color have long been deeply engaged in justice movements, and in the 20th century, Black women in the US organized contemporary feminist theories with some of the most transformative ideas in the history of feminist thought. The Combahee River Collective Statement took identity politics as its foundation and argued for the "development of integrated analysis and practice based upon the fact that the major systems of oppression are interlocking."[53] This idea is the bedrock of intersectional analysis. In 1989, Kimberlé Crenshaw coined the term "intersectionality" to connect theories on race, class, and gender discrimination. These theories had been circulating widely for some time in both the US and abroad, but had not yet been harnessed collectively to analyze privilege and oppression. Crenshaw combined them as a cohesive theoretical method. She explains:

> Black women are sometimes excluded from feminist theory and antiracist policy discourse because both are predicated on a discrete set of experiences that often does not accurately reflect the interaction of race and gender. These problems of exclusion cannot be solved simply by including Black women within an already established analytical structure. Because the intersectional experience is greater than the sum of racism and sexism, any analysis that does not take intersectionality into account cannot sufficiently address the particular manner in which Black women are subordinated.[54]

Intersectional analysis accompanied feminism long before it had a name. It's evident in Pauli Murray's "Jane Crow" and early Black and Indigenous feminisms. After Crenshaw named it, it grew to be the primary feminist analytical method. NOW's updated purpose is taking "action through intersectional grassroots activism to promote feminist ideals, lead societal change, eliminate discrimination, and achieve and protect the equal rights of all women and girls in all aspects of social, political, and economic life."[55] Note the key word, intersectional.

So, what *is* intersectionality and how does it work? Intersectionality is an analytical method for understanding the systemic nature of inequity. In their book *Intersectionality*, Patricia Hill Collins and Sirma Bilge say that although there are varied understandings, most would agree on the following:

> Intersectionality is a way of understanding and analyzing the complexity of the world, in people, and in human experiences. The events and conditions of social and political life and the self can seldom be understood as shaped by one factor. They are generally shaped by many factors in diverse and mutually influencing ways. When it comes to social inequality, people's lives and the organization of power in a given society are better understood as being shaped not by a single axis of social division, be it race or gender or class, but by many axes that work together and influence each other. Intersectionality as an analytic tool gives people better access to the complexity of the world and themselves.[56]

An intersectional analysis, then, begins by recognizing that women don't share one universal experience simply by virtue of anatomy or gender. If one woman is heterosexual, white, and wealthy, while the other is homosexual, Afro-Latina, and middle class, there are distinctive and predictable differences in the kinds of problems the two women will face. We could jump to the conclusion that intersectionality simply combines identity categories. We might think that the more "minority" identities one fits, the greater the oppression. But, as Collins and Bilge explain, intersectionality isn't simply a formula for adding up oppressions, but an act of critical inquiry that involves adapting questions and explanations to suit a given scenario. They call this "a special kind of relationality, one where the interaction or cooperation of two or more entities produce a combined effect that is greater than the sum of their separate parts." Because of this, intersectionality "can produce important new knowledge and/or practices."[57]

While gender as the foundation of feminism might make sense in white patriarchal culture, everything changes if we include a historical perspective that recognizes slavery, Manifest Destiny, and the existence and influence of matriarchal and gender-balanced cultures. For such cultures, gender was never a problem until invasion. With invasion, race was introduced, which was at least as pressing as newly imposed gender norms. Also, displacement from homelands led to poverty, and celebration of wealth displaced sharing values, so class became a major issue.

Recognizing that different groups are more pressed by some norms than others is a first step. The second step is recognizing that identity categories don't stand alone as singular factors. Addressing them one by one ignores the unique ways they function together. For these reasons, an additive approach is inadequate and an intersectional approach works better. As Crenshaw says, when identities intersect, the result is more than the sum of their parts. When we recognize that, we can examine how hierarchical systems create limiting grids that connect and maintain inequity.[58] Intersectionality also considers how multiple factors—race, class, gender, and more—are the result of an overarching history of domination by one mode of thinking. As we saw in Part Two, domination as a way of life isn't a given, and as we also saw, beliefs and values blend, conflict, and change unevenly. Our next tool provides a way to think about these factors as moving targets.

We've discussed how race was invented, how class is important in some cultures and almost non-existent in others, and how ideas of gender and ability vary greatly across time and place. We've examined how evaluative binaries structure norms in Western culture. They are so prevalent in our taken-for-granted thinking that analyzing them can illuminate all kinds of situations. They demonstrate why cultural schemas like race, class, and gender have a special place in any feminist toolbox. These schemas are sometimes called vectors of identity, vectors of analysis, or simply, vectors. We'll break down how this technical-sounding term contributes to intersectionality as a theoretical method.

Vector is a mathematical term, usually shown as an arrow indicating magnitude and direction. Magnitude means size or quantity and direction is movement from point A to point B. A vector could be used to calculate an object's motion or to predict what will happen when two objects collide. The clue to locating a vector is the fact that it differs according to time and place. Because norms are susceptible to change between point A and point B, they qualify as vectors. We need to address how they change to understand how they intersect or collide.

Let's review a few vectors in Western culture. Race didn't exist as a concept until a few hundred years ago, and that concept changed after slavery and continues to change as we address civil rights. Ideas of class have also changed, moving from fixed positions of aristocrat or peasant by birth, to moveable positions of elite, middle class, or working class according to income or resources. Working–class advocacy led to child labor laws, a 40-hour work week, overtime pay, and other protections such as Medicare, Medicaid, and Social Security. We've also seen gender norms change due to three or four waves or an unstoppable river of feminisms. But today, all these protections are under attack. The continual force of historical processes makes norms into vectors that move at varying speeds and in varying directions.

Vectors distinguish factors that are *components* (race, class, gender) of our *subject of analysis* (inequity) from the *method* of analysis (intersectionality).

If you break your arm, the *subject of analysis* is your injured arm. The *components* of the subject include bones, muscles, ligaments, blood vessels, and tendons, and there is stand-alone information about each of these. Though they can be measured individually, these components function together to enable your arm to do a task. Their relationships change when your arm is broken and change again as your arm begins to heal. Each component, and therefore your arm, heals more or less quickly depending on various factors. Do you need surgery? How old are you? Do you have access to good nutrition? Have you been offered physical therapy?

Vectors make the invisible visible so we can do more accurate analyses. X-rays and MRIs make invisible fractures and tears visible, allowing your doctor to prescribe appropriate *methods* of healing (surgery, cast, physical therapy). However, this analogy only goes so far, because the body is a natural system and societies are cultural systems. The problem of a broken arm is immediately evident, and the health of the arm is measured by a fixed set of normal functions. On the other hand, there is a wide range of ways we can live human life and what is normal in one time/place may be abnormal in another. Societies can go on for millennia without realizing there are different and/or better ways to function. When the way we function places people in perpetual inequity, the outcome is privilege and oppression.

Applying Vectors in Intersectional Analysis

Gender inequality in the US differs from the 19th century to now, and both differ from global examples. The women's movement in India is deep and dynamic. In 1927, women in India formed the All India Women's Conference, a nongovernmental "organisation dedicated to the upliftment and betterment of women and children." Twelve years before NOW, the National Federation of Indian Women was formed in 1954 to stand up against gender inequities fostered by British colonialism. But gender doesn't stand alone. In the US, we claim to be a classless society, but our nation began by granting citizenship to white landowners only. We saw how race figured in the slow progression of voting rights and how wages are still affected by gender, race, and class. India, on the other hand, had a rigid caste system based on birth that wasn't abolished until 1950 and is still a human rights problem today.[59]

By thinking of norms as vectors that are always in motion, we're reminded that they don't stand alone and can examine how they work together in different times and places. Our case study uses intersectional analysis as a method for tracing the roots of an important contemporary issue. Because stereotypes (along with their phobias and isms) are an extremely effective master's tool for maintaining norms and authority, it's useful to trace how they change.

Case Study: Racial Stereotypes

Let's look at schemas of race, gender, and class before and after the US Civil War. We'll examine them one by one, consider how they worked together, and trace how changes to one schema, class, altered the intersection of race and gender, changing stereotypes of Black masculinity.

Step 1: Schemas: Recall that Civil War era gender schemas were based on the idea that "Power in America has always been about aggressiveness . . . that's American manhood." The masculine norm was strong, dominant, aggressive, and sexual. According to this schema, men "can't help" their sexual urges. The opposite pole of that schema is womanhood, idealized as weak, submissive, gentle, and spiritual. Although there are positive and negative aspects to both poles, male is evaluated as superior to female, justifying female submission. According to Manifest Destiny, a man's role was rough-and-tumble conquest, and his helpmeet's role was civilizing. According to race schemas, recall that Africans at this time were considered sub-human and primitive. The class schema at the time allowed one group of people, wealthy white men, to control other groups of people. Poor white men couldn't vote until just before the Civil War, and Blacks were "property" until abolition.

Step 2: Intersections: We can see that schemas work together when we look at how race was entangled with class to justify slavery. Let's also look at how race and gender intersected. Since European gender was evaluated as the superior norm, African gender-balance was evaluated as abnormal and inferior. This led to the stereotype that Black women were aggressive and sexual—hence, more masculine—than white women and Black men were submissive and gentle—more feminine—than white men.

Step 3: Change (Schemas act as Vectors): Schemas never function alone. The evaluative binary knots intersections together, so that when one changes it pulls on the others, sometimes disconnecting them. With the abolition of slavery, whites lost a major source of wealth, and Blacks were legally free to earn and build wealth, which meant the class schema was no longer supposed to be locked to race. Jelani Cobb explains how whites responded:

> During slavery, the stereotypes of Black men were that we were happy-go-lucky, mostly lazy individuals who really needed the benign tutelage of the slave institution. After slavery, in order to justify the physical violence that would be required in order to *prevent us from exercising our rights,* that stereotype changed into the lawless, dangerous, buck . . . it was almost like a template that they shaded in and said "this is what Black men will be now" [emphasis added].[60]

Figure 7.7 Black Male Stereotypes.[61]

When we take history into account, still snapshots (schemas) become moving pictures (vectors) that unfold as changing narratives. As the speed and force of the Civil War changed slavery to freedom, whites changed stereotypes to maintain class authority. Black men, previously painted as submissive and gentle—feminine qualities—were suddenly described as domineering and violent, or "hypermasculine." Portraying Black men as rapists justified constant terrorism, such as beatings, home and business burnings, and lynching, which made it harder for them to establish financial independence. Still, some built towns and wealth. An example is "Black Wall Street" in Tulsa, Oklahoma. Sparked by the new stereotype, a Black man was accused of assaulting a white woman, and in 1921, the community was attacked with bombs, planes, and rioters. Along with massacre and homeless survivors, there was destruction of Black property that would be worth $31 million today, speaking directly to the role class played in this event.[62]

Sometimes, maintaining a stereotype supports domination better than changing it. During slavery, white men used the stereotype of the over-sexed African woman to justify raping enslaved Black women. The class motivation is obvious: in 1807, importing Africans was prohibited, and rape became a way to produce more "property"; the man who raped a Black woman "owned" (and often sold) his half-Black children. After the Civil War, the stereotype that Black women were over-sexed remained intact to prevent Black women from gaining rights over their own bodies—you may recall how Spillers relates this to sexuality earlier in this chapter—while the stereotype of Black men underwent a radical change from peaceable to violent to assure Black men didn't gain fiscal rights. In both cases—changing one stereotype, maintaining the other—deeply vested economic interests were at stake. Vested interests help explain why some stereotypes change quickly and easily, while others endure. Those with the authority over media—at this time it was newspapers—more easily shape cultural narratives. Still, we can change things from the grassroots up, and "Black is beautiful" is an example.

The hidden evaluator driving Western narratives about race, class, and gender is the belief that ranking is a valuable way to organize society and that domination indicates superiority. Because of this underlying belief in the right to dominate, slavery didn't completely end when it became illegal. It continued long after the Emancipation Proclamation through careful, and not so careful, concealment of its aims. In July 2018, unmarked graves were found of 95 men thought to be prisoners of a convict-lease program at the Imperial State Prison Farm in Sugar Land, Texas. Inmates were almost exclusively Black men who had been arrested for minor crimes like "vagrancy, flirting with white women or petty theft." This ties directly to both the content of the new stereotype (they were flirting) and its effects (they couldn't earn a living). Prisoners were "leased by the state to private businessmen and forced to work on plantations, in coal mines and railroads, or on other state projects—such as building the entire Texas Capitol building from scratch."[63] The convict-lease system lasted into the 20th century. Some estimates suggest that more African Americans were literally worked to death by the convict-lease system than killed by lynching.[64]

Stereotypes are transmitted from generation to generation through obvious and subtle means. They can then rise like a threat from the subconscious where cultural schemas live and lead to irrational actions. In Ferguson, Missouri, on August 9, 2014, when 6'4" white police officer Darren Wilson looked at 6'4" Black teenager Michael Brown, he didn't see an unarmed kid about his own size who he could arrest but "a demon." He said he felt "like a five-year old holding onto Hulk Hogan" and shot him to death.[65] Another event had a happier ending. In 2009, Henry Louis Gates Jr. was arrested because someone called 911 when they saw the Black Harvard professor trying to open the jammed door to his own home. A request for proof of Gates's address could have ended the event, but instead officer James Crowley assumed Gates was dangerous and arrested him. Charges were dropped and President Obama invited them to the White House to discuss the incident over beers.

Knowing how stereotypes from media and early education worm their way into our emotions, it is worth pondering: did Darren Wilson ever see his mother clutch her purse close or cross the street when she saw a Black man approaching? Did this unconsciously influence his feelings about Brown? We'll never know, but we do know he almost certainly saw things like this repeatedly. Did racial profiling of the stereotypical "lawless buck" (in modern terms, Black man = gangster/thug) affect Wilson and Crowley's actions? Statistics tend to the conclusion that, whether they were consciously stereotyping (or racial profiling) or not, they almost certainly did.

In this example, the main vectors of analysis are race (Black) and gender (male). Class status did not initially help Gates, a well-to-do Harvard professor. He was treated as a criminal due to his race and gender alone. Vectors of analysis can identify the active parts of any issue in order to measure privilege and oppression. In sum, when a cultural group dominates cultural others, those others suffer not only from beliefs about them, but also from actions based on those beliefs. You can test this thesis by applying intersectional analysis to any issue that concerns you.

This chapter introduced you to feminist theories on gender, sexuality, race, class, and disability, and culminated with intersectionality. We found that theories about the social construction of gender cannot accurately analyze all women's experiences. Each feminism has theories particular to its stakes, and intersectionality is nimble enough to address them all. Once you can apply the intersectional method, you'll be able to incorporate other theories to research and analyze feminist issues in different times and places. You'll be able to add theoretical premises of your own that reflect your personal experiences. Ideally, this is just the beginning of examining and intervening in the world around you. There is no single feminist theory that you have to follow, just like there is no loyalty oath you have to sign to be a feminist. Knowing there are many ways to think, and things to think about, empowers you to act in line with your concerns.

Notes

1 "Theory." *Oxford Dictionaries.com*. Oxford U Press. 2019, https://en.oxford-dictionaries.com/definition/theory.
2 "Katherine Johnson Biography." *NASA.gov*. Last modified Aug. 6, 2018, https://www.nasa.gov/content/katherine-johnson-biography.
3 Ashley Graham. "Plus Size? More Like My Size." *TEDx Berklee Valencia*. 2015, https://www.ted.com/talks/ashley_graham_plus_size_more_like_my_size.
4 "Just 8 Men Own Same Wealth as Half the World." *Oxfam*. Jan. 16, 2017, https://www.oxfam.org/en/pressroom/pressreleases/2017-01-16/just-8-men-own-same-wealth-half-world.
5 Christopher Ingraham. "The Richest 1 Percent Now Owns More of the Country's Wealth Than at Any Time in the Past 50 Years." *The Washington Post*. Dec. 6, 2017, https://www.washingtonpost.com/news/wonk/wp/2017/12/06/the-richest-1-percent-now-owns-more-of-the-countrys-wealth-than-at-any-time-in-the-past-50-years/.
6 Gloria Anzaldúa. "How to Tame a Wild Tongue." *Borderlands/La Frontera: The New Mestiza*. Aunt Lute. 1987, p. 81.
7 "Racism." Merriam-Webster. https://www.merriam-webster.com/dictionary/racism.
8 Beverly Daniel Tatum. *Why Are All the Black Kids Sitting Together it the Cafeteria?: and Other Conversations About Race*. Basic-Perseus. 1997, p. 7. David Wellman's book is *Portraits of White Racism*.
9 Ibid., p. 11.

10 "Racism." Merriam-Webster online.

11 Allan G. Johnson. "Social Oppression." *The Blackwell Dictionary of Sociology: A User's Guide to Sociological Language.* 2nd ed. Blackwell. 2000, p. 293.

12 Peggy McIntosh. "White Privilege: Unpacking the Invisible Knapsack." 1988, http://www.racialequitytools.org/resourcefiles/mcintosh.pdf.

13 David A. Fahrenthold. "Statistics Show Drop in U.S. Rape Cases." *The Washington Post.* June 19, 2006,
    http://www.washingtonpost.com/wp-dyn/content/article/2006/06/18/AR2006061800610.html.

14 Rape and Incest National Network. "Statistics." *RAINN*, 2019, https://www.rainn.org/statistics/victims-sexual-violence.

15 Leah Fessler. "The Poorest Americans Are 12 Times as Likely to Be Sexually Assaulted as The Wealthiest." *Quartz.* Jan. 3, 2018.

16 Ibid.

17 Ibid.

18 "Prevalence Rates." End Rape on Campus. 2009, http://endrapeoncampus.org/new-page-3/.

19 Rape and Incest National Network.

20 Ibid.

21 Fiona Lloyd-Davies. "Why Eastern DR Congo is 'Rape Capital of the World.'" *CNN.* Nov. 25, 2011, https://www.cnn.com/2011/11/24/world/africa/democratic-congo-rape/index.html.

22 Nina Wilén and Bert Ingelaere. "War-Torn Congo Has Been Called the 'Rape Capital of The World.' Here is How Fighters Think about Sexual Violence." *The Washington Post.* Aug. 31, 2017, https://www.washingtonpost.com/news/monkey-cage/wp/2017/08/28/what-do-rebels-think-about-sexual-violence-in-congo-we-asked-them/?utm_term=.23378b7055d2.

23 Owen Bowcott. "Congo Politician Guilty in First ICC Trial to Focus on Rape as a War Crime." *The Guardian.* Mar. 21, 2016, https://www.theguardian.com/world/2016/mar/21/icc-finds-ex-congolese-vice-president-jean-pierre-bemba-guilty-of-war-crimes.

24 Hortense Spillers. "Interstices: A Small Drama of Words." *Pleasure and Danger: Exploring Female Sexuality.* Ed. Carol Vance. Pandora-HarperCollins. 1984.

25 Gayle Rubin. "Thinking Sex: Notes for a Radical Theory of the Politics of Sexuality." *Pleasure and Danger.* Ed. Carole Vance. Routledge & Paul Kegan. 1984, pp. 267–319.

26 Nepal Pride Parade, Mitini Nepal 2/14/2019, Creative Commons, https://commons.wikimedia.org/wiki/File:Nepal_Pride_Parade4.jpg.

27 Carolyn Epple, "Coming to Terms with Navajo Nádleehí: A Critique of 'Berdache,' 'Gay,' 'Alternate Gender,' and 'Two Spirit.'" American Ethnologist. Vol. 25, No. 2, May, 1998, pp. 267–290.

28 Hijra Protest Islamabad, Arun Reginald, 5/5/2008, Creative Commons, https://commons.wikimedia.org/wiki/File:Hijra_Protest_Islamabad.jpg.

29 Julie McCarthy. "A Journey of Pain and Beauty: On Becoming Transgender in India." *NPR.* Mar. 18, 2014, https://www.npr.org/sections/parallels/2014/04/18/304548675/a-journey-of-pain-and-beauty-on-becoming-transgender-in-india.

30 "List of Nonbinary Identities." Nonbinary Wiki. Last updated Feb. 9, 2019, https://nonbinary.miraheze.org/wiki/List_of_nonbinary_identities.

31 Trans Day of Visibility, 3/31/2016, Pax Ahimsa Gethen, Creative Commons, https://commons.wikimedia.org/wiki/File:Trans_Day_of_Visibility_SF_2016.jpg.

32 Lori Grishman. "What Does the Q in LGBTQ Stand For?" *USA Today.* July 22, 2016, https://www.usatoday.com/story/news/nation-now/2015/06/01/lgbtq-questioning-queer-meaning/26925563/.

33 Ashleigh Shackelford. "Why I'm Nonbinary but Don't Use 'They/Them.'" *Wear Your Voice.* July 7, 2016.

34 H. G. Virupaksha, Daliboyina Muralidhar, and Jayashree Ramakrishna. "Suicide and Suicidal Behavior among Transgender Persons." *Indian Journal of Psychological Medicine.* Vol. 38, No. 6, Nov./Dec. 2016, pp. 505–509.

35 Cost of Living circa 1983, Property of Menoukha Robin Case.

36 Kathleen Elkins. "Here's How Much Money Americans Think You Need to Be Considered Rich." CNBC.com. June 21, 2017, https://www.cnbc.com/2017/06/21/how-much-money-americans-think-it-takes-to-be-considered-rich.html.

37 "How Hollywood Misrepresents the Working Class Featuring Gabe Gonzales." *Decoded with Franchesca Ramsey.* Web series. MTV. S6: Ep. 7, Feb. 21, 2018, http://www.mtv.com/shows/decoded/episode-guide.

38 John Komloss. "In America, Inequality Begins in the Womb." *PBS News Hour.* May 20, 2015, https://www.pbs.org/newshour/economy/america-inequality-begins-womb.

39 Working Class Bulwark, Jacob Burck, 1934 *Daily Worker,* Creative Commons, https://commons.wikimedia.org/wiki/File:Working_Class_Bulwark_by_Jacob_Burck.jpg.

40 Steven Deyle. *Carry Me Back: The Domestic Slave Trade in American Life.* Oxford U. 2005, pp. 59–60.

41 "The Racial Wealth Gap." *Explained.* Creators Joe Posner and Ezra Klein. S1: Ep. 1. Netflix, May 23, 2018.

42 The HOLC maps are part of the Records of the FHLBB (RG195) at the National Archives II.

43 Ibid.

44 Theodora Regina Berry. "Engaged Pedagogy and Critical Race Feminism." *Educational Foundations.* Vol. 24, No. 3/4, Summer/Fall 2010, pp. 19–26.

45 Rosemarie Garland-Thomson. "Feminist Disability Studies." *Signs.* U of Chicago Press. Vol. 30, No. 2, Winter 2005, pp. 1557–1587.

46 "What is the Americans with Disability Act?" ADA National Network. Last updated Mar. 2019, https://adata.org/learn-about-ada.

47 "Disability." ADA National Network. Last updated Mar. 2019, https://adata.org/glossary-terms#D.

48 Rosemarie Garland-Thomas. "Integrating Disability, Transforming Feminist Theory." *NWSA Journal,* Vol. 14, No. 3, Fall 2002, p. 20.

49 "Harriet Tubman: Superspy." Dir. & Writer Derek Waters. Performance by Octavia Spencer and Crissle West. *Drunk History.* S3: Ep. 4. Sept. 2015, http://www.cc.com/video-clips/2qw47o/drunk-history-harriet-tubman--superspy.

50 *The Commonwealth.* Boston. Vol. 1, no. 45, July 10, 1863, http://www.harriettubman.com/tubman2.html.

51 "The Combahee River Collective Statement." 1977, https://combaheerivercollective.weebly.com/the-combahee-river-collective-statement.html.

52 *Feminists: What Were They Thinking?* Dir. Johanna Demetrakas. Netflix. Oct. 12, 2018.

53 Ibid.

54 Kimberlé Williams Crenshaw. "Demarginalizing the Intersection of Race and Sex: A Black Feminist Critique of Antidiscrimination Doctrine, Feminist Theory and Antiracist Politics." U of Chicago Legal Forum. Issue 1, Article 8, 1989, p. 140.

55 "About NOW." National Organization for Women. 2019, https://now.org/about/.

56 Patricia Hill Collins and Sirma Bilge. *Intersectionality*. Polity, 2016, p. 4.

57 Ibid., p. 33.

58 "Feminism 101: Patricia Hill Collins, Black Feminist Thought in the Matrix of Domination." *Mind the Gap*. Feb. 15, 2008, https://mindthegapuk.word press.com/2008/02/15/feminism-101-patricia-hill-collins-black-feminist-thought-in-the-matrix-of-domination/.

59 "India: 'Hidden Apartheid' of Discrimination Against Dalits." *Human Rights Watch*. Feb. 13, 2017, https://www.hrw.org/news/2007/02/13/india-hidden-apartheid-discrimination-against-dalits.

60 Byron Hurt. *Barack & Curtis: Manhood, Power, and Respect*. 2008. BHurt.com. 2019, http://www.bhurt.com/films/view/barack_and_curtis.

61 Toy Bank. http://www.tradecards.com/articles/mb/jollyn.html; Racist Glassware. "Decoding the American Racial Imagination: 1988 and William Horton." *Medium.com*. Dec. 10, 2016, https://medium.com/@maweber/decoding-american-racial-fear-1988-andwilliam-horton-d7ed2a0f628a.

62 Rao Sameer. "Remember the Tulsa 'Black Wall Street' Massacre through Its Last Known Survivor." *ColorLine.com*. June 1, 2018, https://www.color lines.com/articles/remember-tulsa-black-wall-street-massacre-through-last-known-survivor.

63 Meagan Flynn. "Bodies Believed to Be Those of 95 Black Forced-Labor Pris-oners from Jim Crow Era Unearthed in Sugar Land After One Man's Quest." *The Washington Post*. July 18, 2018, https://www.washingtonpost.com/news/morning-mix/wp/2018/07/18/bodies-of-95-black-forced-labor-prisoners-from-jim-crow-era-unearthed-in-sugar-land-after-one-mans-quest/?utm_term=.d414db7e7bf2.

64 Ibid. See, in particular, the books with Meagan Flynn references: Douglas A. Blackmon's *Slavery by Another Name* (2008) and Robert Perkinson's *Texas Tough: The Rise of America's Prison System* (2010).

65 Josh Sandburn. "All the Ways Darren Wilson Described Being Afraid of Michael Brown." *Time*. Nov. 25, 2014, http://time.com/3605346/darren-wilson-michael-brown-demon/.

8   Feminisms and Theorists

#WTF: What's That Feminism

Intersectionality is rooted in a long-lived idea. We saw its beginnings with Sojourner Truth, its articulation by Claudia Jones, its application in plays by Lorraine Hansberry, the exposition of its philosophy by the Combahee River Collective, and its naming by Kimberlé Crenshaw. Intersectional analysis has become the primary method employed by feminist scholars. Almost all advanced WGSS books and articles rely on it, but they often don't explain how they use the method. As you continue in WGSS, look for vectors to better understand and practice intersectional feminism in scholarship and activism.

A sign of intersectionality's widespread effectiveness is how it's become a buzzword among both feminist and their detractors. A good search reveals everything from celebratory articles to the Urban Dictionary's smear campaign: "radical feminists hate all men. But intersectional feminism teaches us that it is only OK to hate white cisgender men."[1] Some misunderstand intersectionality as reverse hierarchy that privileges the devalued pole of the binaries in Table 3.1. They state, "I don't fit any of the intersections so you're taking away my authority." But whether we fit the valued or devalued pole of a norm, all intersections affect us. But intersectionality isn't about reversing who's in charge or privileging the most oppressed by adding up identities. This additive notion misses how discriminations are interconnected. When we examine racism, for instance, we're never *just* talking about racism. Classism and sexism are always part of the mix. Also, the point isn't to upend the hierarchy but to create equity. Just as matriarchy isn't the reverse of patriarchy, equity isn't achieved by reversing the power structure.

Stereotypes and misunderstandings obscure what intersectionality can reveal about how lives at the intersections of vectors vary. For example, ethnicity, one of many vectors addressed by intersectional feminists, can include cultural practices as well as historical and political events. Chimine Arfuso describes how the unique experiences of Cuban women require a new feminism.

A Case for a Cubana Feminism
by Chimine Arfuso

Latina Feminism in the US was primarily pioneered by Chicana scholars, but, as we learn more about intersectionality, it is important that we do not generalize about all Latin American descendants. While the following themes do not speak for all Cuban-American experiences, they are found abundantly among Cuban and Cuban-American novelists and memoirs, and I believe are foundational in defining a Cuban-American Feminism.

History: Cuba is indigenous American land of Taíno and Ciboney tribes. It was first colonized by Spain in the late 1400s and was an early site of African diaspora via slavery. To this day, Cuban-Americans are trying to reconcile oppressive systems based on race from colonialism. Cuban-American experiences are impacted by Fidel Castro's rise to power in 1959, the Cuban-American diaspora, and US and Cuba foreign policy relations. It was only during the Obama administration that the over 40-year trade and travel embargo was slightly lifted from Cuba, a move recently reversed by Trump.

The Diaspora: Diaspora has been defined as a mass displacement of people from their country. Prominent diasporas include the Transatlantic Slave trade and the Holocaust. Recent scholars have argued that the combination of the mass exodus of Cubans from Cuba in the 1950s and 1960s with fear and political complications in returning home should be considered a diaspora. This disconnect from our home country is significant for Cuban-American feminism.

Religion: Religious politics in Cuba are also complex. Spanish colonialism brought in Catholicism. The people displaced from Africa and enslaved in Cuba introduced African Spirituality such as Lucumí (also known as Santería), Palo Mayombe, Ifa, and others. Additionally, there are still Indigenous Taíno populations with their own unique spiritual practices. As a result, there is a wide range of spiritual beliefs varying between African and Native American spirituality and Catholicism. Because of Catholic religious imperialism, many elements of Indigenous Spirituality are demonized and given names such as witchcraft and voodoo. This conflict between indigenous practices and Catholicism and how or whether or not native traditions survived the Cuban-American diaspora is foundational in the Cuban-American perspective.

Why a distinction: Decentralizing the predominantly Chicana lens on Latina Feminism makes space for the complex and interconnected racial politics that women from other Latin countries face. In Cuban-American perspectives, Latina Feminism, Black Feminism, Indigenous Feminism, and Womanism can intersect based upon our individual standpoints. While no one theory can cover the range of experiences among women across Latin countries, allowing for more nuance helps us as feminists practice in the spirit of Crenshaw's intersectionality.

Digital feminism refers to the enormous amount of feminist practice taking place over internet venues such as Facebook and Twitter. Media today offers grassroots connections on a global level. With the advent of hashtags, people can easily find others who share their concerns, ranging from broad topics (#IntersectionalFeminism, #ClimateJustice) to specific events (#WomensMarch).

When academics study the way the Humanities (languages, literature, philosophy, history, religion, art, and music) are expressed online, it's called Digital Humanities, and digital feminism is a subset of that field. You can use the tools that identify beliefs, values, vested interests, and issues to navigate the world of digital feminism. These tools can place individual experiences in historical and cultural context and help us understand the dynamics of what John Trudell called authority and what most academics call power. They reveal that authority isn't just about personal skills, strengths, talents, and accomplishments, but about how social venues either constrict or nourish employment of those skills, strengths, talents, and accomplishments. Because social media allow individual digital feminists to bypass authority's top-down grip on distribution of information, online campaigns apply social justice theories about power dynamics in real time.

Ayana A.H. Jamieson, founder of the Octavia E. Butler Legacy Network,[2] explains that Black activists

> have been forerunners in . . . digital humanities. While [some have formal digital humanities scholarly training,] many participants in the subculture dubbed "Black Twitter" are grassroots organizers, concerned citizens, and members of groups with . . . shared experiences. Considerable overlap and collaboration between scholars and regular folks who are users of twitter occurs regularly, commenting on topics from . . . #BlackLivesMatter [to #SayHerName]. . . . These activists have diversif[ied] digital humanities (#transformDH) and contributed to more accurate media portrayals of all community members.
>
> As digital humanities scholar Moya Bailey notes:
>
> The ways in which identities inform both theory and practice in digital humanities have been largely overlooked. [. . .] By centering the lives of women, people of color, and disabled folks, the types of possible conversations in digital humanities shift. [. . .] [They offer an] opportunity to . . . expose implicit assumptions about what and who counts . . . as well as . . . structural limitations that are the inevitable result of an unexamined identity politics of whiteness, masculinity, and ablebodiness.[3, 4]

Feminist activists use image and video-rich digital media to spread information, organize events, and rally support. The millions who attended recent years' Women's Marches in Washington, DC and throughout the world gathered almost exclusively due to online exposure. Organizers used digital means to address intersectionality and diversify representation at the march. The debate about whether this effort was successful also took place in online venues and continues to be a subject of debate on social media today.[5]

Cyberfeminism by Alice Lai

Although cyberfeminists love their computers, they are not content simply to play with the new toys, but to make use of them for political purpose and to develop critique of their abuse and problems.[6]

Cyberfeminism does not treat technology as a neutral tool; rather, they argue that it is embedded in structures of power, is often described and understood in gendered terms, and can shape the ways in which gender is constructed and performed in cyberspace.

Cyberfeminism emphasizes the interplay among technology, gender/women, and activism. Cyberfeminists advocate practicing feminism with a technological slant, including a thorough critique of gender inequality, collective activist approaches, and creative cultural productions. These individuals continue to use all kinds of technology (such as the Internet, cyberspace technology, social media, and creative tech tools) to fight against women's oppression and gender stereotypes as well as the inequalities associated with technology. One notable example of cyberfeminism is subRosa (2011), a group of artists who combine "art, activism, and politics to explore and critique the intersections of new information and biotechnologies in women's bodies, lives, and work."[7] They perceive cyberspace and technologies as opportunities not only for information/experience sharing, but also for consciousness-raising and female empowerment.

Cyberfeminist pedagogy would employ digital connectivity, critique, and creativity to achieve feminist goals that may be based on individual, community, or historical context. Through such a pedagogy, students learn to advocate for women, use technology to place women at the center of activism, and form coalitions with diverse social groups across genders, races, classes, sexualities, religions, and nationalities. Moreover, Richards (2011) asserted that "cyberfeminist pedagogy would attend to the ways in which digital technologies both subvert and reinscribe gender, race, and other corporeal hierarchies in virtual space; it would be attentive to the productive and ironic play of cyberfeminist activism and theory."[8] Cyberfeminists in the field of art education question gender assumptions and disparities associated with art technology and their effects on the education of art teachers and artists in today's digital age.

Cyberfeminists' critique of digital gender inequality, therefore, is aimed at critically analyzing how/why women might be affected by gender inequality embedded in the world of technology[9]; for example, how/why women and men might approach technology creation and usage differently;

how/why technology creation and usage might perpetuate a patriarchal system; how/why women might be marginalized or oppressed by technology; and how gender divides in technology-driven educational settings and industries might hinder women's educational, social, and economic advancement.

#WTF Who's That Feminist

Rhianna Rogers

"What Are You?": Living as a Multiracial Woman

As I reflect on what it means to be a multiracial woman, I am drawn back to a memory I had as a three-year old child at KinderHaus (a German kindergarten my parents sent me to.) We were playing with crayons and the teacher asked us to draw a picture of our families. I wanted my picture to look like my family, so I choose a white crayon for my mom, a black crayon for my dad, a white crayon for my sister, and a burnt sienna crayon for myself and my brother. I remember a student asking me why I chose burnt sienna and not black and I responded, "Obviously, because I am not black, I am burnt sienna."

As a 30-something multiracial woman of two multiracial parents (i.e., my mother predominately identifies as American, English, and German and my father identifies as American and Cajun-Creole), I was brought up to believe that I could identify racially however I wanted to. Thus, my racial and cultural individuality was strongly encouraged. My parents always stressed to me that learning about all of my racial/ethnic backgrounds was important and that no one could tell me what ancestry was more important than another. I can clearly remember my mom telling me, "Sweetheart, we want you to be proud of who you are and all the cultures that make you up as a person. Don't let anyone ever tell you otherwise." My parents encouraged me to study my heritage(s) and they regularly took me to cultural events that dealt with all parts of my ancestry.

Even though I grew up in a progressive part of California (an hour north of Los Angeles), my racially pluralistic upbringing was quite unique in the early 1980s. Very few people had openly identified themselves as multiracial at the time, though I did meet a few growing up. Because my approach to race and ethnicity was so unique, I faced a lot of adversity from different groups of people. Some felt I was "too white" or "too black" for certain cultural behaviors, while others just wanted me to pick "a side" and be done with it. I ignored these pressures and continued to pursue a more pluralistic view of my own identity. In my own worldview, I believe that my identity was not shaped by my skin tone, but rather the cultures that were a part of my upbringing and surrounding. Being raised this way made me proud of all my ancestors. The cultural freedom that my parents gave me allowed me, from a young age, to develop emotional intelligence around diversity and race that was quite different from my peers. My parents encouraged me to learn the "truths" about history (e.g., slavery, racism, limitations on gender roles) which allowed me to confront difficult concepts very young, like why some of my ancestors enslaved others or why some of my other ancestors were enslaved. Confronting difficult topics like this at a young age allowed me to look deeper at myself and society and understand how behaviors were created in those around me.

Looking back, I can see just how much this upbringing influenced me to be curious about cultures and pursue a degree in Anthropology and Cultural Studies. My curiosity about culture ultimately led me to decide at the age of six that I would become a professor, an archaeologist, and an expert on culture (amazingly, I actually did just that!). If you were to look back at my academic course work, you would find that I have always been mesmerized by culture. I did focused studies on my ancestry (e.g., US History; English, German, Irish Studies; Cajun-Creole Studies; African and African–American Studies; Cherokee and Native American Studies; and French Studies) so I could understand my personal history. Looking back, my parents' forward thinking led me to be the scholar I am today.

Though I feel privileged to have been given the opportunity to develop a multiracial worldview, I found many instances where my views conflicted with mainstream US views of race and identity. Case in point, because my physical features and behaviors cannot clearly be distinguished as belonging to a particular racial group, I regularly get asked "Where are you from?" or "Where are my people were from?" In most cases, Los Angeles, California, clearly wasn't the answer they were looking for, so these conversations continue until I say something like "Why is it so important for you to know my ancestry and to have this conversation?" Usually, this gets them to reflect (but most of the time it makes them uncomfortable). In cases like this, the undercurrent of their question was, "You aren't white, but you aren't black. What are you?" Being confronted by their own biases is not always easy for others to acknowledge.

Since mainstream US culture tends to force people into racialized groups, my pluralistic ideals of race were (and are) odd to some people. However, recent research indicates that this trend is changing; in fact, there is a growing number of US people who identify as two or more racial or ethnic identities.[10] Coupling this data trend with the increased representation of multiracial peoples/couples in media and marketing in the 2000s and beyond, we are starting to see an increasingly visible and active multiracial nation. Yet the extent to which multiracial people have impacted US culture is a bit skewed. This is because it was not until the 2000 US Census that multiracial classifications were included as an option, which means many others, like myself, were excluded from previous US racial data sets. This did not mean we didn't exist.

In a recent conversation, my father (who externally could be classified as a black man but has always self-classified as multiracial) told me that he hates labels. As he said, "why must I be defined by others' perceptions or insecurities? My name is Tony and that is how I would like to be labeled." I find myself feeling the same way as an adult. Labels feel confining and place limits on who and what I am. I don't believe that anyone else has the right to place a label on me, yet due to others' discomfort, I find myself trying to find labels I can tolerate, shifting and code switching between my various racial and cultural identities, and shying away from multiracial conversations in order to gain acceptance in various groups. The frequency that I feel I have to shift cultures (especially in a professional work environment) on a daily basis gives way to a feeling of racial and ethnic ambiguity in myself. There are times that I feel like an outsider always looking into every cultural group I belong to, which can be exhausting. Having a background in anthropology has helped me cope with these feelings as well as contextualize why they exist, yet there is more work that needs to be done to help multiracial people feel accepted in mainstream culture.

Compounding these internal issues are the external culturally constructed stereotypes I face as being labeled a woman of color. Though I internally do not care to be labeled as anything but "Rhianna," I cannot ignore that society does not classify me the same way. It is worth noting that scholars have found five major experiences faced by multiracial peoples: (1) external racial and ethnic pressures that result in internalized racial shifting/code switching; (2) racial/ethnic ambiguity; (3) feeling like an outsider; (4) seeking community and (5) feelings of racial classification resistance or anti-labeling.[11] In short, research confirms a collective multiracial experience, one with direct ties to the social and environmental pressures associated with having a multifaceted identity in a color-conscious society. I can personally attest to this experience and feeling. As a woman of color in the US, I have faced constant stereotypes (the Jezebel: a sexualized, aggressive black woman whose goal is to conquer men; the Mammy: a lovable, non-threatening, unattractive black woman who is meant to comfort others; and the Headstrong Black Woman: a loud, sassy, argumentative woman who does what she wants and is there for entertainment). These one-dimensional portrayals of women of color, especially black women, has been the most difficult part of US culture for me to grapple with as a multiracial person. Since I don't classify myself by my skin tone (though others do), I find myself breaking these stereotypes often, which makes others around me uncomfortable or confused.

I would like to illustrate this with another example: Based on my mom's love of horses and experiences as a barrel racer, I grew up loving cowboy culture. From an early age, I would wear cowboy boots as often as I could. As a product of Southern California, I was also heavily influenced by Hispanic *ranchero/cowboy* culture, and I loved going to rodeos, listening to *mariachi* music, and riding horses. One year, I remember my parents bought me a very expensive pair of cowboy boots as a gift. I was so proud of my boots that I wore them to school to show everyone; however, I remember being confronted by a classmate (a woman of color) who told me that I was "being white" and proceeded to make fun of me. I was so hurt by this experience that I immediately took off my boots and walked around in socks the rest of the day. I remember returning home and asking my mom why this happened and she said that people will not always understand my view of culture and how I think. Though I would not have handled this situation the same way today, my experience illustrates how multiracial individuals respond to societal pressures in order to conform to traditional means of categorizing others by race.[12] My hope is that as we progress as a society, multiracial identities are understood and celebrated rather than marginalized in mainstream US culture.

Alice Lai

I Became a Digital Feminist

I begin my story by reflecting on my experience with computers and technology. I consider myself a digital immigrant as I did not grow up with computers, iPhones, the Internet, or digital cameras. My first use of a computer was in my mid-teens when I took a computer class. I still remember that my teacher constantly reminded us (especially girls) that logical thinking and skills are essential for a computer programmer. The final project of that class was to create a tree or circle using computer code. I managed to create a tree not by using computer code but by arranging fonts into a tree-like graphic. Toward the end of that class, most boys were encouraged to take a second computer class to learn advanced computer programming. Girls who were still interested in computers were encouraged to use computers for writing or bookkeeping projects. I discovered that I enjoyed creating computer graphics, but I might not have strong logical skills to master computer programming. This early computer experience taught me that computers and technology were a boy's domain.

I eventually earned a Bachelor's degree focusing on computer graphic design and began my job as a graphic designer in the mid-1990s. I noticed that women were the minority in this field. While I did not feel uncomfortable or belittled in my line of work, I felt that I needed to perform not just as a designer but also a technology expert in order to be part of this male-dominated industry.

While working as a computer graphic designer, I entered a graduate-level art teacher preparation program. There, I began taking courses focusing on teaching with technology and creating my own art teacher websites to present my lesson plans, artist portfolios, and digital storytelling projects. The majority of students and instructors in the program were women, but only a few of the students and instructors were experienced users of computer or art and design software. With this in mind, the instructors typically asked the students to use novice-friendly software, such as Microsoft FrontPage, to create personal webpages. Although a few women, myself included, were able to edit webpages using HTML and additional design software, we were occasionally regarded as "geeks" or exceptions in the class. We were often advised to focus more on content writing rather than other more technical aspects of website creation, which I deemed more interesting and important for improving the usability, readability, and navigation of the site.

As I moved on to a doctoral-level art education program in a large university, I noticed that when undertaking group projects, my male colleagues who shared similar design and technology backgrounds to myself were encouraged to, or quickly volunteered to, be in charge of the component that required the learning and use of advanced media production technologies, such as video, sound, game, and animation programs, to enhance artistic quality. Although I was also interested in learning new technology and exploring its creative and technical capacity, I felt that as a female art education student, unlike the male media arts students, I belonged to and should choose to participate in the teaching, content creation, and presentation elements of the group projects.

These male colleagues, under the tutelage of a male professor, eventually developed one of the department's first online art education courses from scratch. However, none of these creators were asked to, or indeed were able to, teach the online course successfully. Because I had an opportunity to conduct a case study, which included interviewing students about their experiences with this online course during its very first run, I learned from the six students who withdrew from the endeavor that the lack of teaching presence, difficulty in navigating the course, and problems in using the multimedia arts embedded in the course had rendered their online learning unsatisfying. The professor then invited me to teach the course and granted me editing access with which to customize it. I made modifications to allow frequent and easier teaching and social presence, while disabling a few multimedia features that required external downloading of plugins. These changes, in turn, strengthened teacher-student and student-student bonds and reduced students' anxiety over using online technology.

In the field of art education, digital technology plays multiple roles: as a new art medium, tool, and context for enhancing creativity, instruction, and knowledge construction. As I continue to learn new technology and use technology to create digital art and teach online art classes, I become more and more aware of the gender disparity in the technologized art and educational context. Thus, since 2010, I have been focusing my academic publications on digital gender inequality and cyberfeminist pedagogy. For example, I research the intersections of cyberspace/cybertechnology, pedagogy and gender, women's online learning experiences, the quality of women's cyber activities or products, and women's level of satisfaction with their experiences with and use of cyberspace/cybertechnology. In my art classes, I have encouraged students to critique digital images portraying gender stereotypes and create digital images portraying their experiences as women in the digital age. I have become a cyberfeminist who uses technology as a tool for female empowerment and feminist consciousness-raising.

Feminist Theorists

Feminists have written theory about every vector and combination of vectors in Table 3.1. For example, *Hikane: The Capable Woman* (1989–1995) was a journal by and for lesbians with disabilities. It offered personal testimonies and theories about the effects of race, class, and other vectors in the lives of its authors and readers. In this chapter, we address race, class, gender, age, immigration, and disability theorists. Today, immigration and religion have become central issues largely due to the Trump administration's direct attacks on Mexicans and Muslims as well as a rise in neo-Nazi backlash against Jews and immigrants of color. Some of this is new to some readers, but it's not new ground to feminist theorists. These theories have been in the works for a long time and if you get a chance to look at the books we refer to, you'll find they're quite advanced, not introductory like this book. But by now, you've learned enough to take on the challenge.

Feminist theories provide context about and offer remedies for isms and phobias. Analyzing and dismantling isms and phobias is a crucial step in re-establishing egalitarian societies. Among the feminists highlighted here are those who developed the theories we've discussed.

Gender and Sexuality Theorists

The number of women contributing to gender and sexuality theories is enormous. To start your research, here are a few theorists whose work dismantles sexism, heterosexism, and homophobia.

Simone de Beauvoir (1908–1986)

Beauvoir was raised by a wealthy Catholic family. By age 14, she had become an atheist and existentialist, the latter a philosophy based on free will and personal responsibility. She attended the Sorbonne (French university) in the 1920s and became a scholar and writer. She was prolific, but her 1949 book, *The Second Sex*, is best known. It offers a nearly 1,000-page critique of patriarchy and its history, and is considered the rallying cry that initiated second wave white feminism. Beauvoir's ideas were so controversial that the Vatican banned *The Second Sex*. In fact, it's still banned, but that didn't stop it from becoming the basis of much feminist thought.

Kate Millett (1934–2017)

Millett was active in feminist, human rights, mental health care reform, and civil rights movements. Many of her books are autobiographical, reflecting her own challenges in some of these areas. Her work contributed to the theory that personal testimony is valuable to activism. Her 1970 book, *Sexual Politics*, is considered "the first book of academic feminist literary criticism."[13] In it, she examines authors like DH Lawrence, Henry Miller, and Norman Mailer to expose how Western literature reflects and promotes patriarchy and male hegemony.

Susan Brownmiller (1935–)

Brownmiller, a journalist, was active in the Civil Rights movement in the early 1960s. Later in the decade, she joined a group called New York Radical Women, who helped initiate the Women's Liberation Movement. She is among the "Women's Libbers" who drew so much criticism from the patriarchy. She was one of the earliest feminists to write about rape culture, publishing *Against Our Will: Men, Women, and Rape* in 1975. While that analysis remains highly valuable, as feminists learn more about older non-Western cultures, her assumption that rape is a natural biology drive intrinsic to primitive cultures has become controversial. She wrote:

> Man's discovery that his genitalia could serve as a weapon [dates] to prehistoric times, along with the use of fire and the first crude stone axe. From prehistoric times to the present, I believe, rape has played a critical function. It is nothing more or less than a conscious process of intimidation by which all men keep all women in a state of fear.[14]

This is based on assumptions discussed in Chapter 4:

- Women have been universally oppressed by men throughout time and across places.
- If we believe men have universally oppressed (and in this case, raped) women, we must believe this is human nature.
- If we believe it is human nature, we must believe that working for gender equity is a battle against nature.

However true it may be that patriarchy is a rape culture, not all cultures are patriarchal. As described in Part Two, older cultures tend to be matriarchal or gender-balanced. Respect of women is the core of both, and they say rape before colonialism was so rare and unacceptable that it was punished by death (Yoruba) or exile (many Native North American tribes). Nevertheless, Brownmiller's work holds keys for understanding sexual assault in Western cultures and helped shape anti-rape movements.

Judith Butler (1956–)

Butler is a feminist philosopher whose work influences gender and queer theory. Building on theories about the social construction of gender, her early work focused on the roles of speech and action in that construction. Butler explains that we are not naturally gendered; rather, we "do" gender by repetitively acting out cultural gender norms. Our everyday performances (the "feminine" and "masculine" things we habitually say and do in response to peer expectations) lead to the illusion that gender is natural. This creates a cultural feedback loop, meaning the very acts and statements that construct gender are then believed to be evidence of gender.

Class Theorists

While many feminists address class (e.g., bell hooks in *Where We Stand: Class Matters*), there are feminists whose focus on classism, including Marxist feminists, economic feminists, and socialist feminists. The work of Karl Marx (1818–1883) is the foundation of all three. Women were not his main concern because to Marx, gender was but one of the many ways that owners could exploit workers. He did believe, though, that women's status was a measure of a society's development. He was also critical of gender's designation of a woman's value according to her function rather than as an individual valuable in and of herself. And some of the basic principles of Marxism—that economic inequity is inhumane, that exploitation of workers is wrong, that workers should unite across differences—are valuable to feminists concerned about how the vector of class shapes our experiences and opportunities. This branch of feminist theory led to data that reveals pay inequity.

Economic feminists draw on Marx as well as other sources to theorize how material conditions—what we have, how we live—affect women. Socialist feminists go beyond criticism and suggest political remedies. Socialist feminists also pointed out the unpaid economic contributions made by women in the home.

Western authors and their key texts include Gayle Rubin, "The Traffic in Women" (1975); Michele Barrett, *Women's Oppression Today* (1980); Nancy Hartsock, *Money, Sex, and Power* (1983); Zillah Eisenstein, *Capitalist Patriarchy and the Case for Socialist Feminism; Feminism and Sexual Equality* (1984); Donna Haraway, *Simians, Cyborgs, and Women* (1991); and Rosemary Hennessy, *Materialist Feminism and the Politics of Discourse*

(1993). Worker exploitation is a crucial issue to transnational feminists like Chandra Mohanty, "Under Western Eyes: Feminist Scholarship and Colonial Discourses," (1984) and Gayatri Spivak, "Can the Subaltern Speak?" (1988).

Contemporary feminists continue to address class issues and have put forth many women candidates through the Democratic Socialists of America. The party offers a Socialist Feminist Working Group that addresses "issues that especially impact working class and poor women."[15] With Social Security and Medicaid under attack, many of the poor are elderly.

Ageism Theorists

Ageism has been theorized in many fields since the word was coined in 1969 by physician Robert Butler. In "Ageism within Feminism," Joanne Pohl (University of Michigan School of Nursing) and Carol J. Boyd (Institute for Research on Women & Gender) describe how a range of feminisms age.[16] University of Wisconsin English and Philosophy Professor Leni Marshall has published and presented extensively on ageism. Even popular economic magazines like *Forbes* discuss age discrimination and offer data that "[Proves] It's Worse for Women."[17] Discussion of ageism began with concerns of the elderly and came to include discussion of stereotypes about children and teens. However, because youth don't have the same legal rights as adults (ageism), it's harder to collect hard data on how ageism affects them.

Disability Theorists

Some key theorists and texts on disability studies include Susan Wendell, *The Rejected Body: Feminist Philosophical Reflection on Disability* (1996); Rosemarie Garland-Thomson, *Extraordinary Bodies: Figuring Physical Disability in American Culture* (1997); and Alison Kafer, *Feminist, Queer, Crip* (2013). Kim Q. Hall edited the book *Feminist Disability Studies* in 2011. It contains essays that address a range of topics

> at the intersection of feminist theory and disability studies [such as] . . . the meaning of disability, the impact of public policy on those who have been labeled disabled, . . . how we define the norms of mental and physical ability . . . and how historical and cultural perceptions of the human body have been informed by and contributed to the oppression of women and disabled people.[18]

"Temporarily able-bodied" and other key ideas in feminist disability studies are an active topic of discussion in both academic and popular venues, such as the journal *FWD/Forward* (feminists with disabilities for a way forward).[19]

Nationalism Theorists

Nationalism (hatred of nationalities other than one's own) and xenophobia (fear of strangers) affect immigrants as well as citizens of color who may appear to be immigrants to those consumed with such fear. The first frame of a widely circulated cartoon shows a white man observing a brown woman talking on her cell phone in a grocery store line. In the second frame, he says, "Excuse me Miss, I didn't want to interrupt while you were talking, but I heard you speaking a foreign language. This is America. If you want to speak Spanish you should go back to Mexico." In the third frame, the woman replies, "Sir, I was speaking Navajo. If you want to speak English, you should go back to England." But being identified as a national other is no joke. In Minnesota, one of many true stories is that of a skinny brown Ojibwe boy who got beaten up regularly in middle school. Sometimes, the assailants called him Mexican, sometimes Arab, sometimes Indian (they finally got it right). The situation was so bad that he had to attend high school online.

The point is, brown or Black people of any nationality may be attacked. However, those who are actually immigrants have their own specific challenges. In "Private Fists and Public Force: Race, Gender, and Surveillance," Annanya Bhattacharjee describes how brown immigrant women are in danger because they cannot report crimes for fear of deportation, including assaults on them or their children.[20] They also cannot safely report sexual harassment, mistreatment, or exploitation on the job. Theories about xenophobia, therefore, include the vectors nation, race, class, and gender.

Religion Theorists

Religious bias is an intersectional issue that can involve race, class, and nation. It especially affects practitioners such as Orthodox Jews or Muslims who may be identified on sight by traditional dress. Sikhs and members of other religions whose attire is non-Western are often mistaken for Muslims and subjected to attack.

Islamophobia has grown since 9/11, especially affecting those who wear traditional clothing. The tradition of Arab feminism described in Part Three continues with scholars such as Halef Afshar and Asmar Barlas. Afshar, a member of the British House of Lords, has over a dozen publications, including *Islam and Feminisms: An Iranian Case Study* (1998). Barlas began her career as a Pakistani diplomat. Her positions caused her to seek political asylum in the US where she was founding director of Ithaca College's Study of Culture, Race, and Ethnicity. Her scholarship on religion includes numerous articles and books, including *"Believing Women" in Islam: Unreading Interpretations of the Qu'ran* (2002).

Bias against members of African and American Indigenous religions also constricts or endangers practitioners. Both groups may worship outside the normal church, temple, or mosque, sometimes due to lack of economic resources but more often because nature-based ceremonies take place outdoors at sacred sites such as rivers and mountains. The African Diaspora outgrowth of Yoruba religion, called Lukumi or Santería, had to go all the way to the Supreme Court to assert their freedom of religion. Yet practitioners still get arrested when performing ceremonies today. Indigenous American religious practice was illegal until the 1978 American Indian Religious Freedom Act, and it is now protected. Yet Water Protectors at Standing Rock in 2016 experienced arrests during ceremonies, and many of their sacred items were confiscated and destroyed. Theorists who clarify and defend Indigenous religious freedom include Paula Gunn Allen (see Part Two), Jacqui Alexander (*Pedagogies of Crossing: Meditations on Feminism, Sexual Politics, Memory, and the Sacred*, 2005), and Teresa N. Washington (*Our Mothers, Our Powers, Our Texts: Manifestation of Àjé in Africana Literature*, 2005).

A possible exception to religious bias being grounded in racism and classism is the 6,000-year-old bias against Jews, because it didn't evaporate even for those who, over those millennia, established financial security or eventually came to be seen in Europe and the US as whites. In Spike Lee's 2018 film, *BlacKkKlansman*, a Jewish undercover policeman, who's successful partly because he's perceived as white, is endangered by anti-Semitism in the Ku Klux Klan (KKK). Revealing white supremacist texts, the film shows clips from the films *Birth of a Nation* and *Gone with the Wind*, and quotes a forgery published in 1903 that led to an unusual form of classism. White supremacists believe the book *The Protocols of the Elders of Zion* documents "the" Jewish plan for world domination, but it's plagiarized from earlier political satire and novels. Due to the spread of lies in this book, when nominal Christians like Donald Trump or even Blacks like Oprah Winfrey become wealthy, it's celebrated, but when Jews become wealthy, it's thought of as a conspiracy.

Scholars like Maria Brettschneider (*Jewish Feminism and Intersectionality*, 2017) address issues particular to being a Jewish feminist, and many secular Jews like Emma Goldman, Betty Friedan, Susan Brownmiller, Shulamith Firestone, and Gloria Steinem were among second wave feminist theorists.

Feminist Critical Race and Intersectional Theorists

As we can see, isms and phobias don't stand alone, but act together in different ways. Many people contributed to feminist critical race theories and intersectional theories that address this phenomenon, and you can research them and read their work as you continue WGSS Studies. Here are a few key players.

Combahee River Collective and Kitchen Table: Women of Color Press Members: Audre Lorde, Gloria Anzaldúa, Barbara Smith, Chrystos, Cherríe Moraga

The Combahee River Collective, an Afrocentric feminist group, was convened in 1974. Members committed to ending race, sex, gender, and class oppression were among the first to articulate theory about how these problems interlock. The Collective established a press that published works by women of color. Writers like Freidan had access to major publishers, but these women did not, so they created their own press. Major publications include *Home Girls: A Black Feminist Anthology* in 1983 and the *This Bridge Called My Back: Writings by Radical Women of Color* in 1984.[21]

Audre Lorde (1934–1992)

Lorde was born a poor, Black, female, lesbian child of immigrants and was legally blind. Being on the devalued side of pretty much every American norm gave her a perspective on difference that has powerfully re-shaped feminist thought. She put the value of identity upfront, self-describing as a "Black lesbian mother warrior poet," and rather than working on any one ism, she focused on ways to form coalitions between those subject to different issues. Along with poetry, she is best known for groundbreaking essays that theorize positive responses to oppression. She writes of the power of poetry, of transforming silence into language and action, and of uses of the erotic and of anger. Her essay "The Master's Tools Will Never Dismantle the Master's House"[22] inspired the dedication to this book, and we've quoted her extensively. Perhaps, most inspiring is her writing and work that teaches us to both value and bridge differences. She brought us feminist tools that we can share. A 2002 film, *The Edge of Each Other's Battles: The Vision of Audre Lorde*, documents a celebration of her contributions in the "I Am Your Sister" conference that brought together 1,200 activists from 23 countries.[23] Lorde performed the title poem at the conference:

> I choose the earth
> We choose the earth
> And the edge of each other's battles.
> The war is the same.
> If we lose
> Someday
> Women's blood will congeal
> On a dead planet.But if we win –
> If we win
> There is no telling.[24]

Gloria Anzaldúa (1942–2004)

Anzaldúa wrote about Chicana, feminist, and queer concerns in essays and poems. Her most famous single-author book is *Borderlands/La Frontera: The New Mestiza* about her experiences growing up on the Texas-Mexico border. She carefully attended to the nuances of being marginal, mixed, and in-between. In doing so, she drew attention to the fixity of social norms in comparison to the fluidity of lived reality. Themes in her work include spirituality, language, health and the body, sexuality, and feminism. She also co-edited *This Bridge Called My Back* with Cherríe Moraga.

Barbara Smith (1946–)

Smith, daughter of a librarian, is an avid reader. She went to graduate school so that she could teach African American literature. She found that Black Studies and Black literature classes were about male experiences and the new field of Women's Studies was about white women's experiences. She was one of the first to teach Black Women's Literature in 1973. This was the impetus for founding Kitchen Table Press, the first US publisher for women of color, which opened the mainstream to many women of color writers who are famous today. She and her colleagues in the Combahee River Collective originated Black Women's Studies and the term identity politics. Today, Smith's activism involves urban policy with coalitions that address poverty and violence.

Chrystos (1946–)

Chrystos is a Menominee political poet who identifies as Two Spirit, a Native term for gender non-conformists. Menominee is their first language, and like Anishinaabe, it does not gender pronouns. Therefore, Chrystos uses gender-neutral terms like they and their instead of she/he or his/her.

Cherríe Moraga (1952–)

Moraga describes her work as political and literary essays, and she also writes plays. Her experience of a multiracial family and internalized homophobia, she says, alerted her to the complexity of oppression. She is a Chicana activist and theorist, and founder of La Red Xicana Indígena, which advocates for complex identity representation in the arts as well as Indigenous women's rights. Her own art, for example, her writing in *This Bridge Called My Back*, describes the painful effects for light-skinned women of color who are often seen as white, too white, or not white enough. No matter which error is made, part of her is erased. She said that in mainstream art, "We never get to see the complexity of who we are as human beings, so how does art make us well?"[25]

Patricia Hill Collins (1948–)

Collins grew up in a working-class Black Philadelphia family. As she pursued her studies, she found that she:

> . . . was increasingly the "first," "one of the few," or the "only" African American and/or woman and/or working class person in my schools, communities, and work settings. I saw nothing wrong with being who I was, but apparently many others did. My world grew larger, but I felt I was growing smaller. I tried to disappear into myself in order to deflect the painful, daily assaults designed to teach me that being an African American, working-class woman made me lesser than those who were not. And as I felt smaller, I became quieter and eventually was virtually silenced.[26]

She found her voice in academic achievements, beginning with the award-winning book *Black Feminist Thought* (1990) that laid out the method called intersectionality. She revisited the state of the method today with Sirma Bilge in *Intersectionality* (2016). Collins began with Black feminism because, like the Combahee River Collective, she found Black women's experiences to be a "crucial lens for understanding systems of oppression generally . . . [as well as] issues of globalization and nationality."[27] She added the intersection of knowledge to feminist discussion, describing how a small elite group with authoritative knowledge—only 2% of Americans have a PhD—often invalidate and dismiss the knowledge of the majority. While the elite may claim to be neutral observers, they are subject, like anyone else, to cultural bias. Scholars must, therefore, practice critical self-reflection (such as our reflexivity exercise) to determine how their beliefs and values affect their perception. Doing this helps scholars understand people as the experts on their own experiences, supporting the feminist value of testimony.

Kimberlé Crenshaw (1959–)

Crenshaw was born in Ohio and attended Harvard Law School. She is a civil rights activist and academic. She founded a variety of terms (intersectionality) and organizations (Columbia Law School's Center for Intersectionality and Public Policy, the African American Policy Forum) as well as the field of critical race theory. While the Combahee River Collective and Collins laid out the philosophy of intersectionality as a method of analysis, Crenshaw gave it its name in *The University of Chicago Legal Forum*

1989 article "Demarginalizing the Intersection of Race and Sex: A Black Feminist Critique of Antidiscrimination Doctrines, Feminist Theory and Antiracist Politics." In it, she examines data about the way Black women's legal claims are dismissed by courts because they differ from complaints expected from white women (about sexism) and Black men (about racism). Crenshaw's TED Talk tells us about "The Urgency of Intersectionality" today.[28]

bell hooks (1952–)

hooks was born to a working-class Black family in segregated Kentucky as Gloria Watkins and changed her name to honor her maternal ancestors. She has been called "one of America's most accessible intellectuals."[29] *Where We Stand: Class Matters* (2000) describes her personal and intellectual development from growing up in a patriarchal home to life as a poor student in a largely wealthy white college community when she attended Stanford University. Much of her work focuses on the intersection of race, class, and gender applied to a range of issues, from media criticism to personal healing, to education, and includes children's books. She is one of the most prolific feminist writers having published over 30 books, including *Feminist Theory: From Margin to Center* (1984), *Sisters of the Yam: Black Women and Self-Recovery* (1993), *Teaching to Transgress: Education as The Practice of Freedom* (1994), *Feminism is for Everybody: Passionate Politics* (2000), and *Writing Beyond Race: Living Theory and Practice* (2013). hooks states that "popular culture is where the learning is"[30] and has appeared in numerous television shows and films, and her work on media theory and popular culture includes the book *Reel to Real: Race, Sex, and Class at The Movies* (1996) and with Sut Jhally the film *bell hooks: Cultural Criticism and Transformation* (1997).

Indigenous feminists have also contributed outstanding work to intersectional feminist theory. They address topics like boarding school abuses, violence against women, and ecological degradation, while at the same time expanding the possibilities of egalitarian societies by addressing traditional women's roles, Indigenous ecological knowledge, and sovereignty. For example, this discussion of the Great Lakes entails issues of gender, sovereignty, and Natural Law (such as the rights of water):

> Given the connections between leadership and gender, many Indigenous peoples interpret discriminatory norms such as sexism as attacks on self-determination and nationhood . . .. Indigenous legal orders may ascribe moral concepts to nonhuman entities or beings that do not make sense within the moral frameworks of settlers' societies, such as viewing "water" as having personhood, moral responsibilities, or rights . . . In one case, an Indigenous

multiparty organization, Anishinabek Nation, created a Woman's Water Commission to increase influence of Indigenous women's leadership roles in water governance in Ontario . . . Many Indigenous persons saw this representation as an expression of far older forms of governance, stewardship, and laws.[31]

Winona LaDuke (1959–)

LaDuke, a member of the White Earth Band of Ojibwe, was born to an Ojibwe father and Jewish mother in Los Angeles, California. Her father was an actor and activist and her mother was an arts professor. After receiving a degree in economics from Harvard in 1982, she moved to the White Earth reservation. She was mentioned in previous chapters and her extensive environmental activism will be addressed in Chapter 10. She is also politically active and was the Green Party's nominee for US vice president in 1996 and 2000. Here, we will focus on her journalism, public presentations, and scholarly contributions to intersectionality. Much of her non-fiction (*All Our Relations*, 1999; *Recovering the Sacred*, 2005) addresses the intersections of race, class, gender, and nation, with a focus on sovereignty as well as women and the environment. Her novel (*Last Standing Woman*, 1997) is an intergenerational journey that chronicles how colonialism changed women's roles in Ojibwe culture.

Brenda Child

Child is a member of the Red Lake Nation of Ojibwe. As an Ojibwe historian, her scholarship about women was spurred by a valued heirloom, her grandfather's wild rice harvesting sticks. She found out they represented a change in gender roles, since before 1940 rice had been harvested by women. She notes, "As Ojibwe people, as Native people, we have to take a very long view of history in order to see gender and women's place in society."[32] This is what she undertakes in one of her books, *Holding Our World Together: Ojibwe Women and the Survival of Community* (2013). Based on the stories of specific women, she theorizes the political and economic power of women in the gender-balanced Ojibwe culture.

Andrea Smith

Smith states that she was raised Cherokee, but because she isn't tribally enrolled her claim of indigeneity has been contested. However, traditional Native tribes did not measure membership by blood quantum. That was an invention of the US government in order to maximize land theft and minimize how many people were eligible for treaty rights. Policy declared that "mixed bloods" could sell their land, and economic restrictions often forced their hands to do so. Also, only "full bloods" or those with a certain percent of Native heritage were eligible for treaty rights, so the less Natives were tribally enrolled, the less the government would owe.[33] This requirement for Native blood contrasts with the contemporaneous "one drop" law for Blacks, in which even one drop of Black blood meant one was still subject to slavery and later to segregation.

Traditional membership in tribes was based on responsible participation in community. Smith is an anti-violence activist who started the Chicago chapter of Women of All Red Nations (WARN), co-founded INCITE! Women of Color Against Violence with Nadine Naber, and founded The Boarding School Healing Project. She represented the Indigenous Women's Network and the American Indian Law Alliance at the UN and was nominated for a Nobel Peace Prize in 2005.

Smith's scholarship includes a half dozen books that helped bring women's issues into Native American Studies and Native American issues into Women's Studies. For example, *Conquest: Sexual Violence and American Indian Genocide* (2005)

> reveals the connections between different forms of violence— perpetrated by the state and by society at large—and documents their impact on Native women. [She connects] state-sanctioned boarding schools from the 1880s to the 1980s . . . and other examples of historical and contemporary colonialism to the high rates of violence against Native American women . . . Smith also outlines radical and innovative strategies for eliminating gendered violence.[34]

This groundbreaking book brings an Indigenous perspective to the violence debates that are part of the critiques of Brownmiller.

Leanne Betasamosake Simpson

Simpson is a First Nations (Canadian) Michi Saagig Nishnaabeg scholar, poet, speaker, musician, and activist. She is one of a group of writers who design their research methodology around their group's Indigenous philosophy to effectively decolonize the kind of knowledge authority that Collins theorizes. In "Land as pedagogy: Nishnaabeg intelligence and rebellious transformation" (2014), Simpson discussed land as the basis of sovereignty. She has also published eight books. *Lighting the Eighth Fire: The Liberation, Resurgence, and Protection of Indigenous Nations* (2008) includes Renée Bédard's discussion of Anishinaabe women's roles as Water Keepers.

Conclusion: Thought Leads to Action

We've introduced you to key theories and feminists who helped develop them. Theory helps you recognize and think about social structures, but it goes beyond thought. It's a practice, something you do. Being a feminist, too, is something you do, not something you are. In *Undoing Gender*, Judith Butler writes, "theory is itself transformative." But personal transformation isn't enough. For "social and political transformation," she says we also need "interventions at social and political levels that involve actions, sustained labor, and institutionalized practice, which are not quite the same as the exercise of theory."[35] Theory is important because although there is no one belief you must adhere to or prescribed actions you must take to be a feminist, feminism does include action. You can't transform what you don't understand, and you can't act on things you don't recognize.

What it takes to transform our world begins with each of us individually but also requires us to move outside ourselves. Audre Lorde wrote about how this kind of transformation works in her iconic 1977 speech "The Transformation of Silence into Language and Action." Facing a breast cancer diagnosis made Lorde realize she might die having never "spoken what needed to be said, or [having] only betrayed [her]self into small silences, while [she] planned someday to speak, or waited for someone else's words."[36] Lorde came to see that while it was "desirable not to be afraid, learning to put fear into a perspective gave [her] great strength."[37] The words she delivered next are as true today as they were then:

> I was going to die, if not sooner then later, whether or not I had ever spoken myself. My silences had not protected me. Your silence will not protect you. But for every real word spoken, for every attempt I had ever made to speak those truths for which I am still seeking, I had made contact with other women while we examined the words to fit a world in which we all believed, bridging our differences. And it was the concern and caring of all those women which gave me strength and enabled me to scrutinize the essentials of my living.[38]

The reasons Lorde cited for women remaining silent are equally powerful now: "fear of contempt, of censure, or some judgment, or recognition, of challenge, of annihilation. But most of all . . . we fear the visibility without which we cannot truly live."[39] Transformation starts with cultivating self-awareness and the understanding that society can work in different ways. Equally essential are wanting a more equitable world, acting with integrity, and being "woke," a Black term referring to awareness of social justice problems and solutions. It might begin with one small thing you do or say and is kept alive and grows with each decision you make. Nobody can know it all, do it all, or always make the right choices, so we keep learning. Transformation means doing something with the knowledge we gain, and the first step of doing is speaking out.

Speaking out isn't without challenges, especially given the complexity of finding common ground when meanings aren't clear or can't be made clear in English. Adrienne Rich has written about this catch-22: "this is the oppressor's language," she writes, "yet I need it to talk to you."[40] This isn't mere overstatement. On the 2018 International Day of the World's Indigenous Peoples, Survival International launched an initiative to raise awareness about Indigenous language loss and why it matters. Many have no idea that "[a]pproximately 600 languages have disappeared in the last century, with one dying every two weeks" or that "up to 90 percent of the world's languages could be lost before 2100, with indigenous varieties those native to a country, or region, deemed most vulnerable."[41] What does this mean when we remember Anzaldúa's quote, "I *am* my language"?

Lorde encourages us to speak, to do *something*, but what? How do we avoid accidentally repeating mistakes? How do we know our vision is better? With all the amazing accomplishments included in this textbook, why *haven't* we made more progress? And why is the progress we do make always in danger? As we move into the final part of *Introduction to Feminist Thought and Action,* it's ok to feel a bit overwhelmed if you're looking at the world somewhat differently and questioning things you haven't before.

The key is that you aren't alone. You are not alone in the questions you're raising, and you don't have to reinvent the wheel to find answers. The more you search, the more you'll find many others have concerns like yours. bell hooks, for instance, has written about both Anzaldúa and Rich and offers this insight: ". . . it is not the English language that hurts me, but what the oppressors do with it, how they shape it to become a territory that limits and defines, how they make it a weapon that can shame, humiliate, colonize."[42] We can learn to sustain ourselves through working productively with others who share similar concerns, for, as Lorde says, "it is not difference which immobilizes us, but silence. And there are so many silences to be broken."[43] In Chapter 9, Activism and Alliances, we show some actions feminists have taken in creating a more equitable, sustainable world.

Notes

1 Knotty Nymphet. "Intersectional Feminism." *Urban Dictionary.* Feb. 6, 2018, https://www.urbandictionary.com/define.php?term=INTERSECTIONAL%20FEMINISM.

2 Ayana Jamieson and Menoukha Robin Case. Content Guide for the SUNY online class African American Experience.

3 Moya Z. Bailey. "All the Digital Humanists Are White, All the Nerds Are Men, but Some of Us Are Brave." *Journal of Digital Humanities.* Vol. 1, no. 1, 2011, http://journalofdigitalhumanities.org/1-1/all-the-digital-humanists-are-white-all-the-nerds-are-men-but-some-of-us-are-brave-by-moya-z-bailey/.

4 Ayana Jamieson and Menoukha Robin Case. "Digital Humanities," for the SUNY online course "American Ethnic History."
5 Rahel Gebreyes. "Women's March Organizers Address Intersectionality as the Movement Grows." *HuffPost.* Jan. 27, 2017, https://www.huffingtonpost.com/entry/womens-march-organizers-address-intersectionality-as-the-movement-grows_us_5883f9d9e4b070d8cad314c0.
6 Susan Hawthorne and Renata Klein. *CyberFeminism: Connectivity, Critique, and Creativity.* Spinifex Press. 1999, p. 9.
7 Ibid., p. 17.
8 Ibid., pp. 6–7.
9 Judy Wajcman. "Feminist Theories of Technology." *Cambridge Journal of Economics.* Vol. 34, No. 1, Jan., 2010, pp. 143–152.
10 Nicholas A. Jones and Jungmiwha J. Bullock. "Understanding Who Reported Multiple Races in the U.S. Decennial Census: Results from Census 2000 and the 2010 Census." *Family Relations: Interdisciplinary Journal of Applied Family Studies.* Vol. 62, Feb., 2013. Nicholas Jones and Amy Symens Smith. "The Two or More Races Population: Census 2000 Brief." *US Census Bureau.* 2001, https://www.census.gov/prod/2001pubs/c2kbr01-6.pdf.
11 Kelly F. Jackson. "Participatory Diagramming in Social Work Research: Utilizing Visual Timelines to Interpret the Complexities of the Lived Multiracial Experience." *Qualitative Social Work.* Vol. 12, No. 4. Apr. 30, 2012, pp. 414–432.
12 Ibid.
13 Patricia Ticineto Clough. "The Hybrid Criticism of Patriarchy: Rereading Kate Millett's 'Sexual Politics.'" *The Sociological Quarterly.* Vol. 35, No. 3. Aug., 1994, p. 473.
14 Susan Brownmiller. *Against Our Will.* Simon & Schuster. 1975.
15 Democratic Socialists of America, Socialist Feminist Working Group. https://www.dsausa.org/feminism.
16 Joanne Pohl and Carol Boyd. "Ageism within Feminism." *Journal of Nursing Scholarship.* Vol 25, No. 3, Fall 1993, pp. 199–203, https://pdfs.semanticscholar.org/bb66/e83f9a23233ced02126d7689dec85ba170c9.pdf.
17 Nancy Collamer. "Age Discrimination: Proof It's Worse for Women." *Forbes.* Dec. 28, 2015, https://www.forbes.com/sites/nextavenue/2015/12/28/age-discrimination-proof-its-worse-for-women/#8f9cb055b60b.
18 Kim Q Hall. *Feminist Disability Studies.* Indiana U Press. 2011, http://www.iupress.indiana.edu/product_info.php?products_id=754705.
19 Laurie Toby Edison and Debbie Notkin. "Guest Post: TAB: Useful, but Not Always True." *FWD/Forward.* Feb. 3, 2010, http://disabledfeminists.com/2010/02/03/guest-post-temporarily-able-bodied-useful-but-not-always-true/.
20 Annanya Bhattacharjee. "Private Fists and Public Force: Race, Gender, and Surveillance." *Policing the National Body.* Eds. Jael Silliman and Anannya Bhattacharjee. Southend Press. 2002.
21 Alexis Pauline Gumbs and Jade M. Brooks. "Book Brilliance & Collaborative Love: Alexis Pauline Gumbs on Continuing the Legacy of Kitchen Table: Women of Color Press." *City Lights.* June 12, 2012, http://www.blogcitylights.com/2012/06/12/book-brilliance-collaborative-love-alexis-pauline-gumbs-on-continuing-the-legacy-of-kitchen-table-women-of-color-press/.
22 Audre Lorde. *Sister Outsider.* Crossing Press, 1984.
23 Jennifer Abod. *The Edge of Each Other's Battles: The Vision of Audre Lorde.* WMM, 2002.

24 Audre Lorde. "The Edge of Each Other's Battles." *Sistah Sinema.* Aug. 3, 2014, https://www.youtube.com/watch?v=zRntvB28CXI.

25 "Cherríe Moraga: Writer and Playwright." *Makers.com. Verizon Media.* 2019, https://www.makers.com/profiles/591f26dfa8c7c425e029ca80.

26 Nicki Lisa Cole. "Biography of Patricia Hill Collins." *ThoughtCo.com.* Mar. 6, 2017, https://www.thoughtco.com/patricia-hill-collins-3026479.

27 Ibid.

28 Kimberlé Crenshaw. "The Urgency of Intersectionality." *TED Talk.* Oct. 2016, https://www.ted.com/talks/kimberle_crenshaw_the_urgency_of_intersectionality.

29 Jhally & hooks. Media Education Foundation. *bell hooks: Cultural Criticism and Transformation.* 1997.

30 Ibid.

31 Kyle P. Whyte, Nicholas J. Reo, Deborah McGregor, MA (Peggy) Smith, James F. Jenkins, and Kathleen A. Rubio. "Seven Indigenous Principles for Successful Cooperation in Great Lakes Conservation Initiatives." *Biodiversity, Conservation and Environmental Management in the Great Lakes Basin.* Eds. Eric Freedman and Mark Neuzil. Routledge. 2018, p. 182.

32 Taylor Rose Payer. *Profile: Brenda Child, Scholar of Native History, Speaks to Her Family's Stories.* Minnesota Women's Press. 2019, http://www.womenspress.com/Content/Features/Profile/Article/Ojibwe-women/1/20/5170.

33 Stephanie Sellers. "Confluences and Crossbloods on Turtle Island." *American E-Journal of American Studies in Hungary.* Vol. XIII. No. 1, Spring 2017, http://americanaejournal.hu/vol13no1mixed/sellers.

34 Book Cover Excerpt. Andrea Smith. *Conquest.* South End Press, 2005.

35 Judith Butler. "The Question of Transformation." *Counterpoints.* Vol. 242, Women & Social Transformation. 2001, pp. 1–28, https://www.jstor.org/stable/42976712.

36 Audre Lorde. "The Transformation of Silence into Language and Action." *Sister Outsider: Essays and Speeches by Audre Lorde.* 1984. Crossing Press. 2007, p. 41.

37 Ibid., p. 41.

38 Ibid.

39 Ibid., p. 42.

40 Adrienne Rich. "The Burning of Paper Instead of Children." *The Fact of a Doorframe.* Norton. 1984, pp. 116–119.

41 David Child. "Indigenous Peoples Day: What Can Be Done to Save Dying Languages?" *Aljazeera.com.* Aug. 9, 2018, https://www.aljazeera.com/indepth/features/indigenous-peoples-day-save-dying-languages-180808201751875.html.

42 bell hooks. *Teaching to Transgress: Education as the Practice of Freedom.* Routledge. 1994.

43 Lorde. "The Transformation of Silence into Language and Action," p. 44.

Part Five

Activism Today

Introduction: Changed and Changing

In the past eight chapters, we gathered stories and ways of thinking from people and places and movements, famous and ordinary, some known all too well and others not well enough. It was a lot to take in and could change the way you look at the world and how you act in it. Don't be surprised if you find yourself feeling unsure about what you can do or are supposed to do next. Applying new or deepening knowledge may even feel like too much to bear. There's a mixture of celebration and burden in knowing how hard and long those who came before us struggled to get us where we are today. Depending on where a culture came from, there have been enormous gains and losses over the past century. We feel urgency and concern for continued struggles faced by women all over the world who have yet to benefit from gains. Especially when we see rights we thought had already been fought over and won in peril, it can feel like no one can ever do enough or be enough.

We might not want to admit it, but we might find ourselves asking, what's the point, and why bother if the struggle will never end? Doubt and apprehension are normal, whether you're opening your eyes to social inequity for the first time, have been keenly aware of it for a while, or are a veteran in struggle. Nearly all of us have those moments where we wonder how much of a difference we can make, if we're doing enough, if what we do matters. Perhaps you've thought to yourself, what can I do? It's a good question, and re-shaping that question can lead to different answers. The problem isn't the question itself, but how many women have been socially conditioned to ask it.

Women raised in some cultures are invariably taught to emphasize the "I": "What can *I* do?" How we tend to answer is also part of our conditioning: *I* can do so little. I don't have enough power. I don't have enough money. My shape, age, skin color, origin, or skills are not impressive. Who's going to listen to me—I'm nobody. And I have too much else I'm responsible for, how can I possibly find time to do one more thing? By design, the question leads us away from the problems and into self-doubt and self-defeat. But there's another way to ask this question. Change the emphasis from "what can *I* do?" to "what *can* I do?" "What *can* I do?" leads to many answers that address one aspect or another of the problem at hand. Focus on what you *can* do in whatever circumstance you find yourself.

Don't confuse focusing on what you can do with the idea that a positive attitude alone will improve things even if you stay silent. After all, this book is called *Introduction to Feminist Thought and Action* for a reason. Action is the goal. As Anzaldúa, Butler, hooks, Lorde, and Rich reminded us, it's not enough to just theorize. We need to break the silence and do something. We need to speak and act because our silence amounts to passive compliance with the structures of oppression surrounding us. But what *can* we do?

For starters, it's useful to acknowledge what we're already doing. By virtue of us researching and writing, and you reading this book, we are doing something together. By being open and willing to learn about experiences outside our own circumstances, we're changing our awareness. The more individual perspectives we're aware of, the more likely we are to perceive the systemic issues that shape them. Cultivating awareness, then, is a necessary action in itself. As the saying goes, you can't change what you don't acknowledge.

Awareness of systemic issues—being "woke," as it's sometimes called—isn't a perpetual condition or a one-time event. It isn't something you *are*, it's something you *do* whenever you make a decision or take an action. Staying woke requires commitment to continual learning and self-reflection. Think about the values and concerns you brought to the beginning of this book. Think about how they may have grown or changed as you learned.

Once you start practicing awareness, the next step is to decide what to do about what you've learned and how to use your energy. Think about the opportunities you'll have to apply what you know when you act. This can include something as simple as what you cook for dinner. For example, activists have started urban community gardens and farmers' markets to bring fresh fruits and vegetables to food deserts. Food deserts are areas of poverty where the only choices stores offer may be snacks and dollar burgers. Buying or helping to grow local produce is a small but potent personal political act.

Not all activism consists of political movements, but they are important because they reflect a collective will. Events like marches can bring awareness to people who had never even thought about an issue.

While one-time events have value, activism is most effective when sustainable. You may raise awareness with a single comment on Facebook about your beliefs or post a hashtag to Twitter, but ideally, you follow up with sustained action. To do this, you need to make alliances with others who are willing and able to do the same. The good news is that in the social media age, finding people who share your views is relatively easy. The more complicated part is practicing compassionate self-reflection skills so you can create successful projects with them.

9 The Power of Activism

#WTF: What's That Feminis(t Movement)?

Below are examples of successful contemporary movements with members who worked to meet the challenges of allying across differences. The first three, Standing Rock, Women's Marches, and Me Too, have become global phenomena. We'll describe the process of creating these events. We'll also re-visit activism in China, Africa, and the Arab Peninsula.

Standing Rock

One of the largest and longest events in American history took place at Standing Rock Sioux Reservation in North Dakota, US. It was part of the No Dakota Access Pipeline (#NODAPL), an ongoing, broad coalition of people from the US and across the world, including Native Americans, US military veterans, Black Lives Matter groups, the Waterkeeper Alliance, international peace movements like Code Pink, and more. #NODAPL is a grassroots movement that expanded via Facebook, Twitter, and other social media to stop the oil pipeline being constructed across sacred burial grounds and under the Missouri River against the express wishes of the Standing Rock Sioux. Approximately 3,000–4,000 camped permanently, with thousands more stopping by to protect the waters for a day, a week, or a month. At its peak, estimates were as high as 10,000 people. As some left the ongoing gathering, others joined, leading to a continuous presence of protectors that lasted well over a year.

Many feared the pipeline, which runs from upper western North Dakota to Illinois, would cause long-term environmental damage. Pipeline failures are inevitable and often catastrophic in outcome. Many saw the Sioux Nation's gathering as one of the best chances to halt the project, since the pipeline would have to go across sovereign tribal land. The originators clearly stated: we are not protestors, we are water protectors. Tribal consensus, therefore, called for peaceful prayer, but DAPL employees and police took a combative approach.

A devastating moment occurred in late November 2016 at Backwater Bridge. For weeks, police had barricaded the bridge, slowing the movement of activists from around the world to Standing Rock. On the night of the 20th, protectors had built several fires to keep warm as the temperatures in North Dakota dipped. Police proclaimed the already barricaded Backwater Bridge unsafe for traffic due to the fires and demanded they disperse. But protectors saw the demand as a deceptive attempt to remove them and stood their ground. Police then used water cannons and tear gas on the crowd, injuring hundreds of people, some of them seriously. Morton County Sheriff Kyle Kirchmeier said that water cannon use "was not a common tactic."[1] Twenty-two-year-old Sophia Wilansky, struck by what those present have described as a grenade, nearly lost her arm. Law enforcement denies it used grenades but confiscated whatever object struck Wilansky.[2]

> Avi Farber, a Taos resident and U.S. Forest Service wildlands firefighter was there and told reporters, "It was a war zone filled with people in prayer. Peaceful water protectors were packed against the razor wire blockade and across the bridge. . . . Police fired rubber bullets the size of your palm into the crowd. They were targeting the faces, heads, and knees of people facing the police, with their hands in the air, who posed no threat."
>
> Farber said that "[a]ll the while the police were drenching water protectors with high pressure water hoses in sub-freezing temperatures. At the end of the night my backpack was a frozen sheet of ice."[3]

According to Water Protectors Legal Collective's Angela Bibens, law enforcement attempts to intimidate them were met with calm and appropriate response. Farber added,

> "It was a very intense scene though in general it was not chaotic. Medics worked efficiently to move the injured to treatment, and water protectors showed an amazing courage, standing, knowing they were in the open to be brutalized . . . Members of the Oceti Sakowin camp are taking time to regroup today [Nov. 21]. It really is amazing to witness the power of the community coming together here."[4]

Unfortunately, the US has not historically honored the many treaties they made with Native nations or respected tribal sovereignty, and while the movement has been successful in building broad coalitions, winning legal battles, and halting work at various intervals, ultimately Standing Rock has been no exception. While one of Obama's last acts as president was stopping the pipeline pending environmental studies, one of Trump's first acts was to sign an executive order (EO) to expedite both the Dakota Access and Keystone XL Pipelines.[5] A federal court later deemed the EO illegal, but in the interim the pipeline was built. Despite this setback, one of the lessons of #NODAPL is the reminder that strong movements are not made or broken by one event. Before the EO, Maidu reservation native Chanse Adams-Zavalla told Wes Enzinna of *Mother Jones* magazine he was in good spirits and knew what he would tell his grandkids about Standing Rock:

> "[e]ven if somehow, someway, they build this pipeline . . . they've inadvertently sparked a whole generation of us indigenous folks and everyone who wants to stand with us to fight for Mother Earth. We're going to inherit this planet, bro, and everyone's welcome to inherit it with us if they want."[6]

The spirit of Standing Rock is allied with similar gatherings around the world.

Women's March(es)

Women across the globe came together on January 21, 2017, to protest the inauguration of Donald Trump. They were responding to the fact that a man who had said "grab 'em by the pussy" was nevertheless elected US president. They were inspired by the phrase "women's rights are human rights," coined in the 1830s by the Quaker Grimké sisters and famously delivered by Hillary Clinton at the 1995 UN World Conference on Women.

Estimates put the total attending the Women's March at its primary location in Washington, DC, and "sister marches" across the nation and globe at five million people, making it the biggest single-day demonstration in US history. There were multiple Women's Marches in every state in the US, totaling 653 altogether. There were also 261 marches abroad, totaling upwards of 350,000 people.[7] Figure 9.1 shows overhead shots of the crowd in DC. People wear pink "pussy hats," hand-knitted by individuals to symbolize opposition to Trump's comment.[8]

Diversity of locations, intensity of motivation, and widespread solidarity makes the Women's March impressive beyond its sheer volume. People overcame mobility issues and serious weather to participate, from

Figure 9.1 Women's March.[9]

Figure 9.2 Various Marches.[10]

marchers hooked up to IVs for cancer treatment in Los Angeles, California, to marchers in 40 below wind chill in Unalakleet, Alaska. Crowds were estimated to be as big as a million in Washington, DC, and as small as one or two individuals in some locations: "[o]ne woman in a Western mountain state was snowed in and couldn't get to the nearby town where she intended to march. Instead of giving up, she held a march of one in her own town."[11] Although there were at least 13 counties in the US where a single person was so motivated that they marched on their own, it was most common for hundreds or thousands to meet, including people from a wide range of backgrounds.[12] Globally, the biggest numbers were in Toronto, Canada (50,000), and London, the UK (100,000), but people from Mexico, Thailand, Uganda, Rwanda, Tanzania, St. Kitts, Norway, South Africa, Japan, Latvia, Australia, and more marched to show solidarity. Sister marches occurred even in places where women's rights and protest in general carry serious risk of government punishment, like in Egypt, Saudi Arabia, and Russia.[13]

This march went on to become an annual event, repeated as of this publication in 2017, 2018, and 2019. Figure 9.2 shows images of activism taken by our authors and contributors in various times and locales.

#MeToo

The Women's March is an example of coalition building in response to anticipated threats. The Me Too Movement, another example of coalition building, was made possible by decades of grueling groundwork by dedicated individuals who did not have the luxury of mainstream traction.

The #MeToo hashtag arose when 87 women accused filmmaker Harvey Weinstein of rape and sexual assault, recounting abuses that spanned decades. On October 15, 2017, after publication of Ronan Farrow's bombshell article about the "open secret"[14] of Weinstein's horrendous behavior, actress Alyssa Milano tweeted, "If you've been sexually harassed or assaulted, write 'me too' as a reply to this tweet."[15] By the next day, over 55,000 people had replied. In only 45 days, "#MeToo . . . made waves across the globe, posted in 85 countries on Twitter and 85 million times on Facebook."[16] From October to November, there were over 1.5 million #MeToo tweets of people discussing their personal stories of rape and assault and showing solidarity for survivors, making #MeToo "one of the most viral and powerful occurrences in social media history"[17] and "a particularly combustible moment for social media activism."[18] But the Me Too Movement actually started decades earlier.

Me Too began in 1997, when Tarana Burke was left speechless after talking to a 13-year-old sexual abuse survivor. "'I didn't have a response or a way to help her in that moment,' Burke said, 'and I couldn't even say "me too."' . . . It really bothered me, and sat in my spirit for a long time.'"[19] Nine years later, she had secured resources and support to create Just Be Inc. and called her movement Me Too.[20] When Milano tweeted the hashtag without attributing it to the movement, Burke was concerned that her focus on helping the most marginalized victims of sexual violence, women of color, would be overshadowed by a universalizing impulse, well intentioned though it was, to say "this happens to *all* women." To be sure, sexual violence is pervasive, but recognizing that some communities experience it more and have less access to support is essential to prevention and recovery. Burke's fears were warranted since historically, when women of color do the foundational work of social justice, white women are often the only ones credited. Their work is co-opted, but their specific concerns are excluded from the conversation.

Other women of color activists were equally alarmed. Journalist Britni Danielle, who had organized #OscarsSoWhite to bring attention to Hollywood's lack of representation for people of color, was among the first to point out it was Burke "who ha[d] been advocating for assault victims & saying #MeToo for years."[21] Nigerian author Luvvie Ajayi tweeted, "Folks who have written pieces on #MeToo. Make sure you've gone back to correct that Alyssa Milano did NOT create it. @TaranaBurke did."[22] Their concern was not only about crediting the correct individual, Burke, but also that women of color's experiences are too often ignored and dismissed.

The day after her original tweet, Milano, having been unaware of its origins, tweeted about Burke as the founder of the Me Too movement and linked to the Just Be, Inc. website. Milano and Burke have since been interviewed together to showcase #MeToo, and many media outlets, like *Time* magazine, quote Burke about its origins and describe the movement as "a framework for how to do the work of ending sexual violence." At their best moments, media highlight Burke's emphasis on "mak[ing] sure that the most marginalized among survivors have access to resources that will help them cross the human journey."[23]

One of the successes of #MeToo was that its primary goals were *not* co-opted or erased by the mainstream. It's a small victory for intersectional feminism that the wealthy, white women who popularized #MeToo supported women of color rather than erasing them.

But sustained coalitions require consistency over time, something that continues to test #MeToo. Nearly a year after it went viral, *People* ran a story crediting Milano with the hashtag.[24] A few months after that, *The LA Times* tweeted "Since Alyssa Milano kicked off the #MeToo movement with a single tweet in October 2017, Americans have been thinking quite a lot about sexual harassment and sexual assault."[25] This time, however, responders, including Milano, called out the *Times* for its error and insisted proper credit be given to Tarana Burke. Moreover, they made clear that they were fed up with Black women's work being routinely erased, demonstrating awareness of social justice that had been missing just a year prior.

China

The #MeToo movement in China faces serious challenges due to state-run censorship. But Chinese women didn't back down. They found innovative workarounds that energized a "firestorm against sexual predation."[26] Journalists Maria Repnikova and Weile Zhou report:

> The Chinese #MeToo movement participants have creatively spread discussions on sexual harassment[,]. . . sav[ing] censored information through screenshots and blockchains. When the hashtag #MeToo was identified by state censors, Chinese netizens started to use other, less immediately recognizable hashtages such as "Woyeshi" (Chinese version of #MeToo) and #Mitu (#RiceBunny, a homophonic of "Me too" in Chinese) with emojis of cute cartoon rabbits eating rice. On another top social media app, WeChat, movement participants spread screenshots of victims' sexual harassment stories, <u>media investigations</u> and <u>commentaries</u>, at times even posting the images upside down to confuse the filtering system.[27]

Just as important has been the collaboration "between journalists, lawyers, victims and social media activists, a practice that defined much of Chinese activism for the past two decades."[28] One of the highest profile cases is that of Zhou Xiaoxuan, who filed a sexual harassment case against Zhu Jun, "a television host and one of the most famous men in China."[29] Her open letter about the incident was circulated online until censors shut it down and state-run media has been forbidden from discussing it. Regardless of the court outcome, Zhou says, "I don't know one day if it could change . . . But my lawyer told me that I must fight to the end because of [those who can't themselves seek justice]. So I will fight to the end."[30]

Liberia: A Women's Coalition to End War

Like Indigenous American struggles, many struggles throughout the world are rooted in political histories of colonialism and imperialism. Liberia was founded in 1822 by the American Colonization Society, a group that believed that the races were incompatible and sent Africans back to Africa. It began as a US colony on land taken from the African Krahn people. Governed by formerly enslaved Americans from multiple African ethnic backgrounds, it declared independence from the US in 1847 but was not recognized until 1862 during the US Civil War.

Despite independence, the US continued to dominate Liberia's economy and played a key role in the infamous "blood diamond" civil wars during the 1990s. Liberian President Charles Taylor enslaved his own people, children as soldiers and men as miners, in order to excavate diamonds to fuel the war economy. Slavery produced a high quantity of diamonds that could be sold cheaply to places like the US, one of the main importers. Philippa Atkinson describes these wars as "a competition for territorial control and economic gain. . . ."[31] Her explanation reminds us how internal and external clashes interact:

> The continuation of the war can be attributed to the interaction of a number of internal and external factors. . . . The fueling of the war through the illegal sale of Liberia's natural resources has been ignored at the international level . . . The internal economic, political and social factors fueling the war are highly complex, involving issues of access to power and resources at local and national levels. Politically-manipulated ethnicity has remained a factor, as Krahn people . . . continued to fight as a group . . . Poverty and lack of opportunity . . . helped promote the attractiveness of fighting as a means for survival . . . The tactics of factions designed to threaten the basic rights of civilians have been highly effective in weakening civilian opposition. . . . The war economy encompasses all activities relating to the illegal extraction, taxation and export of Liberia's natural resources, particularly timber, rubber, diamonds and gold.[32]

While international actors failed to come to Liberia's aid, the women of Monrovia, Liberia, chose to take a unique stand. One of the leaders was Leymah Gbowee, who united Christian and Muslim women, two groups who did not historically join forces. Calling themselves Women of Liberia Mass Action for Peace, thousands of women came together and, wearing all white, participated in marketplace sit-ins, direct confrontations, and even refused to have sex with their husbands and boyfriends until the war was over. They forced President Taylor to arrange peace talks with the various warlords.

Initially, Women of Liberia were excluded from those talks. When they demanded inclusion, Gbowee was threatened with arrest. But she refused to back down. In "Women Fight for Peace," Gbowee recalls saying, "I'm going to make it very, very easy for you to arrest me," taking off her hair wrap and adding, "I'm going to strip naked."[33] In Liberia, a woman deliberately baring her body is a curse meant to shame. Her actions changed the tone of the talks and women became central to the remainder of the meetings. Abigail Disney, producer of *Pray the Devil Back to Hell*, said that while shooting this documentary about the movement she asked one of the warlords at the peace talks,

> "How is it possible in a country where 50% of the women have been raped, where one woman threatening to strip naked to cause such mayhem?" He told her, "You have to understand they were our mothers, and the only way your mother would do that is if she were driven to total desperation." And there was something in that moment there that caused every man in that room, no matter what he'd done during the conflict to ask himself, "what have I done, what have I done to get us here?" And talk about changing the dynamic of the room.[34]

Women of Liberia Mass Action for Peace had the goal of ending war, but continued post-war. One culmination of their movement was the 2006 election of Ellen Johnson Sirleaf, first female president of Liberia. Gbowee, whose leadership earned her the Nobel Peace Prize, has also continued working on behalf of peace. She founded and coordinated the Women in Peacebuilding Network/West Africa Network for Peacebuilding, founded the Liberia Reconciliation Initiative, co-founded and directed the Women Peace and Security Network Africa, founded the Gbowee Peace Foundation Africa (in Monrovia, Liberia), founded the Gbowee Peace Foundation Africa-USA (in New York City, USA), and is the now the executive director of the Women, Peace and Security Program at Columbia University's Earth Institute.[35]

Arabian Peninsula

In Part Three, we discussed several countries that self-identify as Arab, but sometimes the term refers to all the countries on the Arab Peninsula, many with large Islamic populations. Here, we'll look at Saudi Arabia and expand to the peninsula to discuss Israel and Pakistan—Israel because of feminist coalition work going on both within Arab communities and between Jews and Muslims, and Pakistan because women have achieved an enormous level of governmental representation despite the Taliban.

Activism in Arab countries is diverse and complex. Within Saudi Arabia, it ranges from internet activism like Nsawya FM (Feminism FM) to 11 women (9 of them Saudi) whose radio shows are livestreamed from a laptop[36] to increasing presence in the public sphere, such as positions in business and government. Yet, even as the ban on women drivers was about to be lifted, Aisha al-Manea and ten other women who had protested to earn that right were arrested with the charge of "transgressing national and religious principle" and working with "foreign entities," a crime that can incur 3–20 years' imprisonment or even death.[37] On the one hand, notes *AlBawaba News*, women and activism were damaged by this threat, but on the other hand, they were released within weeks.

In sum, Arab activism is thriving from the grassroots to the halls of governance, but still takes great courage and can carry a high price. Palestinian feminist Samah Salaime wrote about gains Arab women have made in Israel. In an article originally published in Hebrew, she described how young Arab women are now 58% of college undergraduates and how older women have worked to increase their representation in Israeli parliament. Also, the first female judge was appointed to Sharia Court in the Israeli Islamic community.[38] Arab feminist organizations "travel from village to village" to increase local governmental representation, and "the Arab-Jewish Hadash party elected a woman to lead its list for elections, setting an important precedent that could serve as an example for other towns." She noted "I . . . stand alongside Jewish women who demand representation . . . and wish them success in their struggle to give Israel's multicultural democracy a facelift."[39] Jewish-Palestinian women's organizations working together for peace include Coalition of Women for Peace, Women's International League for Peace and Freedom, and The Haifa Women's Coalition. Yet, as these women work, war continues.

Pakistani activist Shad Begum is a social worker from Dir, Pakistan. She's the founder and executive director of Association for Behavior and Knowledge Transformation (ABKT), an organization that works in rural tribal areas to increase women's representation. She describes herself as part of the 1% of girls and 5% of boys who were educated, and was elected to local office in 2001. At that time, women representatives were not permitted to sit in council meetings; men would delegate work to them. At one point, they were told to buy sewing machines for community women, but Begum knew that what they really needed was access to fresh water. After succeeding in changing the agenda and providing water for 5,000 families, the women representatives were welcomed to sit in council. This inspired Begum to form alliances with elected women in other regions and focus on getting more women elected. When the Taliban took over in 2007, she persisted but shifted to meet new needs, "establish[ing] four mother-child health care units" that served 10,000 persons displaced by war. ABKT then took on "training around 300 . . .. women . . . for local elections in 2015 . . . and fifty percent of them won."[40] Women voters in her area went from less than 100 in 2013 to 93,000 voters in 2015. The result:

> Change is happening at a local level . . . because women are finding their place in the political process . . . they are now sitting in the councils, taking part actively in the legislation, planning and budgeting. Most of them are now investing their funds on women's health, education, skill development and safe drinking water. All these elected women now share, discuss, and resolve their problems together.[41]

Activists like Begum highlight the extreme importance of representation to feminist activism.

Case Study: US Voting Rights

There are few places that the power of one person means more in the US than the voting booth. But who gets to vote has long been under contention and when we start looking closely at voting rights, major contradictions arise. Did you know that citizens living in US territories, like Puerto Rico, are not eligible to vote in US elections? Similarly, they have no representation in Congress. This lack of representation caused problems when Hurricane Maria, one of the worst natural disasters in American history, devastated Puerto Rico with 2,795 deaths and $43 billion economic impact.[42] Part of what made Hurricane Maria so deadly was the failed federal response, something noted by the US' own Governmental Accountability Office.[43] But the nearly three and a half million US citizens who lost loved ones, homes, and jobs have no chance to respond to these failures in the voting booth.

Voting is one of the most actively protested and litigated struggles, part of no fewer than five constitutional amendments and innumerable laws. Yet who gets to vote remains far more complicated than laws and amendments may suggest.

Let's review some significant voting rights laws enacted in the US.

- The 15th amendment (1870) made it illegal to discriminate on the basis of "race, color, or previous condition of servitude."
- The 17th amendment (1913) allowed voters to elect state senators directly. Previously, state legislatures elected them. The president, however, is still elected through the electoral college. Five presidents have been elected despite losing the popular vote.
- The 19th amendment (1920) gave women the right to vote, but African American and Native American women were still restricted by state and local laws.
- The 24th amendment (1964) abolished the poll tax, a fee implemented after the 15th amendment passed as a "legal" way to disenfranchise African Americans.
- The Voting Rights Act (VRA; 1965) made restrictions to disenfranchise voters, such as literacy and moral character tests, proof of property ownership, and more, illegal. These were targeted at African American voters and affected Native American voters, who only attained legal eligibility in 1947.
- The 26th amendment (1971) lowered the voting age from 21 to 18.

You probably noticed a trend, a ricocheting between inclusive laws to make up for justice gaps in previous eras and new laws after lawmakers find ways to game the system and re-disenfranchise voters. This is because how things work in law (de jure) isn't always the same as how they operate in practice (de facto). Why, for example, would a VRA be needed when the 14th amendment was already on the books? How did the 19th amendment give the vote to only *some* women? How is it that Native Americans, who were here before the nation was even constituted, had to wait nearly 200 years before they were allowed to vote? Why do so few people recognize how unequal the system continues to be?

The VRA isn't a constitutional amendment, but because it requires periodic renewal, it changes over time. Since 1965, amendments have been added, from language assistance to non-English-speaking citizens, to whether a policy results in discrimination regardless of intent. A key change came in 1982. Prior to 1982, states with a record of voter obstruction needed federal review, called preclearance, of their voting rules and facilities. They were required to show that for over a ten-year period, they upheld nondiscrimination policies and actively worked to improve minority voter registration. The 1982 renewal included changes making it possible for "political subdivisions," such as counties and districts and not just a state as a whole, to petition for a "bail out," which meant they no longer needed preclearance to change how they conduct voting. The rationale, ironically, was to incentivize locales to improve their practices after

> the Commission on Civil Rights transmitted a report to the president and to Congress in September 1981 presenting the commission's evaluation of the current status of minority voting rights and again documenting 'resistance and hostility on the part of many citizens to increased minority participation in virtually every aspect of the electoral process,' as well as 'the resistance of numerous local jurisdictions to following either the letter or spirit of the preclearance provisions of the Voting Rights Act.'[44]

The commission found that "'covered jurisdictions have substantially moved from direct, over[t] impediments to the right to vote to more sophisticated devices that dilute minority voting strength.'"[45] Some indirect impediments were "'annexations; the use of at-large elections, majority vote requirements, or numbered posts; and the redistricting of boundary lines [i.e., gerrymandering].'"[46] In plain language, it meant voter disenfranchisement was still rampant. If political subdivisions could apply for a bailout, they wouldn't need to wait for the entire state to improve, and thus VRA compliance and enforcement would, officials argued, improve faster. The opposite happened and set the stage for additional problems.

These problems culminated in 2013 when the Supreme Court gutted the VRA. In a 5 to 4 vote, they invalidated Section 4, which "determined which states must receive clearance from the Justice Department or a federal court in Washington before they made minor changes to voting procedures, like moving a polling place, or major ones, like redrawing electoral districts."[47] Because Section 4 set standards for judging compliance, Section 5, which enforced those standards, was invalidated by default, and preclearance was eliminated. The argument was that the law was outdated and infringed on state sovereignty, or essentially, the success of the VRA made it no longer necessary.

Justice Ruth Bader Ginsburg delivered a scathing dissent from the bench, "an unusual move and a sign of deep disagreement."[48] Ginsburg called the VRA "one of the most consequential, efficacious, and amply justified exercises of federal legislative power in our Nation's history,"[49] noting that the "Supreme Court has long recognized that vote dilution, when adopted with a discriminatory purpose, cuts down the right to vote as certainly as denial of access to the ballot."[50] Ginsburg provided numerous examples of the VRA successfully countering racial gerrymandering, registration schemes, and election subterfuges designed to limit African American voting. "Throwing out preclearance when it has worked and is continuing to work," Ginsburg said, "is like throwing away your umbrella in a rainstorm because you are not getting wet."[51]

One of the primary reasons Ginsburg cited for upholding the VRA was "the evolution of voting discrimination into more subtle second-generation barriers."[52] The 2018 midterm elections show how right Ginsburg was. A key example occurred in North Dakota, where it was expected to be pivotal in the balance of Congressional power. Six years prior, in 2012, Heidi Heitkamp was narrowly elected North Dakota's first female senator, with support from Native American communities putting her over the top. Changes to voter registration requiring citizens to show proof of current residential address, however, imperiled this support as many areas of rural reservations don't have street addresses. A series of court cases over the next two years ensued to counter this bill.

In October 2018, the Spirit Lake Tribe sued, citing House Bill 1369 would disenfranchise Native American voters. Plaintiffs represented a coalition of Native American tribes, including residents of the Spirit Lake Turtle Mountain Band of Chippewa Indians and Standing Rock Sioux. Plaintiffs had all been denied access to absentee ballots, turned away at the polls for not having "correct" information despite showing their government-issued tribal IDs, and feared that they would be prevented from voting on Election Day. The court ruled in favor of the Spirit Lake Tribe and issued an emergency motion for a temporary restraining order halting implementation of the proposed law. The court stated,

> The careless implementation of this law—seeking to confirm the physical address of every voter when the State *knows* there are many unmapped areas, conflicting address systems, and conflicting addresses even within its own system—imposes undue burdens on those with qualifying IDs with addresses the State won't recognize and on those who have been assigned 911 addresses that are themselves incorrect.[53]

The strongest wording in the decision declared the law a "clear and imminent risk of irreparable harm" and stated "the deeply flawed system implemented by North Dakota . . . will result in the widespread denial of the right to vote for qualified Native voters. Indeed, Native voters are already being denied access to the ballot."[54] The ruling was seen as a major victory in a long history of Native American discrimination, made possible through successful coalition building. The coalition had formed, after all, largely at Standing Rock.

Unfortunately, the ruling was overturned on November 1, 2018. The appellate court ruled that the upcoming election was so soon that halting the law would cause "confusion and chaos on the eve of an election."[55] It's important to note the rulings were not overturned because the courts found the bill to be nondiscriminatory. In fact, two courts ruled the law *was* discriminatory. The reason given for overturning those cases was not based on the merits of the bill. It was simply easier to continue racist policy.

Meanwhile, in Florida, voters overwhelmingly approved reinstatement of voting rights for felons who've completed their sentences. The legislature, however, is delaying implementation to the nearly 1.5 million citizens affected. The argument for stalling is that the new Republican governor must first be sworn in and that they are "waiting to see if the Florida Legislature might need to weigh in on the measure," even though the amendment voters already approved "does not call for involvement of this kind."[56]

In sum, how we vote, for whom we get to vote, and how our votes are implemented are susceptible to the many ways people in authority strive to retain dominance. Voting rights are a clear map of the continual tension between the impulse toward equity and the impulse toward dominance.

US 2018 Midterm Elections: A Clear Message

Figure 9.3 Contributor Katharine Ransom Campaigning in Virginia.[57]

The 2018 US midterm elections exemplify political feminism. More women were elected to office than any other time in history, making 2018 yet another "Year of the Woman." The first "Year of the Woman" was in 1992, when 28 women were elected to congress. Twenty-six years later, we've shattered that record. As of January 2019, 102 women are in the house and 25 are in the senate. The diversity of those women is also a record; as Deb Haaland said, 2018 could also be called "the year of women of color."[58] Here are a host of important firsts:

- On local, regional, and state levels, over 50 Native American women ran for offices; 14 of them won. On the national level, for the first time ever, 252 years after the "founding" of the US, two Native American women were elected: Laguna Pueblo Deb Haaland (Democrat (D)-NM, house) and Ho-Chunk Nation Sharice Davids (D-KS, house). Davids is also an openly gay woman.
- Kyrsten Sinema (D-AZ, senate) became the first openly bisexual member of Congress.
- Angie Craig (D-MN, house) became the first openly gay married person and first same-sex mother, beating an opponent who said he wished he could call women sluts.
- Rashida Tlaib (D-MI, house) and Ilhan Omar (D-MN, house) became the first Muslim women in Congress. Omar is also the first Somali-American member and first to wear a hijab on the house floor.
- Ayanna Pressley (D-MA, house) became the first Black woman elected from Massachusetts.
- Veronica Escobar (D-TX, house) and Sylvia Garcia (D-TX, house) became the first Hispanic women from Texas to be elected to Congress, despite the fact that nearly 40% of the state population is Latinx.
- Alexandria Ocasio-Cortez (D-NY, house) became the youngest woman to be elected to Congress. She beat an incumbent Republican who spent $3.4 million on his campaign to her $194,000, 74% of which came from small individual contributions.
- In addition to historic firsts, more women than ever ran for office, and many of those elected took nontraditional paths to get there and gained seats they were typically unlikely to win.
- Lucy McBath (D-GA, house), a flight attendant turned congressional representative, ran because her son, Jordan, had been killed by gun violence. A spokeswoman for Moms Demand Action for Gun Sense in America and a Mother of the Movement, she beat the incumbent Republican.
- Laura Kelly (D-KS, senate) upset sitting governor Kris Kobach, who instituted some of the strictest voter ID laws in the nation and supported Donald Trump's false allegations that over three million illegal

votes were cast in the 2016 election. Kobach was also notoriously anti-LGBTQ+ and one of Kelly's first EOs as governor was to extend nondiscrimination protections to LGBTQ+ state workers.

- Danica Roem (D-VA, house) became the first openly transgender person elected to Congress. She beat anti-LGBTQ+, 13-term Republican Robert Marshall who authored a bill that restricted transgender people's rights to use the bathroom corresponding to their gender identity. Marshall was against abortion in all circumstances and Roem was endorsed, like many of the women above, by Emily's List, a grassroots political action committee that supports pro-choice candidates.

The overall message delivered by voters was a rejection of bigotry and a desire for greater equality. Haaland is one of many women who ran for office "after thinking a woman would become president in 2016 and feeling let down."[59] Stronger representation for women is a start, but Haaland's decision to run ultimately rested on understanding the challenges of her own community and a desire to "have influence over people who are making decisions for one of the most vulnerable communities in our country."[60] For example, in a 2005 decision regarding land restored to the Oneida Tribe in a majority decision written by Ginsburg, the Supreme Court ruled that they "preclude the Tribe from rekindling embers of sovereignty that long ago grew cold" (*City of Sherrill v Oneida*). From an Indigenous perspective, sovereignty remains a living flame.

Despite intensified voter suppression, the 2018 midterms had the highest voter turnout in nearly a century, reversing the lowest turnout in 72 years in the 2014 midterms.[61] The numbers alone are a rebuttal to the Trump administration's divisive rhetoric and assault on human rights at home and abroad. American voters made clear that they won't return to an era of fewer rights or reinvigorated white male dominance.

The messages sent by this election vary according to location and circumstances. There are many remarkable people whose stories we didn't include who are well worth researching. If you live in the US, pay attention to who ran and/or was elected in your local area—maybe you'll be inspired to help register eligible citizens to vote (see #WhenWeAllVote and Whenweallvote.org) or maybe even run for office yourself! After all, despite the increase in women holding office, US numbers are still globally low. If you Google "Women in National Parliaments," you'll find that as of December 1, 2018, the nation with the highest percentage of women holding elected office is Rwanda with 61.3%; Cuba, Bolivia, Mexico, Granada, Namibia, Sweden, Nicaragua, Costa Rica, and South Africa round out the top ten. The US' position on the list might surprise you.[62]

In this chapter, we've talked about movements that were not seamless or easy. Next, we'll talk about the work of making change happen and keeping it going.

Notes

1 Cody Hooks. "DAPL Dispatch: Water Cannons Injure Hundreds in Below-Freezing Standoff." *Taos News*. Nov. 24, 2016, https://www.taosnews.com/stories/dapl-dispatch-water-cannons-injure-hundreds-in-below-freezing-standoff,20421?

2 Josh Nathan-Kazis. "She Still Can't Use Her Hand, A Year After a Grenade Injury at Standing Rock." *Forward.com*. Nov. 17, 2017. https://forward.com/news/387898/a-year-after-a-grenade-blew-up-her-arm-at-standing-rock-sophia-wilansky-is/.

3 Hooks. "DAPL Dispatch: Water Cannons Injure Hundreds in Below-Freezing Standoff."

4 Ibid.

5 Rebecca Leber. "Trump Resurrects Keystone XL and Dakota Access Pipeline." *Mother Jones*. Jan. 24, 2017, https://www.motherjones.com/environment/2017/01/trump-signs-executive-orders-keystone-and-dakota-access/.

6 Wes Enzinna. Photographer Zen Lefort. *Mother Jones*. Jan./Feb., 2017, https://www.motherjones.com/politics/2016/12/dakota-access-pipeline-standing-rock-oil-water-protest/.

7 Erica Chenoweth and Jeremy Pressman. "This is What We Learned by Counting the Women's Marches." *The Washington Post*. Feb. 7, 2017, https://www.washingtonpost.com/news/monkey-cage/wp/2017/02/07/this-is-what-we-learned-by-counting-the-womens-marches/?utm_term=.987f47da8ad8.

8 Photo 1: Women's March 2017-01.jpg. *Wikimedia Commons*. Jan. 21, 2017, https://commons.wikimedia.org/wiki/File:Women's_March_2017-01_(04).jpg; Photo 2: "View of the Women's March on Washington from the Roof of the Voice of America Building." *Wikipedia*. Washington, DC. Jan. 21, 2017, https://en.wikipedia.org/wiki/2017_Women%27s_March#/media/File:Women%27s_March_2017-01_(12).jpg.

9 Photos by Allison V. Craig.

10 Photo on left by Allison V. Craig; photo on right by Sara Shulman Riddington, used with permission.

11 Ibid.

12 "Crowd Estimates." *Chenoweth and Pressman*. Last modified Jan. 26, 2017, https://docs.google.com/spreadsheets/d/1xa0iLqYKz8x9Yc_rfhtmSOJQ2EGgeUVjvV4A8LsIaxY/htmlview?sle=true.

13 Ibid.

14 Ronan Farrow. "From Aggressive Overtures to Sexual Assault: Harvey Weinstein's Accusers Tell Their Stories." *The New Yorker*. Oct. 10, 2017, https://www.newyorker.com/news/news-desk/from-aggressive-overtures-to-sexual-assault-harvey-weinsteins-accusers-tell-their-stories.

15 Nadja Sayej. "Alyssa Milano on the #MeToo Movement: 'We're Not Going to Stand for It Anymore.'" *The Guardian*. Dec. 1, 2017, https://www.theguardian.com/culture/2017/dec/01/alyssa-milano-mee-too-sexual-harassment-abuse.

16 Ibid., n.p.

17 JR Thorpe. "This Is How Many People Have Posted 'Me Too' Since October, According to New Data." *Bustle*. Dec. 1, 2017, https://www.bustle.com/p/this-is-how-many-people-have-posted-me-too-since-october-according-to-new-data-6753697.

18 Sandra E. Garcia. "The Woman Who Created #MeToo Long Before Hashtags." *The New York Times*. Oct. 20, 2017, https://www.nytimes.com/2017/10/20/us/me-too-movement-tarana-burke.html.

19 Ibid.

20 According to Garcia's article, Just Be, Inc. is described as "a nonprofit organization that helps victims of sexual harassment and assault."

21 Britni Danielle. *Twitter post.* Oct. 15, 2017, https://twitter.com/BritniDWrites/status/919770187179556865.

22 Luvvie Ajayi. *Twitter post.* Oct. 17, 2017, https://twitter.com/Luvvie/status/920369861670424577.

23 Alix Langone. "#MeToo and Time's Up Founders Explain the Difference Between the 2 Movements—And How They're Alike." *Time.* Mar. 8, 2018, http://time.com/5189945/whats-the-difference-between-the-metoo-and-times-up-movements/.

24 "Alyssa Milano Reveals How She Found the Confidence to Send the First #MeToo Tweet." *People.* Aug. 7, 2017, https://people.com/tv/alyssa-milano-reveals-how-she-found-the-confidence-to-send-the-first-metoo-tweet/.

25 @latimes. "Since Actress Alyssa Milano Kicked off the #MeToo Movement with a Single Tweet in October 2017, Americans Have Been Thinking Quite a Lot About Sexual Harassment and Sexual Assault." *Twitter post.* Dec. 21, 2018, https://twitter.com/latimes/status/1076207654907899904.

26 Maria Repnikova and Weile Zhou. "#MeToo Movement in China: Powerful Yet Fragile." *Aljazeera.com.* Oct. 22, 2018, https://www.aljazeera.com/indepth/opinion/metoo-movement-china-powerful-fragile-181022082126244.html.

27 Ibid.

28 Ibid.

29 Tom Cheshire. "China's #MeToo Movement Will Soon Get Its Day in Court." *News. Sky.com.* Feb. 17, 2019, https://news.sky.com/story/chinas-metoo-movement-to-get-its-day-in-court-11639871.

30 Ibid.

31 Philippa Atkinson. "The War Economy in Liberia: A Political Analysis." Relief and Rehabilitation Network, Overseas Development Institute. May 1997, https://odihpn.org/wp-content/uploads/1997/05/ networkpaper022.pdf

32 Ibid.

33 *Bill Moyers Journal.* "Women Fight for Peace." *PBS.* S13, Ep. 10. Last updated 2019, https://www.pbs.org/video/bill-moyers-the-journal-women-fight-for-peace/.

34 Ibid.

35 "Our Founder—Leymah Gbowee." *Gbowee Peace Foundation Africa USA.* 2018, https://www.gboweepeaceusa.org/our-founder/.

36 Alma Hassoun. "'We are Real': Saudi Feminists Launch Online Radio," *BBC News.* Aug. 19, 2018, https://www.bbc.com/news/world-middle-east-45181505.

37 "Veteran Rights Activist Aisha al-Manea Released from Saudi Jail." *Albawaba News.* The New Arab. May 24, 2018, https://www.albawaba.com/news/veteran-rights-activist-aisha-al-manea-released-saudi-jail-1136578.

38 Samah Salaime. "The Quiet Feminist Revolution in Arab Society in Israel." *+972.* Mar. 8, 2018, https://972mag.com/the-quiet-feminist-revolution-in-arab-society-in-israel/133687/.

39 Ibid.

40 Shad Begum. "How Women in Pakistan are Creating Political Change." *TedWomen.* 2018, https://www.ted.com/talks/shad_begum_how_women_in_pakistan_are_creating_a_political_revolution/transcript.

41 Ibid.

42 Associated Press. "Puerto Rico Lost $43 billion after Hurricane Maria, According to Govt. Report." *NBC News*. Dec. 4, 2018, https://www.nbcnews.com/news/latino/puerto-rico-lost-43-billion-after-hurricane-maria-according-govt-n943441.

43 US Government Accountability Office. "2017 HURRICANES AND WILDFIRES: Initial Observations on the Federal Response and Key Recovery Challenges." Sept. 2018, https://www.gao.gov/assets/700/694231.pdf.

44 Paul F. Hancock and Lora L. Tredway. "The Bailout Standard of the Voting Rights Act: An Incentive to End Discrimination." *The Urban Lawyer*. Vol. 17, No. 3, SPECIAL CONFERENCE ISSUE: Voting Rights and the Democratic Process: Where Do We Stand Today? American Bar Association. Summer 1985, pp. 379–425, p. 404, https://www.jstor.org/stable/27893307.

45 Ibid., p. 406.

46 Ibid.

47 Adam Liptak. "Supreme Court Invalidates Key Part of Voting Rights Act." *New York Times*. June 25, 2013, https://www.nytimes.com/2013/06/26/us/supreme-court-ruling.html.

48 Ibid.

49 "*Shelby County v. Holder.*" 570 U.S. 529. Judge Ginsburg Dissenting. June 25, 2013, pp. 12–96. p. 3, https://www.documentcloud.org/documents/717244-supreme-court-decision-in-shelby-county-v-holder.html#document/p32.

50 Ibid., p. 6.

51 Ibid., p. 33.

52 Ibid., p. 36.

53 *Spirit Lake Tribe, et al. v. Jaeger*. US District Court for the District of North Dakota, Western Division. Civil No. 1:18-cv-00222-DLH-CSM, Oct. 31, 2018, p.13, https://www.narf.org/nill/documents/20181031spirit-lake-jaeger-memo-tro.pdf.

54 Ibid., p. 18.

55 *Spirit Lake Tribe, et al. v. Jaeger*. US District Court for the District of North Dakota. Case No. 1:18-cv-222. Nov. 1, 2018, p. 2, https://www.courthousenews.com/wp-content/uploads/2018/11/SpiritLakeNDVoterID-troORDER.pdf.

56 Mariana Alfaro. "Florida Lawmakers Might Not Give Voting Rights Back to Felons, Even Though 64% of Voters Want Them To." *Business Insider*. Dec. 13, 2018, https://www.businessinsider.com/florida-lawmakers-might-not-restore-voting-rights-to-felons-2018-12?fbclid=IwAR3JsAduAw0rQNcw4LeE3f51LmGQUh1jTJFYBnep0DQwWPtrn5vrC0yCxko.

57 Photos property of Katharine Ransom, used by permission.

58 Leila Fadel and Talia Wiener. "Record Number of Native Americans Running for Office in Midterms." *National Public Radio*. July 4, 2018, https://www.npr.org/2018/07/04/625425037/record-number-of-native-americans-running-for-office-in-midterms.

59 Ibid.

60 Ibid.

61 Emily Stewart. "2018's Record-Setting Voter Turnout, In One Chart." *Vox.com*. Nov. 19, 2018, https://www.vox.com/policy-and-politics/2018/11/19/18103110/2018-midterm-elections-turnout.

62 "Women in Parliaments." Inter-Parliamentary Union. As of Dec. 1, 2018, http://archive.ipu.org/wmn-e/classif.htm.

10 #WTF I *Can* Do

Movements discussed in this edition are contemporary through early 2019. By the time this book goes to press, there will be more to say on each of them, more movements, and more activists. At some point, what we've written about will become history, but the past can guide you at any time. As you research the past and determine your path into the future, keep in mind movements have long roots that run deep. For example, while the roots of Tarana Burke's "me too" may be the 18.8% of Black women raped in the US, the history of raping women of color is rooted in slavery and colonization—as we saw, rape of Native women is at 34.1%. In both cases, the new nation's economic desires for unpaid labor and land drove the history fueling current statistics. Causes of each movement are systemically connected to all the others.

Because of systemic connections, imbalances and injustices are everywhere we turn. Though overwhelming, understanding these connections allows people to form coalitions. You'll discover many opportunities to work toward change as you explore what you *can* do, but it can also be daunting to determine where to apply your energy and skills. No matter where you decide to act, the principles and strategies in this chapter will help you do what you can.

The Challenging Work of Coalition

It's important to apply intersectional methods when working across differences. In a *Red Table* episode, "The Racial Divide: Women of Color and White Women," Jada Pinkett Smith and guests—her mother, Adrienne Banfield-Jones, and daughter, Willow Camille Reign Smith—describe how that work can begin. Their conversation demonstrates reflexivity: Banfield-Jones explains that working with white feminists "forced [her] to examine [her] own way of thinking." Pinkett Smith's experiences led her to identify not as a feminist but as a womanist. Pinkett Smith invites a white camerawoman to talk about some differences in how Black and white women see the world. As they explain the challenges they face, the camerawoman says, "I never thought of it that way . . . I don't know about being Black." Smith then invites white diversity educator Jane Elliott to join the conversation. Elliott gained notoriety for separating her all-white,

1970 Iowa classroom by eye color to teach students about discrimination and later for her brutally honest delivery in teaching mostly white adults about their roles in racism. Her first comment to the *Red Table* camerawoman is true to form: "What do you mean you don't know about being Black? Can you read?" When the camerawoman affirms she can, Elliott shoots back, "Then why don't you?"[1]

Not everyone can or should be as direct as Jane Elliott, but reflexivity and research can take us far toward understanding each other. Of utmost importance is listening to those directly experiencing an issue. This helps everyone contribute their best to movements that traverse race, class, gender, age, ability, religion, and nation. The truth is that it's easier and more complicated than we probably think. Thanks to social media, we can connect with others with shared concerns more easily than in decades past. But social media's ease and speed has its downsides. Creating lasting social change takes more than sharing concerns, more than likes and quick responses—it takes coalition building.

A coalition is "a single group or alliance formed by a number of separate groups, states, people, etc., to further a common interest or achieve a shared purpose."[2] Feminist coalition building predates any single person or time period, but Bernice Johnson Reagon popularized the idea in 1981 at the West Coast Women's Music Festival. In "Coalition Politics: Turning the Century," Reagon noted there are many ways to work together, but it all starts with balancing our relationship to the issues and people around us. "Most of us," she says,

> think that the space we live in is the most important space there is, and that the condition that we find ourselves in is the condition that must be changed or else. That is only partially the case. If you analyze the situation properly, you will know that there might be a few things you can do in your personal, individual interest so that you can experience and enjoy the change. But most of the things that you do, if you do them right, are for people who live long after you are long forgotten.[3]

Reagon argued for creating coalitions with room for many different struggles, warning against people or

> groups that can only deal with one thing at a time. On the other hand, learn about space within coalition. You can't have everybody sitting up there talking about everything that concerns you at the same time or you won't get no place.[4]

People who only interact with people like themselves often mistake it for safety. They "bar the door" and keep others out. But the others are still out there, and "[t]here is no chance that you can survive by staying *inside* the barred room."[5] Reagon asserted that "in order to take the next step [towards social justice] we've got to do it with some folk we don't care about too much."[6] Her point about joining forces with those who don't share our exact concerns is applied intersectionality, recognizing and bridging differences to form alliances.

Effective coalition members recognize that strength comes from joining others who have similar, not necessarily the same, concerns. When it comes to fighting oppression, those in power, Reagon tells us, "ain't ever gonna give you what you ask for."[7] Effective coalitions recognize victories and setbacks as part of the process and share knowledge with others who can do the work in different locations, who will continue the work after we're gone.

If this idea seems familiar, it is. You may recognize similar coalition building from the Haudenosaunee Confederacy, a coalition with mixed success. Uniting around a single language group and pitting themselves against other tribes may have prevented the broader coalition needed to slow the tide of colonization. Today, the Haudenosaunee Confederacy takes a "think global, act local" approach. At the request of Clan Mothers, their Faithkeeper, Oren Lyons, is active in environmental and Indigenous concerns at the UN. The UN itself is a coalition instituted to work for global peace and security and it too has mixed effectiveness. As Reagon noted, if a coalition is too complex, some concerns will be overlooked. A balanced coalition is both effective and sustainable.

Even effective coalitions face difficulty, especially when long-standing laws and policies work against their aims. One of the most difficult lessons in cultivating a more socially just world is recognizing that change can be exceedingly slow and even small gains are hard fought. Learning to build strong coalitions that endure and continue over time may be more important than single actions.

Like Gbowee's, coalitions can shift venues as conditions change. They can also broaden as people learn to listen. At the 2016 Chicago Humanities Festival, political commentator Melissa Harris-Perry discussed how many progressives lament "what do I tell my children" about the Trump era's overt misogyny and racism. While she sympathized with this position, it revealed something those progressives had long overlooked:

> While I have enormous empathy for the feeling of "what am I gonna tell my children," I must ask you, what the hell have you been telling your children? At what point did it become intolerable for us to think about young people having to grow up next to other people who they are going to have to interact with who may at any point cause them physical, emotional, psychic, personal harm unto the death, because, quite honestly, that's like Tuesday for me, like any Tuesday, not just Election Tuesday. Every single time a black woman who is a mother tries to rent an apartment or buy a house or send her kid to

a public school that her tax dollars pay for, she has to ask that same question. [. . .] I get it, but I want to remind us the ways it's so easy to erase and fail to remember that this is not some brand new thing. And I'm telling you this not to harangue you but hopefully to give you hope that this is not a brand new situation.[8]

At the Othering and Belonging Conference the following year, an audience member asked why it was so difficult to reconcile her identity and challenges as a woman with those as an African American. Harris-Perry responded that many stories—about racism, police brutality, health, and more—are told well in the Black community. "We tell the story of Emmett Till so we know what to do when we see Trayvon Martin," she said. But stories about Black women are told less well:

> "We tell none about rape, sexual assault, or the patriarchy, and as a result . . . we understand each one of those experiences individually, rather than within broader political framework," Harris-Perry said. "We don't know that rape is part of a thing, when babies die in our arms we don't know it's part of thing."

The solution, she concluded, is in "uncovering, recovering, and putting our stories at the center."[9]

Reflecting on the Women's March through Harris-Perry's perspective provides insight about organizing feminist coalitions. The Women's March made much-needed coalition-building progress that some found uncomfortable. While not fully resolved, conversations led to positive changes in how the event was planned and enacted. These changes stemmed from difficult and contentious debates, online and face-to-face.

Initially, the march was organized largely by white women. The original plan was modest: "Frustrated by the 2016 election results, [Teresa] Shook invited 40 of her friends to a March on Washington. When she awoke the next morning 10,000 additional names had joined the group and there were 10,000 interested in coming."[10] The enormous interest that followed brought concerns, especially from Black women who felt frustrated that it took white women so long to see the dangers affecting communities of color. Because of the history of suffrage, abolition, and feminists who ignore(d) or were ignorant of women of color's issues as well as the scarcity of whites supporting movements like #BlackLivesMatter, many doubted white women would follow through with claims of solidarity. Harris-Perry's comment about the need for better stories about Black women is significant because in the history of feminist movements, particularly in the US, Black women have often been remembered as supporting white women, even when they were taking the lead.

When white organizers initially called for people to lend their support and physical bodies to march on Washington, they didn't actively seek out minority participation in leadership roles, continuing the all-too-familiar routine of favoring white women's concerns at the exclusion of minority concerns. Because women of color bear the most immediate and severe brunt of oppression and because of the need to tell better stories of Black women, women of color "advised 'white allies' to listen more and talk less . . . [and] chided those who . . . were only now waking up to racism because of the election."[11]

Some white women felt so uncomfortable with these difficult conversations that they cancelled plans to march. One white woman said she felt alienated from attending after a Black woman march volunteer, likely frustrated by some white women only being drawn to action after they themselves felt personally threatened, told her, "[you] don't just get to join because now you're scared too. I was born scared."[12]

Ultimately, white co-founders Vanessa Wruble and Bob Bland took intersectional critiques to heart, and Perez, Sarsour, and Mallory stepped in. Harry Belafonte, LaDonna Harris, Angela Davis, and Dolores Huerta also became honorary co-chairs, creating a more diverse and balanced coalition. Tamika Mallory is a Black feminist active in Black Lives Matter and active in gun control. Carmen Perez, a Latinx woman, is the director on The Gathering for Justice, founded by artist/activist Harry Belafonte, which is involved in "many of today's important civil rights issues, including mass incarceration, gender equity, violence prevention, racial healing and community policing."[13] Linda Sarsour, a Muslim woman, was director of the Arab American Association of New York and became involved with Black Lives Matter and the Democratic Party. Their participation helped foreground issues beyond the "pussy grab," such as the new president's racial slurs against Latinx people and Muslims along with proposals for a wall and a ban.

As they planned for the second Women's March, issues of inclusiveness still tested the coalition. Mallory was subject to controversy due to her relationship with famously anti-Semitic Black Muslim minister Louis Farrakhan. Alyssa Milano, who popularized Burke's #MeToo slogan among white celebrities, said she would not speak at the next march if Sarsour and Mallory did not condemn Farrakhan. A Black cultural worker, Ernesto Mercer, responded:

> I have my issues with Farrakhan as well, but he is [Mallory's] family friend [since childhood] and . . . support[ed] her when her brother was murdered. [. . .] Tamara isn't making any pro-Farrakhan speeches and he isn't a part of [her] organizations. [She] has stated many times that she does not support all of . . . [his] policies. [. . .] I also hear Tamara's continued response to this as a very good one: You have to be able to talk to folks in "difficult spaces."

Mercer offers examples in mainstream politics of participants who hold difficult or contradictory positions, but nobody demands that they clarify their stance. "There is a double standard," he concludes.[14] In fact, considering the complex global issues at stake and the fact that the march, initiated in response to a US election, has become global, we are, by default, in a "difficult space" where we need to listen to each other and bridge differences. March organizers, therefore, responded to Milano by "condemning anti-Semitism while standing with Sarsour and Mallory."[15]

Including multiple voices at all levels may have led to the Women's March being the biggest and most peaceful single-day protest in US history. Both the inaugural and subsequent marches included diverse speakers, including Angela Davis (Black activist, see Conclusion for profile), Janet Mock (Black transgender activist), LaDonna Harris (Comanche activist and politician), and Sophie Cruz (Mexican activist). Transcripts of their speeches are available online.

It remains to be seen whether lessons learned from the Women's March will endure. Many questions remain: What will it take for white women (and men) to continue to ally in meaningful ways with communities of color? If the threat to their personal concerns passes, will they stay woke? What will it take for people to care about the suffering of others without needing to personally experience that suffering? How do we support our leaders without making them into such grand-scale heroines that any flaws are magnified and seen as disqualifying?

Coalition-building means applying intersectional theoretical methods. It means acting from thoughtful consideration of different but connected experiences. Coalition is stronger when built together. Balanced, strong coalitions engage in more than just lip service, but when someone has the privilege of the public's ear, speaking out is helpful. At the 75th annual Golden Globes, actresses and social activists walked the red carpet together to draw attention to Time's Up, "a solution-based, action-oriented next step in the #MeToo movement. The organization's aim is to create concrete change, leading to safety and equity in the workplace."[16] Stars who walked with activists to reach millions of viewers were:

- Tarana Burke and actress Michelle Williams
- Ai-Jen Poo (director of the National Domestic Workers Alliance) and Meryl Streep
- Marai Larasi (founder of black feminist organization Imkaan) and Emma Waston
- Rosa Clemente (organizer, lecturer, and journalist) and Susan Sarandon
- Monica Ramirez (worker's rights advocate and Alianza Nacional de Campesinas co-founder) and Laura Dern
- Calina Lawrence (Native American and human rights activist) and Shailene Woodley
- Billie Jean King (women's rights advocate and one of the all-time winningest tennis professionals) and Emma Stone
- Saru Jayaraman (Restaurant Opportunities Center United president) and Amy Poehler.[17]

Time's Up recognized that sexual harassment occurs in many workplaces, especially affecting vulnerable populations like women agricultural workers (see Part Two). Therefore, in solidarity with the US women's farmers association, Alianza Nacional de Campesinas, organizers published an eight-page letter in *The New York Times* that started "Dear Sisters." In the letter, 300 Hollywood celebrities acknowledged their privilege to "access enormous platforms to amplify our voices" and noted, "[n]ow, unlike ever before, our access to the media and to important decision makers has the potential of leading to real accountability and consequences."[18] Their "Open Letter from Time's Up" in *The New York Time* detailed their goals and strategies.[19]

Another example of a highly effective coalition involves youth activists who united because a gunman killed 17 students and staff in Marjory Stoneman Douglas High School. They developed a gun control platform—such as universal background checks, a high-capacity magazine ban, and funding for gun violence research—and held a "March for Our Lives," including a 20-state tour called "The Road to Change." When they reached Chicago, they heard from youth in largely Black areas who have lived in constant fear of gun violence. The causes of this violence are at the intersection of race, class, and location, rooted in how Chicago's long-time segregation limits Black students' educational and economic opportunities. Emma González of Parkland invited D'Angelo McDade of the Chicago Peace Warriors to join the tour. While the Parkland students had primarily addressed political issues in speeches at rallies and on social media, the Peace Warriors were trained in on-the-street skills, such as peer mediation and "peace circles" to diffuse potential violence. The Parkland students insisted that from then on, they would only speak along with Chicago teens because

> the press was biased toward the privileged children of Parkland, paying too much attention to them and to school shootings, instead of focusing on the coalition they were trying to build, in which every gun death was equal in its tragedy and emergency, no matter the cause or context.[20]

Since organizing, 69 gun control laws have been passed.[21]

Parkland and Chicago Peace Warriors offer a blueprint for intersectional coalition-building. Each movement has a specific focus and develops skills and resources accordingly, but no one's identity or concerns is resolved by any one issue alone. We build common ground among our differences to work together.

Coalitions require confronting the issue of relative privilege. Audre Lorde was born Black, poor, female, immigrant, lesbian, disabled, and became non-Christian, so she had lived what it means to be on the negative side of pretty much every norm. But most of us have mixed experiences.

Almost all of us have one privilege or another and are at risk for one oppression or another. Therefore, everyone is in a position to reflect on the meaning of privilege, but not everyone does.

Sometimes, people expect to maintain their privilege, even if they also face discrimination. For example, in a *New York Times* article, a white woman stated she didn't attend the Women's March because critiques of privilege made her feel unwelcome.[22] Had she taken an intersectional approach, she could have reflected on how women of color and differently gendered people feel unwelcome in many venues every day. Attending would have put her on more equal footing with them and perhaps furthered the work of coalition.

Sometimes, developing awareness of privilege leads to guilt. Guilt, while understandable, stifles progress. What helps, according to antiracist educator Tim Wise, is awareness, commitment, responsibility, and informed actions.[23] Wise uses the analogy of pollution to address inequity. We aren't individually responsible for putting toxic waste in the air or water or lead paint in houses, but to make our environment healthy, we must clean it up. The same goes for unearned privilege that harms some while elevating others. Just because I didn't individually cause someone else to suffer doesn't mean I should ignore that suffering. Guilt, he says, is "what you feel for what you've done; responsibility is what you take . . . to live ethically." Such responsibility taking is necessary, because "If we don't do it, no one does it. We're the only hope we have."[24]

Doubt and Fatigue are Normal

It can feel exhilarating to take action, but it's also hard work, and if you do it long enough, you'll likely feel doubt and fatigue. In fact, anywhere in the process, you may start to question the value of your activism. Is this really working? What difference am I actually making? Are we doing enough? Will it ever be enough? But rest assured, you aren't alone in this feeling. Even those who've had major impacts go through this on occasion.

Tarana Burke discussed how long and difficult her work in developing Me Too had been:

> In 2006, 12 years ago, I laid across a mattress on my floor in my one-bedroom apartment, frustrated with all the sexual violence that I saw in my community. I pulled out a piece of paper, and I wrote "Me Too" on the top of it, and I proceeded to write out an action plan for building a movement based on empathy between survivors that would help us feel like we can heal, that we weren't the sum total of the things that happened to us.[25]

Burke confessed she felt exhausted and numb from the collective trauma of victimization. She relies on her understanding of the history of struggle to combat such fatigue: "Those who came before us didn't win every fight," she said, "but they didn't let it kill their vision. It fueled it. So, I can't stop, and I'm asking you not to stop either."[26]

The progress made by #MeToo showed Burke it is "bigger than a moment," and she saw backlash against it as "confirmation that we are in a movement. And the most powerful movements have always been built around what's possible, not just claiming what is right now." "Trauma," she says, "halts possibility. Movement activates it." We encourage you to listen to Burke's "Me Too is a Movement, Not a Moment" on your own, but for now, consider these comments:

> Movements create possibility, and they are built on vision. My vision for the Me Too Movement is a part of a collective vision to see a world free of sexual violence, and I believe we can build that world. Full stop. But in order to get there, we have to dramatically shift a culture that propagates the idea that vulnerability is synonymous with permission and that bodily autonomy is not a basic human right. In other words, we have to dismantle the building blocks of sexual violence: power and privilege. So much of what we hear about the Me Too Movement is about individual bad actors or depraved, isolated behavior, and it fails to recognize that anybody in a position of power comes with privilege, and it renders those without that power more vulnerable. Teachers and students, coaches and athletes, law enforcement and citizen, parent and child: these are all relationships that can have an incredible imbalance of power. But we reshape that imbalance by speaking out against it in unison and by creating spaces to speak truth to power. We have to reeducate ourselves and our children to understand that power and privilege doesn't always have to destroy and take—it can be used to serve and build. And we have to reeducate ourselves to understand that, unequivocally, every human being has the right to walk through this life with their full humanity intact.[27]

Every human, not just some, not just many, not even most, but everyone, should walk through life with their full humanity intact. That's the ultimate goal of feminism and the best reason for you to do what you can do every chance you get.

Kinds of Activism

Just as there are many kinds of feminism, there are also many kinds of feminist activism. Rather than deciding which is "best" (addiction to ranking is part of the problem), think of how different forms of activism are complementary, how multiple actions are necessary to resolve complex problems, and how doing something that helps make a positive difference in people's lives also helps sustain your own participation in the process.

Academia offers formal, methodical analyses of feminist issues. Defined as "the life, community, or world of teachers, schools, and education,"[28] it's known for developing and testing theories based on fact-based evidence in pursuit of better questions to ask, solutions to complex problems, and ever-deepening knowledge. While academia is not always activist, many academics see their work as part of that aim. It's where you are most likely to encounter texts like this book and the many students and professors who contributed to its pages. Himanee Gupta-Carlson explains her approach to feminist research in the academy.

Feminist Scholarship by Himanee Gupta-Carlson

Scholars within Women's, Gender, and Sexuality Studies have come up with many different ways of talking about feminist research. I will discuss one perspective—my own. However, my perspective is informed by the ideas of other feminists whose work I have read over the years, and by the feminist-minded professors with whom I worked in graduate school. More than a decade into my post-PhD teaching and researching life, I continue to read and discuss ideas with other feminists. In this sense, all feminist research shares one thing in common: It values the idea of knowledge as conversation.

What does it mean to think about knowledge as conversation? For starters, this perspective refutes the idea of the sole authorial voice (think of the connection between the words "author" and "authority"). It suggests instead that even if a book or an article or a classroom assignment is written by a single person, that person's knowledge emerged as a result of multiple conversations—sometimes stretching over years or even decades—with others. This is why proper citation of all materials used to prepare any kind of writing, visual, or audio work is important. In a feminist sense, when you create a citation, you are acknowledging debts of gratitude to those who helped you in your learning journey.

Knowledge as conversation also challenges the idea that a scholar (or student) can remain distant from her work. When you read a text, view a video, take notes on a lecture, or interview an individual, you are engaging in a dialogue with the material at hand. Those lines of a text that you highlight, those notes that you scribble in book margins—all of these are aspects of you dialoguing with the work. Even if, perhaps especially if, you write, "I hate this idea," or "I don't understand a word of what I am reading," you are immersed in conversation. That immersion makes you and your experience a part of the research. By becoming a part of the research, you might find yourself itching to use that pronoun you were warned in earlier schooling to avoid: the first person, the "I." Many feminists reach for the "I." They see it as integral to positioning themselves within the research to be presented, as acknowledging to readers that there might be inadvertent bias or subjectivity in the work, and even that the use of the first person is highlighting the fact that all knowledge in some aspects is political (in the sense of being crafted from a particular point of view). A slogan of the 1970s feminist movement captures this idea well: The personal is political, and vice versa.

If you want to write with a feminist perspective in mind, you might keep in mind three ways that feminist scholars have categorized feminist knowledge. One category is often referred to as epistemological or historical. This view holds that prior studies of history, society, economics, politics, science, and even such areas as mathematics neglected to document experiences of women. Researchers dedicated to the epistemological/historical perspective work to recover these lost experiences. A second category is known as "standpoint theory" or, as some jokingly call it, "add women and stir." This view holds that prior knowledge about the human experience will reveal new insights when women are moved from the periphery of those experiences to the center. One fine example of how a feminist uses standpoint theory is seen in Cynthia Enloe's 2000 book *Maneuvers: The International Politics of Militarizing Women's Lives*. In this book, Enloe writes about how a domestic item—a can of soup—comes to be militarized when the noodles are shaped in the form of soldiers and tanks. Women who purchase soup for their families are then subjected to a politics that they can choose to engage with or ignore.

The final category of feminist knowledge often is described as postmodern, genealogical, or even deconstructionist. It is less about delineating separations between men and women or divergences of experience and more about questioning how those separations came to be defined in and of themselves. I feel that post-modern feminism is perhaps the most promising form of bridge-building work within feminist research. It seeks to build alliances across differences and strives to hear and respect multiple ways of thinking about particular topics or matters. Its ultimate goal is not liberation for women but rather justice for all.

Academics teach, write, research, and collaborate. Several of this book's contributors do academic activism specifically aimed toward social equity. Stephanie Sellers directed the Women's Center at her college for many years, and Rhianna Rogers has led several initiatives such as Forum on Race and Policing (FoRaP), Difficult Dialogues, and The Buffalo Project.

Education as activism happens inside and outside academia. At its best, it intersects with many other forms of activism, like marches and art. Emma González provided powerful education during her March for Our Lives speech. Learning moments arose from what she did and didn't say: standing on stage in silence after reading the names of all those killed at Parkland High School emphasized the heightened emotion of having to hide from the shooter, of not knowing what would happen next. Speaking out, testifying, and bearing witness are primary forms of education.

Critical analysis of systems, issues, and events are also educational. Tiffany Dena Loftin led a group from all across the country as part of the NAACP Youth and College Division in order to participate in the March for Our Lives. She explained why it was important for them to attend:

> Number one, what they will not do is ignore Black voices. Number two, what they will be sure to do is include our agenda in the agenda for gun prevention reform. When we talk about legislative issues and solutions for gun violence it has to include the intersections of Black violence. That means guns. that means gangs. That means schools. That means teachers. That means police brutality. That means state violence. It has to include all of that if we're going to do this together. This is not just about white people and school shootings in the classroom. They kill us in churches. They kill us on the streets. They kill us in a car. They kill us when we're traveling. And they kill us in the classroom. This is about all the young Black people that you're looking at here right behind me. [. . .] We here to organize, represent, and show power. And the third thing we're here to do is to make sure we have a great time.[29]

Loftin educated listeners about the need to take the empowerment they feel at events home to organize locally because "that's where it matters."[30]

Art is also a form of activism. Art can be formal (like painting, sculpture, photography, and theater) or informal (like mixed media, street theater, television, and film). There are far too many artists to include in this book, so we encourage you to seek out feminist art. Below, we offer two examples: Judy Chicago (US) and Xiao Lu (China).

Judy Chicago

One of the more famous feminist artworks is American artist Judy Chicago's *The Dinner Party*, "an important icon of 1970s feminist art and a milestone in twentieth-century art."[31] *The Dinner Party* took five years and a collective of artists and researchers to complete. The installation was designed to literally and figuratively set a place at the table for women's stories overlooked and under-emphasized in history. With 39 place settings at the table and 999 "Women of Achievement" on the Heritage Floor, *The Dinner Party* "traces the changeover from matriarchy to patriarchy in the myths, legends, and images of the Goddess" and "takes us on a tour of Western civilization, a tour that bypasses what we have been taught to think of as the main road."[32] It is not intended to be "an adequate representation of feminine history" according to Chicago, because "for that we would require a new world-view, one that acknowledges the history of both the powerful and the powerless people of the world." "A true history," she writes, "would allow us to see the mingled efforts of people of all colors and sexes, all countries and races, all seeing the universe in their own diverse ways."[33]

Xiao Lu

In "China's Female Artists Quietly Emerge," Holland Cotter describes this powerful Beijing moment:

On a February day in 1989, a young woman walked into a show at the National Gallery of Art . . . whipped out a pellet gun and fired two shots into a mirrored sculpture in an exhibition called 'China/Avant-Garde.' Police officers swarmed into the museum. The show, the country's first government-sponsored exhibition of experimental art, was shut down for days.[34]

The sculpture Xiao Lu shot was *Dialogue*, a piece she and Tang Song co-designed. According to Xiao Lu, she did not plan nor get prior approval for her performance, hence, the police response. In an interview about Chinese Contemporary Artists, she told Monica Merlin she had sought approval, but the person with authority was

busy and sent me away—probably thinking that he could disregard me because I was not particularly famous. [. . .] [A]t the time, I was an obscure nobody in their eyes, and a woman too. So I did not have the opportunity to speak to anyone about firing the gun before the exhibition opened.[35]

Xiao Lu said the impromptu decision to shoot her own artwork resulted from feeling "very stifled, really quite suffocated," in large part because she "felt like [she] could not communicate with men. *Dialogue* was about that." Xiao Lu was the only woman in her class and knew women's art in China was deemed inferior to men's but said she had not thought about feminism at the time. After her work was included in the *Bald Girls* exhibit in 2012, she experienced what she calls a transformation and began to think about feminism. Curator Xu Juan asked her if she wanted to include her sculptures "because they showed a feminist consciousness." Xiao Lu was hesitant: "I had not thought about feminism when I created them." But she said, "It doesn't matter. I can write about them from a feminist perspective." And I said, "Sure, write on!"

Xiao Lu began to read "many books on feminism" to get an overview for the exhibit, and "it triggered a change":

Before, I had always been concerned with my own personal experiences, but after *Bald Girls* I started to pay more attention to the lives and experiences of other women. My works were no longer exclusively based on my own situation. This was the transformation. [. . .] *Bald Girl* exhibition suddenly opened a window for me.

After 2012, Xiao Lu focused more on supporting women's rights through feminist art. She continues to challenge the status quo. "Even if you oppress me and apply a lot of pressure," Xiao Lu says, "I will still resist you."[36]

Media: Some media outlets dedicate themselves to activism. For example, during Standing Rock, along with Indigenous media like *Digital Smoke Signals*, it was *The Young Turks*[37] and *Democracy Now*[38] that went to the front lines and shared what was happening.

Art and media reflect as well as change society. Some kinds of media overlap with arts. Films that share human experiences, not just the mainstream Hollywood white hero or heroine, can also be activism. Recently, Black filmmakers have followed in the footsteps of visionaries like Black Afrofuturist writer Octavia Butler with box office hits like *Get Out, Black Panther,* and *Sorry to Bother You.* These are just three of many films that are widening cultural representations.

Marches and arts are combined when marchers make signs or create **performance art**. Global activism group Avaaz arranged a demonstration in Washington, DC, on March 13, 2018, in which more than 7,000 pairs of shoes were displayed on the Capitol lawn, one for each child killed by gun violence in the US since the Newtown school shooting in Sandy Hook, CT. Many family members of victims donated shoes, some of them coming to the Capitol personally, including Tom Mauser, who had worn his son Daniel's shoes since he was killed in the shooting at Columbine High School in 1999.

Eve Ensler's "1 Billion Rising" is a mass action campaign organized in 2012 to end violence against women. The "1 Billion" represents the number of women and girls across the globe who will be raped and beaten yearly:

> Every February, we rise—in countries across the world—to show our local communities and the world what one billion looks like and shine a light on the rampant impunity and injustice that survivors most often face. We rise through dance to express joy and community and celebrate the fact that we have not been defeated by this violence. We rise to show we are determined to create a new kind of consciousness—one where violence will be resisted until it is unthinkable.[39]

Flashmobs, choreographed but unannounced group song and/or dance performances, are informal public events that raise social awareness. They've proven to be powerful ways to draw attention to such issues as water, missing and murdered Indigenous women, and sovereignty, especially when considering that traditional Round Dances, accompanied by song and drum, welcome passersby. In a town near Standing Rock, police even joined in a Round Dance.

Social media is an increasingly important activist venue, partly because you can find community quickly and easily. Another benefit is that those with mobility challenges can participate in ways previously unimaginable. Additionally, because it's less limited by geography, social status, or authority, it can unite across differences.

Of course, social media activism has its drawbacks. One of the primary online communication challenges is how people interact. Just because someone reads and responds to someone with a different viewpoint doesn't mean they do so with an open mind. "Don't feed the trolls" refers to recognizing that insincere and uncivil disagreement and personal attacks don't solve problems. The best evidence won't change someone's mind if they aren't open to hearing it, so, it's better to expend your energy in more productive ways.

One of the biggest limitations of social media is how information is skewed. The power to share information quickly across platforms and geographies can be a drawback too. Judging the accuracy and truthfulness of "viral" information can be difficult. There's also a level of de facto censorship, even on the most open digital platforms. Someone has to make information available online, and the people in charge of those choices have their biases. More important, social media often operates like an echo chamber. Because of confirmation bias (seeking out evidence for what you want to be true and ignoring other possibilities) and the availability heuristic (believing something to be true regardless of its falsity because it feels familiar), people tend to follow those who agree with them and ignore those who don't.

A final challenge of social media is access. While it's easier to upload information online than to share in print, putting materials online still requires resources and access. In her graduate thesis, Christian Pippins, of Texas A&M University-Texarcana, explores that challenge. She writes:

> The current #metoo movement is not the first time that women have spoken out against harassment, inequality, or injustice. The speeches of women like Fannie Lou Hamer, Ella Baker, and Mamie Till Mobley remind us that women of earlier generations and civil rights movements have sacrificed and given their lives to the fight for justice and equality. [. . .] Recovering the voices of these black women forces a modern audience to confront why they have been forgotten or silenced while also considering presence and treatment of diverse voices in the modern #metoo movement.[40]

In researching the stories of earlier activists, Pippins ran into trouble. Sources were available in historical archives but had not been made digitally available online. Working and going to school, Pippins didn't have time or financial resources to travel to personally view the documents. Such obstacles highlight how what we know is always shaped by the information available, and some information is overlooked, inaccessible, hidden, and even censored, as we saw in China's Me Too movement.

Social inequality doesn't persist only because of lack the information; it persists because conveying the importance of information to those who can't or won't acknowledge they're resisting change is hard. Yet it offers the opportunity for change, even when people believe in false information. Social media reveals we need to communicate more effectively and direct our efforts to areas that maximize positive social change.

Direct Action: Marches, Protests, and Voting

Social media's superpower is generating **direct action**. The most obvious form of direct action is the **vote**. Did you know that thousands of people registered to vote at the film *Black Panther*, at the Women's March, and at the March for Our Lives? As 11-year-old Naomi Wadler said at the March for Our Lives, "in seven short years, I will vote."[41]

Grassroots organizing provides crucial support to candidates and legislative issues. Organizers often use digital petitions, letters, and calls to elected officials to demonstrate a collective voice. People also use donation platforms to support their work. In the case of one fundraiser supported by Digital Smoke Signals and #NoDAPL, filmmaker Myron Dewey raised nearly $60,000 from individual and group contributions. Some donated as little as $5 while others, like the Students of Color Environmental Collective from UC Berkeley, donated $762.[42] Dewey's film, *Awake, A Dream from Standing Rock* combines art and education and is now on Netflix.

An extreme form of activism is the **hunger strike**. When a bill in Canada threatened Native lands and waters much as DAPL threatens Standing Rock, Chief Theresa Spence fasted for six weeks: "[h]er hunger strike consisted of a liquid diet of lemon water, medicinal teas, and fish broth—a historical survival diet for indigenous communities facing poverty and food shortages from land loss and colonial policies."[43]

Clearly, all these forms can be combined to powerful affect, and being an activist isn't restricted to marching in protests. There are many ways to participate, and if it's new to you, it's often best to start small and get more involved as you learn. You don't have to be a capital "A" activist to make a meaningful difference in the world. You don't even have to have a Facebook, Twitter, or Snapchat account to read and learn about social media savvy movements like Black Lives Matter, Me Too, or No Dakota Access Pipeline. And whether or not you're part of social media, art and music have historically been a vital part of social movements. Bernice Johnson Reagon did, after all, give her famous coalition talk at a music festival. Academic work is often deeply inspired by and directed toward social change, and with the move to make education more accessible, there are numerous ways to learn, from online TED Talks to free online courses called MOOCs. In the US, reduced or free tuition is available to those 60 years and older. Globally, many countries, like in Scandinavia, have little to no cost for education. If organized education isn't the route you want to go, consider other forms of art activism, like making a film or documentary. Technology now makes it possible to shoot and edit a movie on your own phone.

Many of the most inspiring, long-standing, and change-making movements start with ordinary people joining together to create change. Just think of the 2010 Arab Spring, where dictatorial regimes were toppled because individuals banded together to resist authoritarian control. A key principle to remember when it comes to activism and alliances, however, is that while instances like Arab Spring dramatically changed the Middle Eastern landscape, single actions rarely make sweeping change. More often, social change is slow-going and hard won. And when a radical shift occurs, it's easy to forget it was less likely due to one acute action and more likely a tectonic plate-like shift, where ground that had been subject to building pressure finally gave way. All the pressure applied over time—all the previous actions, and struggles, and movements—combined to make a difference.

Notes

1 "The Racial Divide: Women of Color and White Women." *Red Table Talk by Jada Pinkett Smith*. S1: Ep. 14. Nov. 12, 2018, https://www.facebook.com/redtabletalk/videos/343064719835818/?t=633.

2 "Coalition, n.1." *OED Online*. Oxford University Press. July 2018.

3 Bernice Johnson Reagon. "Coalition Politics: Turning the Century." *Home Girls: A Black Feminist Anthology*. Ed. Barbara Smith. Kitchen Table: Women of Color Press. 1983, pp. 356–368, p. 365.

4 Ibid., p. 363.

5 Ibid., p. 368.

6 Ibid., p. 368.

7 Ibid., p. 366.

8 Melissa Harris-Perry. *Chicago Humanities Festival*. Chicago, IL. Nov. 10, 2016, https://www.youtube.com/watch?v=Wi5RXtHC2Dg.

9 Sarah Grossman. *Othering and Belonging: Expanding the Circle of Human Concern*. Oakland, CA. May 2, 2017; Melissa Harris-Perry Closing Keynote. "The Stories We Tell About Who We Are: Race, Gender, Making American Politics." http://conference.otheringandbelonging.org/melissaperry-keynote/.

10 Meredith Woerner. "Who Started the March? One Woman." *Los Angeles Times*. Jan. 21, 2017, http://www.latimes.com/nation/la-na-pol-womens-march-live-who-started-the-march-one-1485033621-htmlstory.html.

11 Farah Stockman. "Women's March on Washington Opens Contentious Dialogues About Race." *The New York Times*. Jan. 9, 2017, https://www.nytimes.com/2017/01/09/us/womens-march-on-washington-opens-contentious-dialogues-about-race.html.

12 Ibid.

13 Carmen Perez. "Our People." *The Gathering for Justice.* http://www.gather ingforjustice.org/carmenperez.

14 Ernesto Mercer. Facebook. Nov. 11, 2018.

15 "Women's March Statement Condemns Anti-Semitism While Standing with Leaders Linda Sarsour and Tamika Mallory." *Jewish Telegraphic Daily.* Nov. 12, 2018, https://www.jta.org/2018/11/12/news-opinion/womens-march-state ment-condemns-anti-semitism-while-standing-with-leaders-linda-sarsour-and-tamika-mallory.

16 Shirley Halperin. "Here Are the 10 Activists Who Shared the Oscars Stage with Common and Andra Day." *Variety.com. Variety.* Mar. 4, 2018, https://variety.com/2018/film/news/oscars-activists-common-andra-day-stand-up-for-something-performance-1202716939/.

17 Booth Moore. "Women's Rights Activists to Walk Golden Globes Red Carpet with Actresses." *The Hollywood Reporter.* Jan 7, 2018, https://www.hollywoodreporter.com/news/golden-globes-2018-activists-walk-red-carpet-actresses-1072300.

18 "Open Letter from Time's Up." *The New York Times.* Jan. 1, 2018, https://www.nytimes.com/interactive/2018/01/01/arts/02women-letter.html.

19 Ibid.

20 Emily Witt. "Launching a National Gun Control Coalition, The Parkland Teens Meet Chicago's Young Activists." *The New Yorker.* June 26, 2018, https://www.newyorker.com/news/dispatch/launching-a-national-gun-control-coalition-the-parkland-teens-meet-chicagos-young-activists.

21 Maggie Astor and Karl Russell. "After Parkland, a New Surge in State Gun Control Laws." *New York Times.* Dec. 14, 2018, https://www.nytimes.com/interactive/2018/12/14/us/politics/gun-control-laws.html.

22 Farah Stockman. "Women's March on Washington Opens Contentious Dialogues About Race." *New York Times.* Jan. 9, 2017, https://www.nytimes.com/2017/01/09/us/womens-march-on-washington-opens-contentious-dialogues-about-race.html.

23 Tim Wise. "Guilt or Responsibility." *Michigan Roundtable for Diversity and Inclusion.* Nov. 4, 2010, https://www.youtube.com/watch?v=XhOh_EGe41Y.

24 Ibid.

25 Tarana Burke. "Me Too is a Movement, Not a Moment." *TEDWomen 2018.* Nov. 29, 2018, https://www.ted.com/talks/tarana_burke_me_too_is_a_movement_not_a_moment/transcript?language=en.

26 Ibid.

27 Ibid.

28 "Academia." *Merriam-Webster.com.* Merriam Webster. Feb. 6, 2019, https://www.merriam-webster.com/dictionary/academia.

29 Eric Roberson. Interview with Tiffany D. Loftin. March for Our Lives. Washington, DC. *Facebook post.* Mar. 25, 2018, https://www.facebook.com/BlueErroSoul/videos/10155587542398250/?t=32.

30 Ibid.

31 "The Dinner Party by Judy Chicago." Exhibitions. Elizabeth A. Sackler Center for Feminist Art. *Brooklyn Museum.* https://www.brooklynmuseum.org/exhibitions/dinner_party.

32 Judy Chicago. *The Dinner Party: A Symbol of Our Heritage.* Anchor-Doubleday. 1979, p. 56.

33 Ibid., p. 56.

34 Holland Cotter. "China's Female Artists Quietly Emerge." *The New York Times.* July 30, 2008, https://www.nytimes.com/2008/07/30/arts/design/30arti.html.

35 Monica Merlin. "Women Artists in Contemporary China." *XIAO LU. Tate Modern.* 2013–2014, https://www.tate.org.uk/research/research-centres/tate-research-centre-asia/women-artists-contemporary-china/xiao-lu.

36 Ibid.

37 Jordan Chariton. "Standing Rock Indigenous Activist: You Don't See Me." *The Young Turks.* Sept. 11, 2017, https://www.youtube.com/watch?v=eSEKLw4ejPI.

38 Amy Goodman. "Dakota Access Pipeline Company Attacks Native American Protesters with Dogs & Pepper Spray." *Democracy Now.* Sept. 3, 2016, https://www.youtube.com/watch?v=kuZcx2zEo4k.

39 "What is 1 Billion Rising?" *OneBillionRising.org.* Last modified 2019, https://www.onebillionrising.org/about/campaign/one-billion-rising/.

40 Christian Pippins. "Black Women's Rhetoric and the Civil Rights Movement." Abstract. *Pathways Research Symposium.* Nov. 1–2, 2018, http://pathways.wtamu.edu/christian-pippins-texas-am-university-texarkana/.

41 "11-Year-Old Naomi Wadler's Speech at the March for Our Lives." *NBC News.* Mar. 24, 2018, https://www.youtube.com/watch?v=C5ZUDImTIQ8.

42 Myron Dewey. *Gofundme.com.* Last modified Apr. 2018, https://www.gofundme.com/waterissacred.

43 Leanne Simpson. "Think Chief Spence Is On a 'Liquid Diet'? I Think You're Ignorant." *HuffPost.com.* Jan. 20, 2013, https://www.huffingtonpost.ca/leanne-simpson/fish-broth-chief-spence_b_2517450.html?ec_carp=%207148420245016630599.

Conclusion: Feminism Is

The intertwining of activists and movements drive feminist thought and action. We hope your travels through this book have revealed the importance of these connections. We conclude this journey by weaving together information and first-person voices to summarize key points that may help you frame your own thoughts and choose your own actions. This is how we began, and similar to what you'll encounter in the world when you have conversations, online or in person, can help change perceptions and shape joint efforts.

By now, you have the tools to think through what you'll find here. As in Part One, narratives reveal how our experiences interrelate and how we can help each other. As in Part Two, narratives educate us about how different cultures and philosophies clash, change, and blend. Thinking about what each of us can do and where to put our energy recalls internal and external pressures discussed in Part Three. We are also reminded that many movements that began in previous centuries are ongoing and continue to change as conditions change. Making nimble, sensitive changes calls on our learning about intersectionality in Part Four. And, as we learned in Part Five, coalitions flourish when we put intersectional theory into action. We also learned how to appreciate the challenges and benefits of coalitions, how to personally apply our energy and skills, and how to care for ourselves and feminist allies for the long haul.

These final voices and theory offer a vision of feminist principles. We hope you'll add your observations, and that your understanding of this overview of feminist thought and action contributes to your decision-making about what you *can* do: what you want to study, do, and be in the world. We hope it helps you reclaim your power and use it.

Feminism Is: Reclaiming Our Power

Remember John Trudell's distinction between authority and power? Authority can be imposed by some over others, but it can never completely destroy a being's intrinsic power. "Being" refers not only to humans but to all creatures as well as winds, waters, and other environmental elements. Though it can cause harm, human authority can't erase the power of our birthright connectedness as co-inhabitants of Earth.

Throughout history, individuals combined their power for social change. We've examined how diverse groups united in 2016–2018 to make changes to US governmental authority. Just after the 2016 election, Trump approved the Keystone pipeline. But a record number of voters elected a record number of women and women of color in the 2018 midterms: to seats in local, state, and national governance, and including the first two Native American women in Congress and dozens of Native Americans in county seats. Those elected were often overt rebuttals of previous policy. For example, an Arikara woman, Ruth Anne Buffalo, was elected over the North Dakota man who sponsored a bill restricting Native American voting rights. Part of Buffalo's success came from crowdfunding that supported workarounds to obtain the newly required IDs for Native Americans, who then voted in record numbers.

This election instantly changed regional and national conversations and affected ongoing decisions. Ruth Buffalo co-introduced a bill that requires the state attorney general's Human Trafficking Commission to train law enforcement on effective response to reports of missing or murdered Indigenous people.[1] Congresswoman Haaland (Laguna Pueblo, NM) immediately called for a federal investigation into missing and murdered Indigenous women, something long called for by #IdleNoMore and #NativeLivesMatter. Many such disappearances are associated with the "man camps" housing pipeline workers. A few days after the 2018 election, a federal judge issued an injunction that stalled the pipelines, stating Trump violated federal law.[2] These are the kinds of results that activism can generate when we reclaim our power.

Feminism Is: Based on Varied Experiences

We've established that our experiences vary—sometimes personally, sometimes politically. We claim our collective power, when each of us, one-by-one, finds inspiration and a sense of connection. Just as individual experiences were a good starting point, they are a good place to return.

Numbers Do Make a Difference
by Menoukha Robin Case

Because I'm 70 years old, ageism is among my concerns. On an individual level, I wonder if I can ever afford to retire—who knows what'll happen to social security, Medicare, and so on. On a community level, I have relatives and friends of multiple ethnicities, sexualities, and religions. Our current political conditions affect everyone and everything I love and care about, whether via erosion of rights or ecosystems. On a global level, I keep hearing about shorter and shorter timelines for successfully turning around climate change. The most recent date is 2030, which is in most of our lifetimes. All of these levels can be addressed through engagement with national politics.

On a national level, I think about the decades my parents experienced collective modes of caring for each other, including social security, Medicare, and laws to protect workers such as child labor laws, overtime laws, and unemployment compensation. Few are aware of what it took to push FDR to promote these programs. Dr. Richard Wolff explains that in response to the Great Depression (1929–1939), millions of people organized in various allied ways. Many unionized to improve working conditions, but about 25% of working-age Americans (around 12 million people) were unemployed.[3] Both unionists and unemployed workers, inspired by the Russian Revolution, proposed radical changes to our political system. Many of them began to work across race and ethnicity lines, even though segregation was still in force. They also began to work across genders, since that line had been breached when women worked in factories during World War II (Rosie the Riveter). Many people with various ideas of how to improve things worked together and organized politically.

These collective allied movements led FDR to raise the Russian Revolution as a specter to convince wealthy individuals and corporations what could happen if they didn't compromise. For those who don't recall, just a decade before our Great Depression the people of Russia, inspired by Karl Marx-proposed fiscal equality, overthrew their Czarist rulers and worked to equalize peasants and former nobles. Because it was a revolution and not a government-driven change, the nobles lost everything, often even their lives. FDR convinced America's "noble" class (corporate magnates) that it was a case of give more or lose it all as massive waves of protest all across the US gathered into a gargantuan tsunami. The wealthy agreed to pay more taxes, sometimes as high as 90%. These high taxes didn't destroy them, as evidenced by the wealthy heirs and robust corporations still active today, thriving despite that change. Economists theorize corporations benefit from the majority of people having a stable income, because otherwise few could afford to buy their goods and services. The taxes FDR instituted funded all the programs noted above as well as the Public Works Administration, where half of the unemployed found jobs in 34,000 projects. They built or repaired roads, bridges, airports, dams, hospitals, and schools. They spent their earnings, and our economy recovered.

Because of historical conditions, my feminism differs from my mother's, which differs from her mother's. Earlier generations suffered greatly before people were able or willing to unite in large enough numbers to matter. This is why it's important to me to choose a line of action in coalition with other groups. Sheer numbers do make a difference.

Elizabeth Beamer Craig describes finding feminism in the aftermath of the period described above. Her experience demonstrates an evolution of white feminist perspective extending beyond gender to include understanding of race and sexuality.

Elizabeth Beamer Craig

I Am a Feminist

Feminism, from the *Encyclopædia Britannica*: (1) The theory supporting the political, economic, and social equality of the sexes; (2) organized activity on behalf of women's rights and interests.

I was born in 1946, part of the baby boomer generation, when, because of World War II, women had more opportunities to join the workforce. Men and women were eager to have earning power to make their lives and their children's lives better and more comfortable than those who had lived before them. Both of my parents were able to get college educations. Even though my mother was born before women could vote and both came from lower economic means, both my parents had strong mothers who instilled in them a love of learning and the discipline to work hard and have big goals. They believed in education as a means to a better, more financially secure life. My mother, who has always been a force to be reckoned with, wanted a family, but she also wanted that college degree that would allow her to pursue a job that she loved as a teacher.

I grew up with two brothers and lots of cousins, both boys and girls. I had strong female grandmothers and aunts as well as supportive uncles who always expressed confidence in my abilities to achieve whatever I sought. My father told me always to reach for excellence. I enjoyed competition and knew I could be a winner regardless of male or female opponents. I always considered education and opportunity to be within my grasp. In short, I grew up naïve and unaware that other girls did not have the same opportunities. I was largely unaware of my black sisters, never seeing or coming in contact with them in my hometown. I did not understand bigotry. I was clueless about diversity.

I have always loved being female. I loved receiving male attention and knowing that I had the power to use my femaleness to procreate and create new life. I never hesitated to embrace and enjoy the power of being female in the sense of becoming a wife and a mother, and creating a family. It seemed, at the time, more valuable than joining the struggle to advance women's rights. But even as a 1960s college student, I considered myself to be a feminist. I just did not consider myself an activist. I did not feel compelled to burn my bra or march in the streets. I would rather flirt with attractive men or beat them on the tennis court or outsmart them in a math class. And then I felt content to raise my children. I did not truly understand the history of male domination until I was much older. I took it for granted. It has always been that way, so why or how could it change? I thought my individual circumstances were the norm. I now attribute a lot of that to not realizing the privilege I was afforded. I was comfortable. I was happy. But at the same time, I raised my children to educate themselves about the changing culture of the times. I pushed them to explore with open minds the new ideas coming with a new diverse era.

I am female, therefore I am a feminist. That is what I think and feel. I am concerned with all aspects of our political and social world that wants to control my thoughts and my body. I abhor men trying to tell me they will decide about my private concerns. I want and deserve the same freedom, the same rights, and the same responsibilities as all citizens in our country.

I am now shocked to look back at the history of this world, and in particular to the history of the USA, and realize how women have been seen, how they have been used, how they have been so disregarded until really just the end of the 20th century. We are not second-rate citizens. We are worthy of all the opportunities for advancement in education, the political arena, and in corporate America as our male counterparts. We should be partners, not adversaries. We should contribute and not be blocked by antiquated norms that have expired and were never true to begin with.

I now wonder about how although my awareness of injustice came at an early age, it took a while to consciously process. When I was ten years old, I lived for two years in Colombia, South America, and for the first time personally witnessed the disparity between rich and poor. I saw rigid social norms between men and women. I saw brown faces instead of the white faces I was used to. I was exposed to a new way of looking at my life and the conditions in which others lived. Spending time in Colombia as a child somehow speaks louder to me now than it did even at the time. I am appalled at the plight of women across the globe. Women are treated abysmally in so many places in the world today and it breaks my heart to think of how Black and Native American women have been treated right here in the US. It is tragic and it is not right. There is so much work to be done.

Sometimes, the work comes to you at an unexpected time, in unexpected ways. I had no understanding of the gay community, for instance, until my son and my daughter came "out" in 1998. Before then, I thought I knew no one gay. I did not know about or understand my children's struggle with their identities. It took their personal courage to come forward for me to start my own journey of understanding. And because of them, it became personal. I started to question myself. What did I really know about homosexuality? Where did my thoughts about homosexuality come from? Why did the prevalent social norms of the time mandate homosexuality as wrong? What caused sexual preference in the first place? It took me no time at all to accept what I probably already knew.

I really liked gay people. My children were smart and honorable and decent and morally strong. They were creative and interesting and fun. They were loving. I had tried to instill in my children the idea that "the truth will set you free," and here they were, willing to stand up and say "this is who I am, this is my truth." They understood that being true to themselves was the most important validation of their worth, as individuals and citizens. I found no fault in them for loving someone of the same sex. As a mother, all that mattered to me was that they had happy and fulfilled personal relationships so they could live productive lives. So I joined P-FLAG to find other parents of gay children. I found many new friends who like me wanted to support their children. I also found that I knew more gay people than I knew. I just didn't know they were gay.

My daughter asked me what made me different from some parents who cannot accept their gay children, but I cannot fathom it. Maybe it comes down to the ability to open our minds and hearts to new ideas and feelings. We have to open up. We have to change. We have to throw away the rubbish ideas of old religions and old customs. We have to hold our government accountable for the protection of rights for all of its citizens. We have to educate ourselves. It all comes down to the truth and how we see it.

Feminism is a good thing. It is a positive way to think about living and moving forward, together. It is a legacy. I am proud to be supported on the shoulders of my grandmothers and my aunts, and especially by my mother. They taught me by both word and deed that I was just as important as any man. They helped create the foundation in me to see the world as it could be, not just as it was, to accept the challenges and responsibilities that come my way so others, like my daughter and sons, will too. Feminism is for the proud, strong, determined women, and men, of the future. We must break down the old stereotypes. We must insist on a new way.

Even if a person was born into a feminist family, multiple positions and experiences can make feminism fraught and complex. Raised in both Jewish and Native American communities, Stephanie Sellers learned two very different ways of thinking and feeling. She found that intellectual principles are not enough to guide actions; in fact, intellect alone can obscure the heart of human concerns. Her narrative, like Beamer Craig's, reminds us that to act across differences and heal cultural dysfunctions we must engage with heart.

Stephanie A. Sellers

Walking in a Burning Fire

At a delicate age, I came to the understanding that the world I had been born to was set up in conflict between girls and boys and that to be a girl meant I needed to fight. I learned that girls were not supposed to beat up boys, though, especially when the girl had very long braids and also enjoyed ballet dancing and pink tights. This ideological conflict never stopped me from punching because I recognized that shutting down my anger would never protect me or anyone I loved. I had a vulnerable younger brother to shield who discovered the power of saying to his assailants "If you hit me, I will tell my sister." When I wasn't bloodying the noses of neighborhood bullies, I was burying the round face of my weeping brother into my fourth grade bosom, trying to assure him that school really could be fun. As a child, my career as a fighter began strictly out of Love, and thus began my identity as a feminist.

My feminist identity took on a darker tone as I grew into adolescence and awakened to the human world around me on television, radio, in the adult relationships I saw, and, most importantly, in books. At the age of 11, my mother gave me a copy of Marilyn French's book *The Women's Room* and within those desolate pages I learned that as a girl I was to hate men, to be wary of them, and to expect suffering when I grew up. Mother believed in education, and within that book was her core teaching to me about being a woman: expect disappointment and loss—personal, societal, eternal. I came to be proud of the slogans of the 1970s from popular culture like "The more I know about men, the better I like my dog." I sang all the words to "Delta Dawn" by Helen Reddy and blended it seamlessly into what it meant to be a woman: I would grow up to be alone, waiting for love that would never come, like the character Mira from French's book, and hence I should never care about men who are sources of pain. As a child-feminist, I proudly rooted for Billy Jean King and remember the thrill of Ali's "Rumble in the Jungle"—both were fighters, like me. I intervened on groups of adults without batting an eye when I saw persecution of an animal, like a horde of grown-ups at the seashore digging shells off thrashing horseshoe crabs. To me, this is what it meant to be a feminist: being responsible for the oppressed and the bullied. Everywhere I looked around me as a child of the second-wave, I saw the pain of women.

At 11 years old, though, I was unable to understand that it was mother, not a man in my future, who I was already waiting for and who would ultimately never arrive to love me. As a budding feminist, I could never have considered that my greatest battle for equity would be bitterly lost and make my efforts of intervening on behalf of the powerless futile attempts at saving myself from my own reality of powerlessness. That lesson would come in adulthood, when I finally realized that no amount of social justice work can make a mother love her daughter. As a child, every evening I waited expectantly for my working-class father to return from work and he did, night after night at 5:00 pm for 17 years, and when I was young I ran into his arms. As a young child I fled to him in illness and injury, and referred to my mother only by her first name. When I refused to let her dress me at three years old, I had already discerned that women would fail me in life, not men, but the world of feminism I would later inhabit claimed otherwise.

The problem with the middle-class feminism I learned in childhood was that my primary source of love was from my father: a man, the very reason, I was told, that I needed feminism. I saved coins to buy tomato plants, and he beamed with pride. I read stories to him from my *Carl Sandberg Treasury* that he could not read himself and he bragged. When mother's abuse escalated and I ran away at ten years old, my father found me. I will never forget the terror on his face as he ran (*ran*) to me; will never forget his tears soaking my hair as he sobbed onto my head. But I had to return, to go back home to the feminist. I was yet too young to understand the idea of being a target for someone else's rage and that I would pay for running away, that I was already paying for dressing myself since I was three. I was still too young to understand the anguish of a mother who was hated for being female and born into a culture that was bent on cutting her down at every turn. I didn't yet understand the devastation she felt when she reproduced herself by giving birth to me, unplanned and unwanted, deepening the spiral of abuse from her family that would never end. At 11, I could not comprehend the practice of retaliation that would subtly escalate for decades until mother totally cut me out of her life and expected everyone in the family to do the same. To me, this behavior was the pinnacle of anti-feminism, and I learned it from the first feminist I ever knew. White middle-class feminism never permeated the armor of mother's trauma that would allow her to love herself and eventually me. Feminism would offer me a lot in life, but never a path to healing the lack of attachment and bond between mother and me because I was born a girl, like her. In the end, feminism failed to save our relationship, though it clearly saved both of us from something worse.

Despite mother's understandable allegiance to the brand of feminism from *The Women's Room*, I was too young to intellectually grasp that social beliefs we argue for, slogans we wear, and protests we participate in can have little to do with the way a woman actually treats other women, especially her daughter. I have a bitter chuckle at so many women's "Resist" slogan on their Facebook pages that have cropped up since Trump was elected: slogans do nothing until we start resisting what is destroying us in our own lives. That's difficult work. That's painful. That's the work we are all running from: personal insight and the battles within our own lives that might lead us to dismantling everything we believed was permanent. Feminism as a political platform can be a doorway to healing, but only if the feminist is willing to walk through the burning fire of her own wounds as a girl first. What does western culture offer women to accomplish that healing? Where do we turn? The personal may be political and vice versa, but I learned in adulthood that a woman can say she is a feminist and still hate herself as a woman and function from male-centric, patriarchal values. Mary Daly called them Fembots. My mother took me to hear Daly speak when I was 25 and afterward we sat in the Lincoln Diner in Gettysburg, Pennsylvania, and smiled at each other. Supposedly, mother and I were both believers, united in our commitment to the right of all women to be treated with dignity and respect. It sounded great coming from her lips and lured me like carrot on a stick to unrelentingly believe that, one day, her beliefs would be applied to me personally. She did my brother's laundry until he was married and told me I was worthless because I don't make enough money. Close range. Point blank. Next sentence: "Did you hear on NPR about how badly that national corporation treats women? Outrageous!" My mother was a tough teacher, but, by god, did I learn.

Because of my upbringing with white middle-class feminism from my mother and the psychological bond that affirmed my inherent worth as a girl from my father, I became an activist at a young age. I marched for women's rights down Constitution Avenue in Washington, DC, and wrote letters to editors of newspapers about the tyranny of homecoming queens and breast enlargement surgery for teen girls. I was already comfortable with conflict and being resoundingly unapproved of and unpopular among my peer group, seeking other fringe people like myself as my community. In every action, I could see my father's silent wink of approval and hear my elderly great-auntie kvetching about those who would speak against me. I signed petitions, made posters, and volunteered in women's shelters answering the hotline. I delivered Christmas gifts to the poor and told the drunken boyfriends of women friends to shove it when they tried to pull their shit with me. As a young adult-feminist, the worst behaviors of men became glue that fused mother and I together and overshadowed a lifetime of her contempt for me. Feminism turned out to be the only bond we ever shared. This is what feminism meant at this point in my life—having a common enemy. In my 20s, I stopped bloodying noses and learned how to use my hands to fight other battles in the ancient war against women. My mother is the person who brought me to that work.

After my formal education at university, I had training, knowledge, and credentials to back up my feminist beliefs, which I began to see were perceived as increasingly radical in this male-privileged world. Men told me to "tone it down"; women said "oh, you're one of them." I had to learn that people who were hostile to me on-sight often pegged me (correctly) as a non-compliant woman, and this was intolerable to them. Increasingly, I began to see that what was only normal to me was considered outrageous to others. My mother was proud of her feminist daughter, as long as I minded my place at the margins of her life. Then, two things happened that changed the course of my life and my brand of feminism: I spent more time with my local Native American and Jewish communities, and I met the man I would marry. I learned ancient teachings of my ancestors and participated in ceremonies. I learned about Mother Earth and Lilith. I was healed in sweat lodges and sang in women-only havdalah ceremonies, with a woman rabbi leading. I received Love and inclusion without having to fight. I pushed my hands into garden dirt and into the soft warmth of bread dough in my own kitchen. The man I married was also born a fighter, so we worked together for social justice. We organized a rally on the square of our hometown to protest a judge's light sentencing of a husband who had stun-gunned his wife 27 times and then beat her. Years later, we marched around that same square in a show of support for

Muslim and immigrant neighbors. We went back to DC with the Nations to protest sexual violence against Indigenous women and the building of pipelines on Native lands. My Welsh protestant husband wore a yarmulke for Sabbath as I prayed in Hebrew in our little cabin in the forest. I scrubbed the kitchen floor on my knees, baked him cakes, and finished my doctoral degree. He nursed me when I was sick, listened to my poetry, and built me a house. I loved every minute of life as a young wife, just as I love my life now as a middle-aged feminist married to a man for 24 years. I am home at last in the world we made together with our many communities. This is how I do feminism, and at its core, it is based in Love and connection, not hate, fear, and loneliness.

I am never going to be Mira or Delta Dawn, not because I have a husband, but because I have woman-valuing ancestral roots, multiple healthy communities, and an unshakeable belief in my own ability to cultivate a meaningful life. This is feminism to me: confidence in being a woman. This is what western culture denies women, and attacks on gender are simply one way to keep all people silent, divided, and full of rage, fear, and hate. Though I found my way out of the personal conflict of my childhood, the problem I had with mother never went away. I am a girl, like her, and in her world happiness was not an option for me. She had raised me well and modeled so many good things about being human, but feminism alone could not transcend the traumas she endured as a girl and woman. Without that transcendence, I could only be her split-apart hated self, her source of every projection of anguish patriarchy dumped on her. Isn't this what the core archetype of Woman is in western culture—an object of terror and the antithesis of a patriarchal framework? Loving me was too transgressive for mother, just as a woman president terrifies many Americans and the Goddess makes the Vatican shudder.

Most Americans' women ancestors were targeted for sexual violence in wars, burned at the stake, politically displaced due to empire, and enslaved for generations. This means that, in addition to the suffering and oppression that women face today and that communities of color, LTQ people, and Indigenous nations face at much higher rates, we are all carrying genetic memories of terror in our DNA for being women. Legally, our grandmothers just got the right to vote and the ability to own property several decades ago. All women in America know a woman who has been raped or beaten, in addition to the violence we have experienced in our own lives. As American women, we have a lot of deeply painful baggage to overcome, and this baggage shows up in our mothering, our professional lives, and our personal friendships with women. When I said "No" to my mother at age three, I was rejecting *her* pain's legacy in my life, but of course, that legacy is far greater and more powerful than either of us. I had hoped we could outrun it together and bask in a different legacy that unites women, that allows for a greater understanding of what women's relationships can be, can become. Now, I am left to do that work without her, still hoping that at least I will someday feel a bit of the bond that I caught glimmers of at times in our laughter together as mother and daughter. We had 40 difficult years together, but now that we are parted, the pain of my trying to breach her misogyny can stop. Before I could walk, she was unwittingly training me to survive being her daughter. For that courageous act, I can only thank her for what made me a feminist. My father's love kept me going and gave me gumption, but my mother's rejection made me invincible.

Feminism Is: Intergenerational

Because of the historic trauma, Sellers describes and continuing tensions between Western and Indigenous principles, activism is ongoing, which means it's intergenerational. When Elder and youth activists of today work well together, they either start with good relationships or do something like the critical work of "walking through fire." People of different ages work together well when each person's power, in Trudell's sense, is respected and when authority is circulated to address each particular issue. Perhaps this is why Indigenous activists, young, old, and in between, have worked effectively together on a variety of causes.

Elder Josephine Mandamin is an early Water activist, who led a ceremonial walk around each of the Great Lakes, accompanied by people of all ages and ethnicities. Mandamin, from Wiikwemkoong Unceded Territory on Manitoulin Island in Canada, is a member of the Three Fires Midewiwin Lodge. Eddie Benton Banai, Chief Elder of Three Fires, said in 2000 that due to pollution, "water will cost as much as gold by 2030. What are we going to do about it?" In Anishinaabe tradition, Water is sacred and women are Water Keepers. It's the grandmothers' role to lead the community in praying for and protecting Water. In answer to the Chief, Mandamin, as a Grandmother, walked nearly 17,000 miles between 2003 and 2017. She received the Lieutenant Governor's Ontario Heritage Award for Excellence in Conservation in 2016.

The following *Water Song* by Elder Doreen Day expresses the heart that motivated the walkers:

> Nibi, Gizaagi'igo (*Nibi, Gee-zaw-gay-i-go*) - Water, we love you.
> Gimiigwechiwenimigo (*Gee-mee-gwe-chi-way-nay-mi-go*) - We thank you.
> Gizhawenimigo (*Gee-zhaw-way-nay-mi-go*) - We respect you.[4]

Idle No More, founded in 2012 by four young women, also began with the purpose of Water protection. The impetus was a Canadian bill that deregulated and polluted waterways via mining, tar sands extraction, and pipelines across sovereign Native lands. Thousands of people from all over the world joined Idle No More, including Elders like Chief Theresa Spence and Winona LaDuke. LaDuke is co-founder of Honor the Earth, today directed by Tara Houska (Zhaabowekwe). Idle No More also inspired youth like Ta'Kaiya Blaney (Tla A'min First Nation), who began her to work as a Water Protector in 2012 at the age of 11 with her song *Shallow Waters*. She, too, has inspired many young people.

Youth in groups like ReZpect Our Water and The International Indigenous Youth Council were the impetus for the 2015–2017 #NoDAPL stand by Water Protectors on the Standing Rock reservation.[5] Support was global, and for over two years, tens of thousands of people went to the Standing Rock reservation. At any one time, the camp hosted up to 5,000 people. Attendants comment on the experience of sharing and caring, of living in peace without need for policing. Case's grandson, Justin Smith (Ojibwe) said he cried happy tears every day because he experienced his grandfather's stories about Mino Bimaadiziwin (A Good Way of Life) in action.

#NoDAPL started when a youth group ran all the way from North Dakota to Washington DC carrying a petition with 350,000 signatures regarding the pipeline. This sparked the movement that drew tens of thousands of Water Protectors to North Dakota and initiated more waves of water protection throughout the Americas. Tokata Iron Eyes, a tribal member, was 13 years old in 2016 when the US government initially announced that they wouldn't issue a permit for the pipeline.

> "You helped start this movement, didn't you?" Social activist and author Naomi Klein asked Iron Eyes . . . "This entire movement was brought up by the youth," . . . Iron Eyes told Klein. "It just started so small and then this entire camp was built . . . the easement for DAPL was denied . . . [I feel] like I got my future back."[6]

Youth like Iron Eyes were supported by grandparents and parents like Tokata's father, Chase Iron Eyes, a lawyer who co-founded the Lakota People's Law Project and the news website *Last Real Indians*. Other Elders, like LaDonna Brave Bull Allard, helped establish and sustain the Water Protector camp on her own land on reservation. The youngsters were the spark and the Elders endured attacks and arrests to protect them so they could carry the future.

While few mainstream journalists covered events at Standing Rock, some, like *The Young Turks*, sent young reporters to cover the story. They may have been inspired by Elder journalist Amy Goodman of *Democracy Now*, who put herself on the frontlines and endured arrest to get the story out. A wide array of communities stood with the water protectors, from young US soldiers to older Veterans who offered a formal protest for the Armed Forces' part in Native genocide, from older celebrities like Jane Fonda to younger actors like Shailene Woodley.

Native Lives Matter (on Twitter @NLMcoalition) and media like *Last Real Indian, Indigenous Women Rising*, and *Digital Smoke Signals* grew out of Idle No More. Because so many First Peoples involved in Idle No More are from tribes in which women are Water Keepers, the movement grew to address #MMIW (Missing and Murdered Indigenous Women), something concerning all tribes due to the wildly disproportionate number of Indigenous women attacked and lost in both the US and Canada.[7] These groups continue to inspire younger people like Christine Nobiss, co-founder of *Seeding Sovereignty*.

Activism in many communities relies on good intergenerational relationships.

Angela Davis (1944–) was born "in the 'Dynamite Hill' area of Birmingham, Alabama . . . name[d] because so many African American homes [there] . . . had been bombed over the years by the Klu Klux Klan." She joined the civil rights movement in response to the 6th Street Baptist Church bombing and was active in political groups in the 1960s, beginning with the Communist Party's work for economic justice and Black Panthers' community support programs. A scholar and educator, she became a UCLA professor of philosophy in 1969.[8] She currently focuses on the school to prison pipeline and has written many books that have inspired thousands of activists.

Maxine Waters, fondly called Auntie Maxine by Black communities to denote her status as an Elder and relative, has been a US Representative from California since 1991. She stood on the forefront of political change for over 40 years. She served on six Congressional committees and chaired the Congressional Black Caucus and Out of Iraq Caucus. Her concerns have always been global. When she was a California assemblywoman, she worked toward divestment from South Africa in protest of apartheid, a Dutch-Afrikaans word meaning "apartness." These are just a few highlights of Representative Waters' groundbreaking career.

After the 2016 presidential election, she continued to speak out in a no-nonsense style, calling our 45th president "a bully, an egotistical maniac, a liar and someone who did not need to be President"[9] and "the most deplorable person I've ever met in my life"[10] and called for his impeachment. A final straw (though there was more hay to come) was the separation and imprisonment of children of asylum-seekers. At a 2018 Keep Families Together rally, she called them "our children," again defining us as global citizens. She urged us to speak out too:

> Members of your cabinets have been booed out of restaurants, who have protesters taking up at their house who say "no peace, no sleep" . . . let's make sure we show up wherever we have to show up, and if you see anybody from that cabinet in a restaurant, in a department store, in a gasoline station, you get out and you create a crowd, and you push back on them, and you tell them they're not welcome anymore, anywhere.[11]

Waters pointed out that as a Black woman, she was well aware of the history of the slavery auction block that separated children from parents.

She may also have been aware that public declarations holding men accountable carries on a powerful African women's tradition described in the Nigerian Women's War and the Liberian Women's Movement.

The president called her a "low IQ person,"[12] called on Congress to censure her, and demanded that she resign. Death threats followed and protestors showed up at her house, but Auntie Maxine stands strong and continues to inspire younger generations of lawmakers such as Lucy McBath. As Yara Shahidi wrote in *Time* magazine,

> Auntie Maxine, has made my generation proud to be nieces and nephews. She is adored and admired by people who care about social justice and is oh so eloquent in letting the world, particularly the white men of Congress who dare test her acumen, know that she is not here for any nonsense.[13]

Davis, Waters, and many others are part of the long heritage of Black women leading the way in resistance, fights for rights, and feminist thinking. They helped inspire the young founders of Black Lives Matter, a group bringing us all awareness of unjustified killings of Black people of all ages.

Feminism Is: Intersectional

#BlackLivesMatter maintains an intersectional, inclusive approach while focusing on one specific issue. It was founded in 2013 after George Zimmerman, who murdered Black teenager Trayvon Martin, was acquitted. The founders are Opal Tometi, who is Nigerian, and Patrice Cullors and Alicia Garza, who are queer. BLM's "Guiding Principles" reflect Black feminism: Intergenerational, Diversity, Collective Value, Empathy, Loving Engagement, Restorative Justice, Globalism, Queer and Transgender Affirming.[14] If you visit their website, though they don't use the term feminist, you'll see a page called "Herstory," a word coined by feminists, and one of their hashtags, #SayHerName, refers to Black women killed by police. BLM foregrounds being "Unapologetically Black" and supports Black Villages, Black Women, and Black Families, much like womanists. Their statement about "What We Believe" echoes that of the Combahee River Collective:

> Our continued commitment to liberation for all Black people means we are continuing the work of our ancestors and fighting for our collective freedom because it is our duty.
>
> Every day, we recommit to healing ourselves and each other, and to co-creating alongside comrades, allies, and family a culture where each person feels seen, heard, and supported.
>
> We acknowledge, respect, and celebrate differences and commonalities.
>
> We work vigorously for freedom and justice for Black people and, by extension, all people.[15]

BLM's inclusion of allies reminds non-Black people to do the work of reflexivity. They address racism as a specific intersectional problem that affects people of diverse genders, ages, and origins in different ways, reminding us that any one issue affects women differently. Anamaria Ross, a women's health scholar, explains how even something as natural as breast-feeding can have varied meanings and effects.

Breastfeeding Activism as Feminism
by Anamaria Iosif Ross

Why is breastfeeding advocacy feminist activism? Because all people who bear children need to be able to achieve healthy futures. Persons of diverse genders may bear, birth, and breastfeed babies as well as nourish and nurture children toward healthier futures: women of all ages, nonbinary persons, transgender men, bio-typical men, or anyone in-between. Is breastfeeding a right or a privilege? Is it more favored by the poor or the rich? Is it a source of daily comfort or stress? Breastfeeding and nurturing babies and children entails culture-bound beliefs and norms. Like most human needs, newborn care is embedded in traditions, social relations, and power struggles.

As mammals, we would have never survived without nursing our newborns. In many societies, babies commonly nursed for two to six years. This has been represented as "backwards" or "primitive." In medieval times, peasant women breastfed the babies of aristocrats along with their own babies. Not breastfeeding was only an option for the wealthy. Breastfeeding became a contested cultural practice and ironically, nowadays it is strongly associated with education, privilege, and upper middle-class status.

Aggressive marketing from formula companies, the medicalization of birth, and the dominance of male health providers contributed to the idea that artificial feeding is scientific progress. Women were strapped to beds to give birth flat on their backs in a hospital setting where men were in charge, and women's knowledge and wisdom were discounted. They were told that manufactured infant formula was equivalent to breast milk and that breastfeeding was unnecessary. Millions of western women aspiring to modernity, personal freedom, and equal opportunity in the workplace turned away from breastfeeding in pursuit of reproductive choice and self-determination.

As research about the health benefits of breastfeeding accumulated, a new movement of female empowerment emerged. Organizations that promote breastfeeding, such as *La Leche League*, have been vilified by some critics as being "Breastfeeding Nazis," a repurposing of the old derogatory term *feminazi*. In the press, disagreement about the necessity of breastfeeding became known as "mommy wars," as controversies erupted. A 2012

Time magazine cover that portrayed a petite mother standing up while nursing her three-year-old son who was standing on a chair drew a lot of media attention. The story, entitled "Are you mom enough?",[16] sparked outrage. More and more people and public health organizations began to advocate for breastfeeding rights and opportunities. Many state governments stepped up to make public breastfeeding a civil right and many states exempted breastfeeding from indecent exposure laws. When mothers were asked to cover up or leave a business, they turned out in droves to nurse in protest or boycott these organizations.

An instance of activism occurred in May 2015, when a woman described on Facebook how an upstate New York cider mill employee asked her to cover up when she nursed her infant son. In no time, social media was abuzz with outrage and solidarity. Mothers with and without babies turned out in droves for a "nurse-in" at the cider mill the Saturday after the incident. The cider mill owner made a public statement in support of breastfeeding and what began as a protest turned into a celebration. Biology gifts us, therefore, the popular slogan: "I make milk. What's your superpower?"

Breastfeeding is truly a female superpower that provides comfort for infant and mother, who synchronize their breathing, heartbeats, sleep cycles, and temperatures. Breast milk has been called "liquid gold" for its irreproducible blend of living nutrients, from antibodies to beneficial microbes, that inhibit infections while providing complete nutritional benefits that last into adulthood. For mothers, extended breastfeeding reduces their risk of breast cancer, diabetes, obesity, and prenatal depression. It also saves money and resources for families and societies by reducing health care costs.

Research shows that formula feeding can lead to chronic health conditions that affect minorities more severely, and various studies have identified breastfeeding as a top priority to address health disparities between ethnic groups. Initiatives like "It's Only Natural" encourage non-Hispanic Black mothers, who breastfeed less often and for shorter periods than other racial-ethnic groups, to embrace breastfeeding. They need access to prenatal care, maternity leave, family support, and community resources. Employers need to provide breaks and spaces for mothers to pump milk. As described in Chapter 1, women of color are typically paid less for the same work than most other women. It is difficult for mothers in hourly, low-wage jobs to get this kind of flexibility. This is especially worrisome because Black women of reproductive age tend to have higher rates of breast cancer, get diagnosed at later stages, and have worse outcomes than whites, Asians, and Hispanics. Exclusive and extended breastfeeding could improve these outcomes. Cultural and health system barriers, like inefficient use of interpreters and lactation consultants, and limited access to quality Baby Friendly birth facilities, limit access to breastfeeding information and support for minority and refugee mothers.

While reproductive choice and education have proven essential to female emancipation, "freedom from breastfeeding" came with unanticipated health liabilities and long-term effects on the health of mothers and children. Breastfeeding is a twining of nature and culture that depends upon environmental, social, and political factors. Mothers cannot fulfill their own breastfeeding goals without ample support from families, communities, legislators, and health care providers. All mothers need to be empowered to advocate for their health, and support needs to be available to all mothers, regardless of origin or social status. Breastfeeding activism needs to address intersectional questions like race and class to be successful.

Feminism Is: Coalitional

While some movements and organizations practice intersectionality *within* a focus on one issue (breastfeeding, Me Too) or one locale (family court), others work *between* issues in broader, sometimes global, context to gather wide support and build on how we're all interconnected. Even groups dedicated to just one event can take an intersectional approach. If they don't start that way, they may learn as they grow, like Women's March organizers. When Angela Davis spoke at the 2017 Women's March, she invoked the crucial role of intersectionality in building coalitions:

> . . . we are collective agents of history . . . The struggle to save the planet, to stop climate change, to guarantee the accessibility of water from the lands of the Standing Rock Sioux, to Flint, Michigan, to the West Bank and Gaza. The struggle to save our flora and fauna, to save the air—this is ground zero of the struggle for social justice. This . . . march . . . represents the promise of feminism as against the pernicious powers of state violence. And inclusive and intersectional feminism that calls upon all of us to join the resistance to racism, to Islamophobia, to anti-Semitism, to misogyny, to capitalist exploitation. . . . We dedicate ourselves to collective resistance. . . . Resistance on the ground, resistance in the classrooms, resistance on the job, resistance in our art and in our music. . . . This is just the beginning and in the words of the inimitable Ella Baker, 'We who believe in freedom cannot rest until it comes.' Thank you.[17]

Notable coalitional resistance took place in Minneapolis and Saint Paul. The "Twin Cities" have amongst their brown and Black residents a disproportionately large population of Native Americans for whom the area is traditional homeland, from the Dakota, Ojibwe, Ho-Chunk, Cheyenne, Oto, Iowa, Sac, and Fox tribes. Because of this, people there have more direct experience of racist violence, arrests, and shootings of Native

Americans than the rest of the US. As Rene Ann Goodrich said, "We're so touched by the loss of our loved ones, or the missing ones, so it's really close to home here in Minnesota."[18]

Perhaps that is why the Twin Cities was the birthplace of AIM (the American Indian Movement) in 1968. AIM began as grassroots gatherings and grew into a group that, like the Black Panthers, provided escorts and police protection, started community businesses, and created culturally appropriate places to teach and care for children like the Red School House. AIM leaders in consultation with traditional Native spiritual leaders have brought successful suits against the federal government and AIM protectors showed up where needed in the larger Native community, such as Alcatraz, California, 1969–1971, Wounded Knee, South Dakota, 1973, and Standing Rock, North Dakota, 2016–2017 .

It's not surprising, therefore, that Minneapolis is the home of seasoned activists like Goodrich, who protests wearing a red Solidarity Shawl with blue and purple fringes to honor Native survivors of historical and contemporary abuse. She's a coalition builder between Native groups like MMIW, Idle No More, and Native Lives Matter. The third annual Women's Memorial March in Duluth, Minnesota, explicitly addressed links between pipelines and murdered women. She also formed a coalition between Native Lives Matter and Black Lives Matter.

Figure 11.1 Rene Anne Goodrich.[19]

Feminism Is: Everywhere and Anywhere

Feminism can take place anywhere and in any form, physically or virtually. But sometimes activism has to take place where you stand. Rhianna Rogers describes the importance of #MeToo in academia.

"Me too," Reflections on Sexual Harassment in Higher Education by Rhianna Rogers

When the "Me too" phenomenon spread through my own social media, I decided it was time for me to join and say "Me too" as well. As a young scholar (in age, not intellect), I was exposed to quite a bit of harassing behavior while in college. It began when I was an undergraduate student. I decided to get a minor in Education because I knew that I wanted to be a teacher, just not at what level. As part of my teacher training, I was required to observe an Elementary School teacher. I was very young at the time, 19, and I was very excited about this opportunity. I was placed with the only male faculty at the school and I got to work being his assistant for the term. Shortly after working with this teacher, I was introduced to another administrator, another male, who worked on campus. He seemed to be very interested in helping me adjust to the school and offered to show me around. Being naïve, remember I was very young, I thought this was a great idea. Over the next two weeks, I began to realize that this individual had ulterior motives. He began asking me out on dates (even though he was married), offering to buy me gifts and to take me home. I felt very uncomfortable about his behavior, but I didn't really have anyone to talk to on campus.

The issue reached a head when I was called into the principal's office and was informed that I needed to change my behavior and dress "more appropriately" because I was generating too much attention at the school. I asked the principal what this was specifically in reference to, and she informed me that a few other faculty members had been gossiping that I was having an affair with this administrator. As would be imagined, I was shocked by this revelation. I decided to speak with my faculty adviser at my university about it, and she was appalled. She immediately withdrew me from my teacher's placement and set up a meeting with University Council to discuss if we should pursue legal action. I was called into this meeting and was asked to recap the overall experience with this individual from beginning to end, which was very traumatic. Once I was done, the University Council said I had grounds to pursue a restraining order as well as action against the school for defamation of character. Though young, I was well aware of the stigma that could be attached to me for speaking out. I clearly remember asking the University Council what chances I had of negatively impacting my teaching career if I were to file this suit. He was very honest with me and said, "There is historical data that indicates those who file suits have difficulty gaining regular employment afterward." I was disheartened by this news and, because of this, I decided to not move forward with any legal action. Instead, I changed my degree in hopes to avoid future situations like this one.

Unfortunately, this was not the only case. While in graduate school, I was introduced to a seasoned professor who was very influential in one of my fields of study. Scholars at the college encouraged me to work with him since his interests were so closely aligned with mine. I was very excited to work with him, given his background. It is important to mention that I was still very young, only 22 years old when I finished my MA degree and began work on my PhD. I remember in my initial meeting with this professor that he asked me out to dinner. This was odd, since I had never had a professor ask me to dinner upon meeting me for a few minutes. However, as a young, naïve, and eager student, I assumed he was asking me out because he was interested in learning about my area of study, my previous work, and academic goals. However, I was still uncomfortable, so I politely declined and hoped that was the end of it. However, as time progressed, I realized his motives were not professional. Still, as the leading scholar at my institution in one of my fields, I felt I needed him to be a part of my graduate studies to move forward. Over the next couple of years, it became clear that this professor's intent was inappropriate and his goal was to control me and my career. Though I reported this behavior to my adviser (who was female) and to the director of my program (who was male), I was never given a direct path to resolve the problem. On the contrary, I received a very harsh email from the Director of the program, who told me that I was exaggerating since he was "a highly respected scholar" who would not engage in this type of behavior with a student.

Realizing that I was not getting support, I then tried to transfer to another university to work with another specialist. Unfortunately, the professor used his power and influence to prevent me from making this move. I realized that I had to either stay or start over elsewhere. I decided that since I had dealt with it this long, I would just put up with him and finish my degree. However, this turned out to me more difficult than I anticipated. On one occasion, he told me that in order to graduate I had to do whatever he said. On another occasion, while on an international research trip, he created a situation where he exposed himself to me. I did not welcome this attention and told him so, but I was unable to leave the international project without losing my research grant because it was under his control. When I returned to the US, he threatened me by saying that if I did not sleep with him, he would ruin my career. I could not take it anymore and I dropped out of school.

Over the course of a year, my adviser regularly reached out to me and asked what had happened, but I hid it because I was ashamed (as most victims are). I kept thinking, "How could I have allowed this to happen to me again?" It was not until I was encouraged by my partner to speak with my adviser in person that I felt confident enough to explain what happened. Once I did, she immediately told me to report this to the dean (who was a woman at this time and a mentor of mine throughout my undergraduate and graduate careers.) Once again, I was asked to recite all of the situations that I had experienced with this faculty member, including the international incident. This meeting, which was comprised of all women, was the first time I felt encouraged to say what happened and did not feel judged. By the end of the meeting, I felt empowered to finish my PhD. They helped me to reorganize my courses, my dissertation committee, and remaining requirements so that I would not have to work with him again. If not for this meeting, I would not be a doctor or professor today.

I tell these two stories to demonstrate the simple fact that situations like this can occur in any environment. Although sexual assault and harassment can be experienced by anyone, it is crucial that we acknowledge how race and class intersect with gender to make some populations more vulnerable than others. As a young, poor college student and a member of a marginalized racial group, I felt I had little choice in either of these situations. In my head, I had only two options: I could either give up and let down the countless people who had helped me get to where I was or continue on and deal with the harassing behaviors I encountered. I may have felt differently if I was better supported while these situations occurred; being taken seriously by female faculty members/advisers is what made me feel empowered to continue in both cases. But resources for those who experience sexual violence can be more difficult to access for young women and women of color; it's not just that race and class shape the likelihood of sexual harassment and assault, it's that they also create barriers for survivors working to recover from the trauma of such experiences. We as scholars need to recognize that these situations occur within academia and that we all need to be aware and ready to empower those who have experienced them.

I know if the academic women mentioned above had not reached out to help me in both cases and pushed me to finish, I would not be in academia today. As such, I wholeheartedly believe that part of my responsibility as an adviser and mentor of both female and marginalized students is to share with them these stories. In my own work, I have consciously searched for highly qualified, female research assistants in order to give them a safe space to grow as scholars and to ensure they can excel in a healthy academic environment, devoid of harassing behaviors. Over the years, I have been very upfront with my female students about the realities of working in male-dominated fields and the unfortunate likelihood that they too may experience various forms of harassment. I use myself as an example of someone who has persevered, despite this environment, with the help of others, to where I am today. When thinking about their futures, I encourage my students to find positive reinforcement in themselves, their significant others, and when selecting mentors. I believe taking these negative situations and illustrating how they have empowered me to help others is an important concept that coincides well with the overall #MeToo movement.

In *Feminists: What Were They Thinking?*, Margo Jefferson says, "For better or worse there is not a situation in one's daily life that does not have feminist subtext ... and one is constantly aware that even when you want to rest it stands up and hits you in the face."[20] Jessica Marsico is a Mom whose experiences in family court led her to increased activism. Court is only one of the many places people often turn, seeking respite or justice, only to find that sexism and racism will "hit you in the face."

Why Family Court Mothers Need Feminists
by Jessica E. Marsico

Every month or so a mom reaches out to me, pleading. She heard I know things, that I once won, that I will listen. Sometimes, it's a friend of a friend or a high school acquaintance. Sometimes, it's a total stranger; I rarely learn how they came to find me. The crisis and need and despair encompass the entirety of their lives, and I fall into it with them. That is the only grace: sharing realities denied by the rest of the world.

With each new story, I fight a tiny death within that would eventually slacken the grip I have on stewarding my own family court trauma so that I can do this work. The tiny deaths begin because, in fact, no story is new; the legitimized violences are thematic, constant, normalized.

We need you to know so many things. That the status quo in family courts is violence against women and their children through police and child protection workers. That privacy within the family and home are not the only dangers: so too are family courtrooms, hospitals. That fathers, social workers, and judges behave eerily similar. That accusing mothers of hysteria is still acceptable. That our failures signal the end of mothering. That we are petrified.

Technically, family courts have jurisdiction over State interference and surveillance of family members. Federalism grants organization to states, and each has some way of hearing and adjudicating custody/visitation; child support; paternity; abuse/neglect; termination of parental rights; adoption; juvenile delinquency; and many other docket types.

But all of this is jargon. It is State-carved classifications with built-in relations reflecting only the dominant reality through an official narrative. It is the language of the oppressor, not the oppressed: the oppressed has no language to speak her intersectional reality, no authority to construct that language, and no means to upend that structural censorship. But how can this actually happen, and who is it happening to?

First, let's lay out who does *not* go to family court. Parents who conform to societal norms of the nuclear family certainly do not, absent the need for an order of protection. Thus, when a couple is both married *and* investing in litigation, they go to Supreme Court. My county seat is New York's original capital, Kingston, and the Supreme courthouse is uptown in a beautiful, historic stone building across from coffee shops and a farmer's market. They fight one another, with or without attorneys, but they never fight the State.

By contrast, the family court in my county is a converted used car dealership, across from a laundromat and on the corner of a main road. It scarcely has any parking, but does have triple-booked court calendars and $75 an hour assigned counsel for poor folk. The people there are mostly mothers, already defeated in many ways, carrying their turmoil into grimy waiting rooms. They often speak with their attorneys, for the first time, within public earshot. There's no dignity to any of it, as if they don't need better because they don't know better. But they know well enough that this is where they will fight for their safety and for their children.

This structure and its laws and policies have barely changed since the 1959 Standard Family Court Act, written by white cis men. It pre-determines what is sayable, by whom, and how, excluding all other values and needs, thus narratively reproducing dominance. It is enforceable, dis-abling the nurturer while emboldening the aggressor. Fifty-seven years later, it is still happening; concrete real-life scenarios, though heartbreak-ing, show precisely how.[21]

1   A young mother is holding her three-year-old daughter's hand at the clerk window begging for protection from the controlling relation-ship she's detailing. The clerk cuts her off with, "What you think is domestic violence probably isn't" and, as the mother's voice grows panicked, the clerk shoots the court officer a look. He puts his hand on his gun and advances toward the mother and child. She backs away wide-eyed and sobs in her car as her child eats dry Cheerios in a booster seat.

2   In a conference room with scarcely enough space for three people, a mother is badgered by two attorneys to agree to the terms of the court and an abuser. She's not confident about fighting: what if she *does* look bad to the judge? What if she *does* lose time with her kids? Free will oaths are always extracted by the judge, and they are always a lie.

3   A mother is warned in a public hallway of family court by her chil-dren's attorney that if she makes one more Child Protective Services (CPS) report against their father and the social worker doesn't be-lieve abuse is occurring, her children will be given, full stop, to their abuser.

4   Racial profiling and a difficult pregnancy flagged a young mother of color as a drug use risk. Her baby tests positive for a narcotic she was prescribed a year earlier. CPS, finding her home unsuitable, takes her six-day-old son until she would move back into the home of her mother and sex-abuser stepfather. She could not, ever. Within a year, family court terminates her parental rights, and her boy is gone to her forever.

5   Demanding her right to a hearing on a protective order petition with proof that her four-year-old son is being sexually abused by his father, a mother is forced out of the courthouse in the rough grip of a court officer.

Feminist legal theory is brimming with decades of thought on all of this: Crenshaw's intersectional feminism; variations on the anti-subordination principle; the differing lenses, on CPS and race, of Roberts and Ashe; Finley on the gendered nature of law and legal reasoning; and Fineman's earlier critiques of liberal legal feminism and her more recent work on vulnerability. These are and have been a rich and necessary progression of thought on maternal subordination and endangerment, but all of these women are lawyers or legal scholars. However well intentioned, they cannot liberate motherhood from the state. Only mothers can do that.

Other work *is* being done. There are calls for family court and CPS abolition, but the clamor of father's rights groups, deafening with ever-fallacious *reverse sexism*, weakens these movements. In-person support groups and resource centers like "The Nurtured Parent" in New Jersey provide information and solidarity. There are also informal and largely undocumented local networks providing whatever the moms in them need and can realistically give: 24-hour crisis phone trees; court appearance "buddies," so no one ever has to go alone; babysitting swaps; trial prep and petition-writing; and validation.

But it is not enough. What mothers need now are the means to develop their own liberation[22]: consciousness-raising; the tools of critical inquiry, thought, and action; access to authorship of new taxonomies; bureaucratic navigational skills; mutual aid; a development of Motherhood as an intersectional identity and experience; and the empowerment to assert that their children belong to them. Without access, they cannot internalize the words of Audre Lorde, words they desperately need: "We can learn to work and speak when we are afraid in the same way we have learned to work and speak when we are tired."[23]

You can help to get mothers there. Use your voice to increase the social acceptability of family court discussions; observe family court waiting rooms; witness any proceedings you can get into; and make space for the untold, marginalized stories through your every affiliation. Write letters to the editor. Engage your families, professors, friends, classmates. Make it their work, too. And use art, like Maxine Kumin, who unwittingly wrote our hearts:

> I am tired of this history of loss!
> What drum can I beat to reach you?
> To be reasonable
> Is to put out the light.
> To be reasonable is to let go.[24]

Some coalitions are everywhere and anywhere at the same time. The HeForShe movement asks everyone to pledge to support gender equity by doing whatever they *can* do wherever they are. Elizabeth Nyamayaro describes how this African initiative became a global phenomenon:

- In three days, more than 100,000 men committed to HeForShe. Within the first week, at least one man in every single country joined.

- In the first week, HeForShe created more than 1.2 billion conversations on social media and received thousands of emails.
- A man in Zimbabwe created a "husband school" for men abusive to their partners.
- In Pune, India, a youth advocate organized 700 cyclists in a rally to share the HeForShe message.
- The French hospitality company, Accor, committed to eliminate the pay gap for all of its 180,000 employees by 2020.
- The government of Sweden committed to close both the employment and the pay gap for all of its citizens within the electoral term.
- United Nations Secretary-General Ban Ki-moon, secretary-generals of NATO and the EU Council, the prime minister of Bhutan, the president of Sierra Leone, all the male EU commissioners, and members of the Swedish and Iceland parliaments signed up with HeForShe.
- One in 20 men in Iceland has joined the movement.
- Hundreds and thousands of students around the world created more than 100 HeForShe student associations.[25]

Activism can reach across time and space to unite people with unexpected differences around a common cause.

Feminism Is: Global

As we saw in Liberia, struggles throughout the world, like Indigenous American struggles, are rooted in political histories of colonialism and imperialism. Eco-activism, transnational activism, and Indigenous activism overlap because global issues like climate change and economic inequity grow from the same roots. Activists around the world have identified how colonial greed to accumulate and control resources has spread out and ravaged continents. The philosophical genesis of this greed persists, creating ongoing problems that threaten life and health.

Forced sterilization and other forms of birth reduction for women of color, earlier addressed by Margaret Prescod, are still ongoing. In Canada, a 2018 report states that Indigenous women who birthed in hospitals weren't permitted to hold their newborns until they agreed to undergo sterilization.[26] Health officials have acknowledged that they were also coerced during the painful process of labor and falsely told it was reversible.[27] A woman who lives in Cherokee country in North Carolina told us,

> almost every Native woman I know has to have a C-section. I began to wonder many years ago why. They tell them their hips are too narrow and I think it is a mandate from government to limit the number of babies in Cherokee families. This means they can only have three. It also means a bigger bill so Tribes have to pay more. It may be that I'm wrong, but I don't think so.[28]

Canada and North Carolina are the tip of the iceberg: "In recent years, the practice has been documented in countries in North and South America, Europe, Asia, and Africa. It has targeted women who are ethnic racial minorities, women with disabilities, women living with HIV, and poor women."[29]

Reasons for forced sterilization vary but share an economic basis. Transnational feminists theorize historical economic consequences of these kinds of practices and clashes. They follow how such problems work their way through contemporary politics and policies. Eco-activists, like Indigenous activists, are concerned with how economic exploitation of the Earth affects ecosystems, including a habitable climate on which all life relies.

These are a few of the many reasons that feminism is global. Whether destruction of Indigenous lives, Indigenous aquifers, control of agricultural resources, or other forms of economic exploitation are at stake, global authority over resources by a wealthy elite remains at the root of many problems.

Final Words

To organize our thoughts and choose our actions, we asked, "How did we get here?" Knowing how we got here allows us to uncover the hidden architecture of the master's house. Knowing how it was built provides us with analytical principles and feminist tools adaptable to changing situations. History, principles, and tools can help you negotiate change. This book offered just a taste of what can be researched and what can be done.

Some tools, like reflexivity, are like a GPS we can use to locate ourselves in the feminist landscape. Individual positions vary, and our experiences change as society changes. Some changes have been for the better (Europeans learned about gender equity from Indigenous Africans and Americans), others for the worse (Europeans imposed patriarchy on Indigenous cultures), but in every case, there has been dynamic interaction. Some issues look familiar for hundreds or even thousands of years, yet change is nevertheless continual, offering hope for reclaiming our power together.

What's That Feminism? Using reflexivity and research, you can locate yourself in the feminist landscape and/or create a feminism or feminisms that support you in being who you want to be, doing what you want to do, and learning how you can work with others—because numbers count!

Who's That Feminist? Maybe it's you.

Notes

1 ND House Bill 1311. *66th Legislative Assembly.* Introduced Jan. 3, 2019, https://www.legis.nd.gov/assembly/66-2019/documents/19-0753-02000.pdf.
2 Indigenous Envtl. Network v U.S. Dep't. of State, 4:17-cv-00029-BMM; 4:17-cv-00031-BMM. MT. Filing 218. Nov. 8, 2018. See also Filing 252. Motion to Stay denied. Feb. 12, 2019.
3 Richard Wolff. "FDR's New Deal, Taxes, Denial." *The Norman Show. YouTube.* Nov. 1, 2017, https://www.youtube.com/watch?v=o-Qkqq5y8Ys.

4 "Nibi Song." *Mother Earth Water Walk.* Last updated Dec. 5, 2017, http://www.motherearthwaterwalk.com/?p=2915.

5 Matthew Green. "The Youth Activists Behind the Standing Rock Resistance (with Lesson Plan)." *The Lowdown.* May 23, 2017, https://www.kqed.org/lowdown/27023/the-youth-of-standing-rock.

6 Alexandra "'I Got My Future Back': One of the Young Leaders of the Standing Rock Movement Sheds Tears of Joy." *Alternet.com.* Dec. 5, 2016, https://www.alternet.org/activism/i-got-my-future-back-13-year-old-behind-standing-rock-movement-sheds-tears-joy-over.

7 "MMIW – Missing and Murdered Indigenous Women." *Coalition to Stop Violence Against Native Women.* 2019, https://www.csvanw.org/mmiw/.

8 Dwayne Mack. "Angela Davis (1944–)." *Black Past.* Feb. 10, 2011, https://blackpast.org/aah/davis-angela-1944-0.

9 Yamiche Alcindor. "'Auntie Maxine' Waters Goes After Trump and Goes Viral." *New York Times.* July 7, 2017, https://www.nytimes.com/2017/07/07/us/politics/maxine-waters-trump-ben-carson.html.

10 Max Greenwood. "Maxine Waters: Trump is the Most Deplorable Person I've Ever Met." *Home News.* Aug. 4, 2017, https://thehill.com/homenews/house/345307-maxine-waters-trump-is-the-most-deplorable-person-ive-ever-met.

11 "Maxine Waters @ Keep Families Together: Protest Rally and Toy Drive." June 23, 2018, https://www.youtube.com/watch?time_continue=61&v=-1Fu3g1MGHY.

12 Wolf, "'Trump' Waters has 'extraordinary low IQ,'" *CNN Politics,* https://www.cnn.com/videos/politics/2018/06/25/erick-erickson-donald-trump-tweet-maxine-waters-sot-wolf.cnn

13 Yara Shahidi. "2018 Time 100 List: Maxine Waters." *Time.* 2018, http://time.com/collection/most-influential-people-2018/5217567/maxine-waters/.

14 "What We Believe." *Black Lives Matter.* Last updated Dec. 20, 2018, https://blacklivesmatter.com/about/what-we-believe/.

15 "A HerStory of the #BlackLivesMatter Movement, Alicia Garza." *The Feminist Wire.* Oct. 7, 2014, https://thefeministwire.com/2014/10/blacklivesmatter-2/.

16 Feifei Sun. "Behind the Cover: Are You Mom Enough?" *Time.* May 10, 2012. http://time.com/3450144/behind-the-cover-are-you-mom-enough/.

17 Lyndsey Matthews. "Here's the Full Transcript of Angela Davis's Women's March Speech 'History Cannot be Deleted Like Web Pages.'" *Elle.* Jan. 21, 2017, https://www.elle.com/culture/career-politics/a42337/angela-davis-womens-march-speech-full-transcript/.

18 Andrew Kirov. "Women's Memorial March Honors Murdered and Missing Native Women." *Fox 21 Online.* Feb. 13, 2018, https://www.fox21online.com/2018/02/13/womens-memorial-march-honors-murdered-missing-native-women/.

19 We have permission from Ms Goodrich but have not been able to get a response from Unicorn Riot who published this photo.

20 Margo Jefferson. *Feminists: What Were They Thinking?* Dir. Johanna Demetrakas. Netflix. 2018.

21 These scenarios are sourced from any of the following: oral histories, non-participatory observation, or my own experience. All occurred in the state of NY between 2008 and 2017.

22 Jessica E. Marsico. "Liberating Motherhood from Family Court: An Interdisciplinary Study to Guide Collaborative Research and Intersectional Theory-Building." *ProQuest Masters & Doctoral Theses.* No. 10812039. 2018.

23 Audre Lorde. *Sister Outsider.* Crossing Press, 1984.

24 Maixne Kumin. "September 22." *The Privilege.* Harper & Row. 1954, pp. 79–82.

25 Elizabeth Nyanmaro. "An Invitation to Men Who Want a Better World for Women." *TEDWomen*. 2015, https://www.ted.com/talks/elizabeth_nya-mayaro_an_invitation_to_men_who_want_a_better_world_for_women/transcript?language=en.

26 Padraig Moran. "Indigenous Women Kept from Seeing Their Newborn Babies Until Agreeing to Sterilization, Says Lawyer." Prod. Idella Sturino and WIllow Smith. *CBC Radio*. Nov. 13, 2018, https://www.cbc.ca/radio/thecurrent/the-current-for-november-13-2018-1.4902679/indigenous-women-kept-from-seeing-their-newborn-babies-until-agreeing-to-sterilization-says-lawyer-1.4902693?fbclid=IwAR0jg2yjQ9qLYpfsNXSrrLPimpvJmNpedDGMX-cdAmt2XvWwCgSHCTyjGzw.

27 Vincent Schilling. "First Nations Women Forced to Be Sterilized Before They Could See Newborns." *Indian Country Today*. Nov. 16, 2018, https://newsmaven.io/indiancountrytoday/news/first-nations-women-forced-to-be-sterilized-before-they-could-see-newborns-kAcg4zOPfkmnM-aKRh31OQ/.

28 Marion Cowart Smith. Personal Communication with Menoukha Case. Nov. 16, 2018.

29 Priti Patel. "Forced Sterilization of Women as Discrimination." *Public Health Reviews*. Mar. 12, 2017, https://doi.org/10.1186/240985-017-0060-9.

Notes on Contributors

Alice Lai is a professor at SUNY Empire State College. She earned her PhD in Art Education from The Ohio State University. At Empire State College, she creates and teaches online courses focusing on women's art history, contemporary art and theories, and multicultural art. Her ongoing research topics include art education, online education, critical theory, and pedagogy (e.g., feminisms, feminist pedagogies, critical multiculturalism, and digital inequality). She has frequently presented her research at national and international conferences. She also has published book chapters and articles in academic journals, mostly in the field of art education.

Anamaria Ross, PhD, MPH, CLC, is a mother of two teenage sons and a faculty mentor at SUNY Empire State College at Utica. She earned a doctorate in medical anthropology from Tulane University, a Certificate of Advanced Study in Health Services Management and Policy from the Maxwell School, and a Master of Public Health from the CNYMPH Program of Upstate Medical University and Syracuse University. Anamaria is the author of *The Anthropology of Alternative Medicine* (2012).

Chimine N. Arfuso is a Cuban, French–Italian, first-generation American, decolonial/feminist scholar/activist. She has centered her experiences as the victim of a violent rape by a serial rapist as a teenager, as the daughter of a Cuban refugee, and as the single mother of twins to fuel her scholarship and outreach. She is also a Zumba instructor, intersectional breastfeeding advocate, and Palera, and integrates these elements into her feminist praxis, most recently in academic lectures at institutions such as the University of California, Davis, Fresno State University, and the University of Nazerbayev in Kazakhstan. She is working on a PhD at California Institute of Integral Studies in Transformative Inquiry, focusing on intersections between Latina, Indigenous, and Black Feminism; Reproductive Justice; Autohistoria-Teoría/Autotheory; Indigenous Cuban/African Diaspora traditions; and Decolonial Research Methodology.

Elizabeth Beamer Craig grew up a baby boomer child during the 1960's chaos of the civil rights movement, Vietnam War, and moon landing, and graduated Phi Beta Kappa from UNC-G in 1968. She is a wife and mother of three amazing children, who she tried to raise with open minds and open hearts, and worked for 38 years in the billing department of an Abingdon, VA, law firm before retiring. She is a devoted supporter of LGBTQ+ rights and passionate about reading, traveling, yoga, and tai chi.

Elizabeth Wiltse is a graduate of SUNY Empire State College with a Bachelor of Science in Historical Studies. She is currently a graduate student at Vermont Law School studying environmental law and policy, with special interest in social and environmental justice, and gender equality. She has served as a graduate legal intern at the New

York State Office of the Attorney General in the Environmental Protection Bureau in Buffalo, NY, and as an AmeriCorps volunteer with Legal Assistance of Western New York. She lives in Western New York with her husband David, her daughter Molly, and their best friend, a 14-year-old Vizsla, Jane. Elizabeth enjoys the outdoors, gardening with David and Molly, and of course, spending time with Jane.

Henry Odun LeBron was ordained as an Interfaith Minister in 1991 at the New Seminary, New York, NY. He was also initiated as a Yoruba/Lucumi priest in 1981 in Brooklyn, NY. He is a spiritually focused holistic practitioner and spiritual advisor. Within the last 40 years, he has counseled and conducted transformative workshops while supporting the journey for equality and spiritual empowerment in the African American, LGBTQ, and Latino communities. He served on the board of the Yoruba Cultural Center, which encouraged Yoruba spiritual beliefs, as well as being an advisor for the Latino Commission on AIDS. He presently sits on the Board of Joint Approach, a Housing cooperative, in Prospect Heights Brooklyn.

Himanee Gupta-Carlson is a writer and professor at SUNY Empire State College, where she teaches historical studies. Her research and teaching practices are grounded in feminist-inspired methods. She takes knowledge as a form of conversation as her starting point. Her book *Muncie, India(na): Middletown and Asian America* (2018, University of Illinois Press) exemplifies this practice through its blending of storytelling, ethnography, and memoir. Gupta-Carlson has published numerous articles on the South Asian diaspora, Hip Hop feminism, and Hip Hop education. She is working on a book-length manuscript on community-based Hip Hop and sustenance farming as interrelated practices toward social change.

I I "Kathy" Chou writes, "I am a woman believer with two cultural roots-Taiwan where I was born and educated up to high school, and New York my home state for over 30 years. Through my grandmother's feminism, I was empowered to truly examine my own life, honor it with meanings, hold it like a flower to be cherished."

Jessica E. Marsico is a legislative advisor, policy analyst, and mixed methods researcher on the NYS Assembly Majority Leader's staff. Her role as cannabis legalization team lead was borne out of a highly selective Graduate Fellowship during the 2018 Legislative Session. Jessica studies and writes about Motherhood as an experience, primarily focusing on intersections of race, girlhood trauma, and variations of social control. She is a poet, sociologist, herbalist, and amateur neuroscientist interested in peripartum epigenetics. Jessica (and her work) can be found on LinkedIn and ResearchGate.

Katharine I. Ransom earned a Bachelor of Arts in Economics from Ithaca College and a Master of Business Administration, with a concentration in Economics, from Southern New Hampshire University. She is currently a Doctor of Philosophy in Transformative Studies student at the California Institute of Integral Studies. She focuses on Feminist Economics research, specifically the economics of matrilineal societies, using Marxist and Transnational Feminist theories.

Lola Rocknrolla is a writer, director, producer with seven short films, two TV pilots, tons of music videos, and an off-Broadway show to her credits. She is currently shooting a doc feature about the gay nightlife legend Dean Johnson. Lola is also in preproduction for a feature based on her off-Broadway hit "Homo the Musical."

MaryNell Morgan is a professor Emerita of Political Science with a PhD from (Clark)-Atlanta University. Her multidisciplinary teaching, scholarship, and singing focus on the life, work, and legacy of W.E.B. Du Bois. She was a consultant to the PBS Documentary "W.E.B. Du Bois: A Biography in Four Voices." She participated in establishing the Du Bois International Pan African Research Center in Accra, Ghana. Among her fellowships and awards are the Sterling Brown Visiting Professorship at Williams College and a Wellesley & Spelman College Women's Center Workshop entitled "Black Women's Studies Curriculum Development." Her academic, community, and creative arts affiliations include The National Conference of Black Political Scientists (Life Member); The African Heritage Studies Association; The Association for the Study of African - American Life and History (Life Member); The Underground Railroad History Project of the Capital Region; and The Peoples' Music Network – Songs for Freedom and Struggle.

Nancy Babbitt writes, "I am a woman who is like flower that had been snipped off from her roots, weakening and wilting until receiving a watering. Water brought forth renewed vitality and with that energy I proceed to scatter seeds. My feminism is as a gardener: I gather, steward, and scatter seeds and then I nurture their emergence and growth - bringing forth abundance of life and beauty renewed."

Patrice Lorna LeBron writes, "I am pursuing a Masters degree in Liberal Studies at the Graduate Center of the City University of New York. My undergraduate studies at Empire State College formed the foundation of my concentration in Africana studies in graduate school. I address leadership among African American and Caribbean women through the lens of literature, biography, and memoir. The most poignant learning in my writing journey, so far, is the importance of transparency as a medium for healing. I address healing through (1) exploring how slavery and post slavery affected African American and Caribbean women's leadership in the 20th and 21st century. (2) examining the heritage of their leadership in global and community context today. (3) performing a feminist inquiry along vectors of analysis such as race, class and gender. In my ongoing excursion with the inner-self, I continue to examine contemporary triumphs of personal, community, and global artfulness, which offer inspirational leadership strategies in the world."

Rhianna C. Rogers, PhD, RPA, is an associate professor in the Department of Social and Behavioral Sciences and the inaugural Co-ordinator of Interdisciplinary and Multidisciplinary Studies at SUNY Empire State College. Rogers is trained as both an anthropological-archaeologist and historian, specializing in Mesoamerica and native cultures of the US. She received a certificate in Ethnic Studies, a BA in Social Sciences (Anthropology Major and History Minor), an MA in History, and a PhD in Comparative Studies (Anthropology, History, and Linguistics Concentrations) from Florida Atlantic University.

Roberto Borrero (Borikén Taíno) is a human rights advocate, cultural consultant, artist, and musician. Roberto has particular expertise in Caribbean and other Indigenous Peoples issues. He is currently the In-ternational Mechanisms Director for the US Human Rights Network and has previously worked for the International Indian Treaty Council and the American Museum of Natural History. He has over 20 years' experience engaging the United Nations system and as an independent consultant worked with UNESCO, PBS, BBC, El Museo de Barrio, Tribal Link Foundation, the Natural Resources Stewardship Circle, and the Smithsonian Institution's National Museum of the American Indian, among others. At the community level, Roberto also serves as President of the United Confederation of Taíno People.

Stephanie A. Sellers holds a doctoral degree in Native American Stud-ies specializing in Women of the Eastern Woodlands. Her most recent book is the co-edited volume with Menoukha Robin Case titled *Weaving the Legacy: Remembering Paula Gunn Allen* (West End Press 2017). Sellers has presented her research on Native American Traditions panels at many national conferences, including the MLA, American Acad-emy of Religion, the National Women's Studies Association, and the Elizabeth A. Sackler Center for Feminist Art in the Brooklyn Museum. Dr. Sellers was the Inaugural Director of the Gettysburg College Women's Center and is a columnist for *SageWoman* Magazine.

Index